CW01558717

A PECULIAR EFFECT ON THE BBC

Bernard Wilkie

A PECULIAR EFFECT ON THE BBC

Bernard Wilkie

A Peculiar Effect on the BBC

This edition first published September 2015 by Miwk Publishing Ltd. Miwk Publishing, 45a Bell Street, Reigate, Surrey RH2 7AQ.

ISBN 978-1-908630-22-3

Copyright © Bernard Wilkie 2015.

The rights of Bernard Wilkie to be identified as the author of this work has been asserted in accordance with the Copyright, Designs and Patents Act 1988.

All rights reserved. No part of this publication may be reproduced, stored in or introduced into a retrieval system, or transmitted, in any form, or by any means (electronic, mechanical, photocopying, recording or otherwise) without the prior written permission of the publisher. Any person who does any unauthorised act in relation to this publication may be liable to criminal prosecution and civil claim for damages.

A CIP catalogue record for this book is available from the British Library.

The publishers would like to thank: Martin Wilkie, Mat Irvine, Mike Tucker, Steve Roberts, Jonathan Helm, Andrew Henderson, Andrew Emmerson and Julian Knott. And of course Bernard and Jack, without whom so much wouldn't be possible.

Cover and book design by Robert Hammond.
Cover photograph © BBC Photo Library,

Printed and bound in Great Britain by Berforts Information Press Ltd (www.berforts.com)

This book is sold subject to the condition that it shall not, by way of trade or otherwise, be lent, re-sold, hired out, or otherwise circulated without the publisher's prior consent in any form of binding or cover other than that in which it is published and without a similar condition including this condition being imposed on the subsequent purchaser.

www.miwkpublishing.com
This product was lovingly Miwk made.

Dedicated to Amelia and Hugo

C o n t e n t s

F o r e w o r d   b y
M a t   I r v i n e

The 1950s were still the very early days of television when Bernard Wilkie, and his colleague Jack Kine, created what became the BBC Visual Effects Department. It started in a somewhat mishmash way by two guys working for the Scenic Design Department producing models for schools productions and devising end captions for light entertainment shows. But this developed into what became for a fair length of time the largest special effects company in the world. Bernard and Jack almost certainly didn't envisage the way it would grow from those early days, but they were ideally placed to develop such a unit, in fact it was almost poetic. After all Jack was an artist while Bernard was an engineer; combined they were definitely the 'Leonardo da Vinci of special effects'.

When I first arrived on the scene, I had a slight similar background to Bernard's. I was very interested in conjuring at an early age and did amateur stage effects, (though I was never let near a blank-firing revolver!). Although I never took up engineering as a full time occupation, my father was an electrical engineer, so a large percentage of his influence must have rubbed off. It was Jack, as Manager of the Effects Department at that time, who gave me a chance – he took me on for a two week trial, and I stayed over 20 years – and one of the first designers I worked with, and continued to work with, was Bernard. It was not 'an apprenticeship' in the actual sense of the word, but was in practice. You learned by example – watch Bernard carefully wiring up pyrotechnics, then you were given your own chance, under his watchful eye. (These circumstances were oddly reversed many years later when Bernard had retired, but was back supervising our regular pyrotechnic training sessions. However he admitted some of his techniques were rusty and so got me to show him how it was currently done!)

Working with Bernard gave me that all-important grounding in effects, which may have occasionally come over as it we were 'making it up as we went along' (though, ahem, sometimes we were…), it was far more down to adaptability – no two effects were ever quite the same. So although experience would have taught you how to basically go about the next effect on the agenda, it could – and would – invariably chuck surprises at you – and you had to be ready for them. I remember going on location with him, with a gaggle of fellow assistants, for such programmes as *Dave Allen at Large* or *Some Mothers do 'ave 'em*, where much was built in-situ; in the middle of a field, or a wood, or on a beach, where you invariably had to improvise, so you had to make sure you always have the basic tools and materials to hand. He is often quoted as saying, 'Never go into the studio without a roll of sticky tape and a tube of Black Bostik'. Whereas the 'tape' was self-explanatory, I admit I never quite grasped the Black Bostik part as all it would do was to leak in your pocket! But what he was actually saying, and whatever the materials, was, 'Doing effects is always down to being prepared – for any eventuality.' So if it can happen, it will happen. And even if it can't possible happen – it will still happen… I think that, more than anything, held me in good stead for the rest of my effects career. Thanks, Bernard.

Mat Irvine
BBC Visual Effects Department 1971 - 1993

I n t r o d u c t i o n

In writing this book I wanted to depict what it was like to work in television when there was only one channel.

I was going to describe the primitive techniques we used, the shoestring budgets we were given – and even explain why viewers had to let their sets 'warm up' before they could get a picture. But most of all I was determined to pay tribute to the people I worked with – colleagues whose amazing talents created the finest television service in the world.

And that's where I came unstuck.

I found that I was trying to tell the stories of dozens of people and, worse still, digging up irrelevant material so that nobody would be left out. I should have seen that I was taking on an impossible task and when it became clear that the whole thing was a mess I pressed the 'Do you realise what you're doing?' button and erased the lot.

Starting afresh, I decided to restrict my story to the exploits of Jack Kine and myself believing that our work and our twenty five-year partnership would suffice to give readers some idea of what the early days were like.

It was an exciting period and Jack and I were there from the beginning. We were there when Television Centre was still only a rubbish dump and Lime Grove was as famous as Hollywood. We were the first designers to work at Ealing Studios and were certainly the first effects men ever to be employed in British television.

And there were the shows: *Monty Python*, *Quatermass*, *A Square World, Nineteen Eighty Four*, *DoctorWho* and so many, many more.

I hope this story of our adventures (and misadventures) will amuse you.

Bernard Wilkie

P u b l i s h e r ' s   N o t e

Typically when we receive a manuscript we edit and provide feedback for the author. With this book, it wasn't possible. Martin, Bernard's son, was very open to us tweaking here and there, but without Bernard here it felt wrong somehow to change his text too much. We moved some chapters around for chronological reasons and fixed some spelling mistakes, but otherwise we've left well alone.

For example, when Bernard speaks of the Daleks in the underground we suspect he's thinking of the Yeti in the underground in *The Web of Fear*. But it's always possible it relates to *Day of the Daleks* where the Daleks do indeed appear in train tunnels. Similarly *Colony in Space* and *Frontier in Space* seem to mesh into one story.

What we instead have is a carefully controlled, beautifully crafted effect with a degree of chaos behind the scenes. What could be more fitting?

T h e   M a g i c i a n ' s   T a l e

When I was eight years old my parents gave me a conjuring set for my birthday. It came in a large cardboard box and contained eight playing cards which could be manipulated to show clubs or diamonds, a magic coin tray, a ball on a string that would perform to spoken commands, a red silk handkerchief that would vanish when rubbed against a billiard ball and a magic wand in ebony black with silver tips. I had never had such a wonderful present and I loved it. I now knew what I was going to be when I grew up: I was going to be a stage magician.

Later that year my parents took me to London to see the great illusionists Maskelyne and Devant and there, for over two hours, I sat entranced by feats of wizardry undreamed of in my experience. By now I considered myself one of the fraternity and felt inordinately proud that my fellow conjurers should be capable of such brilliant showmanship. I don't know what stopped me from asking my father to take me back stage where I might introduce myself and congratulate the stars on their performance. I wished that I'd brought my magic wand and the ball that slid down a string to establish my credentials but perhaps when I grew up I would meet them and discuss magic matters on a professional level. I went home in a trance imagining the day when I too would hold an audience spellbound.

My chance came sooner than expected and my audience, hitherto limited to a row of empty dining chairs, was to become a live one and like Maskelyne and Devant I would perform on a real stage. This elevation to stardom came when our art teacher, who was seeking talent for the Christmas concert, asked our class if any of us could do anything. My hand shot up and bursting with pride I informed him that I was a conjurer. My name was quickly added to his list. He didn't bother to ask what sort of conjurer because he was the poor sod who'd drawn the short straw and would have been grateful to sign up a kid who did Long John Silver impersonations without a parrot and minus a crutch.

Apart from an appearance as a gauze-covered fairy at infants' school this would be my first public performance, but I wasn't worried. I'd seen the experts at work and knew how easy it was to captivate an audience. Wouldn't they love those magic passes with the wand and my command of the billiard ball? Even now in writing about it I squirm with embarrassment. In a sequence of events that was to be repeated throughout my life I had bitten off more than I could chew –1 lived in a dream world, not in the real one. There had been a rehearsal, but for some reason I couldn't attend and so, on the night of the show and after a brief conversation with the art teacher, I found myself on stage. I carried my box, which confidently proclaimed 'Will amaze and delight your friends' and placed it carefully on the table. I removed the lid, hitched up my sleeves and prepared to thrill my audience.

Had I thought about it, even for a second, I would have realised that card tricks performed before a crowd which stretched to the back of the hall was not a good idea. It was even less of a good idea to lay them out on a trestle table placed on a stage which itself was over four foot high. The derisory calls of 'Can't see!' from an audience whose line of sight was several feet below my trick alerted me to action. To give everyone a better view I tipped the table forward.

My box of magic slid gracefully onto the stage depositing amazing illusions all over the place and I had to leave my card trick in order to retrieve my props, some of which had finished up dangerously close to the edge of the platform. Abandoning the card tricks and half my act I brought out my string and ball trick. This had always worked well but had been left in the box with the string screwed in a bundle. I tried desperately to untangle it but my fingers had become thumbs and it took me ages to straighten it out.

I learned a lot from that experience; I learned that whatever happens in life one should never panic even when every fibre in one's body is yearning to faint and I learned that a performer should always rehearse with his props before going on stage.

It seemed to take hours but having unravelled the string I held it vertically in front of me. I explained that the ball would descend stopping and starting at my spoken command. When it refused to budge I shook it and the ball plunged to the end of the string. I think I was saying 'Abracad....' but it was difficult to hear myself above the laughter. There was only one thing for it, I had to bring out my remaining trick – the billiard ball and the handkerchief.

I was saving it for my pay-off but as my entire act seemed to be a pay-off there was nothing else I could do. Completely demoralised and desperately anxious to get off the stage, I made one last attempt to amaze and delight. Somehow I managed to retrieve a tiny bit of self-confidence and prepared to knock 'em in the aisles. The billiard ball trick consists of the ball and a silk handkerchief. The magician holds them high, showing them both clearly, then he rubs them together in his hands and Lo! The handkerchief has vanished! The magician taps the billiard ball to prove that it is solid, puts it in his pocket, bows to the audience and leaves to rapturous applause.

Milking my performance for all it was worth I completed the trick without revealing the fact that the handkerchief was stuffed into a cavity within the ball and put it, not in my pocket, but on the table. It ran forward, fell to the floor and rolled into the auditorium. A corner of the handkerchief was now protruding so that it resembled a one-eared rabbit with a painful hernia. A helpful man in the front row gathered it up and as I leapt from the stage he handed it to me and said sympathetically, 'Well done, Sonny'.

Red-faced I hurriedly returned to the stage, but when I tried to climb back found it was too high. For several seconds I scrabbled around, demolishing the art master's tasteful crepe paper bunting, until I gave up and fled to the prompt corner where a flight of wooden steps led to darkness and oblivion. Two of the masters carried away the trestle table while I gathered my tricks and in shameful humiliation and tears hid in the cloakroom. I had failed to amaze and my performance was lamentably short of delight, but I was told afterwards that people were still chuckling as they left the hall.

In the days before television, visual entertainment was confined to the cinema and the stage. But to enjoy a film we had to leave our home and (rain or shine) walk through the streets to the local 'flea pit', a concrete cavern which always smelled of disinfectant and cigarette smoke. For a stage show we went to The Hippodrome which was huge and smelled of oranges and peanuts (unless it was raining in which case the smell of wet hair overpowered all others). I was a committed cinema-goer but once a month my parents would take my brother and me to 'The Hip' where, seated on concrete tiers of frightening inclination we joined the poor people up in the gods. My family were on hard times and had we opted for real seats it would have meant foregoing the bag of peanuts – and that was unthinkable.

Having lost his two grocery shops to price-cutting competition my father could barely afford to buy the family food and therefore, taking us to The Lewisham Hippodrome once a month must have meant that he sacrificed two pints of beer and an ounce of tobacco. At the Lewisham Hippodrome and the New Cross Empire I saw most of the famous variety acts of the day. The Crazy Gang when they were individual acts, Ernie Lottinger (a master of suggestive *double entendre*, though I had not understood his jokes) and one of my favourite comedians, Leonard Henry, a stand-up comic of considerable charm. One of his visual jokes was to take a handful of white confetti from his pocket and throw it into the air. 'Snowstorm' he would announce. Then he'd reach into his other pocket and produce a handful of red confetti. Flinging it into the air he would say 'Russian Snowstorm'. I was convulsed.

Laughter didn't come easily in those grim days and my love of comedy resulted from the discovery that there were people in the theatre who really could brighten my life – and this to me was a wonderful thing. The cinema also had its laughter makers with comedians like Bob Hope, The Three Stooges, The Marx Brothers, Harold Lloyd and the incomparable Will Hay, who with Moore Marriott, Grahame Moffat and the boys of Narkover epitomised the best of British humour. Cinema or stage, I knew them all to be part of that magical world of show business and I longed to join them. I had proved that I wasn't cut out to be a performer but I felt sure there must be some other role I could play.

Had I been able to look into the future I would have seen that in years to come I would meet and know famous actors and comedians of my own generation. I would work with them, drink with them and joke with them. I would travel all over the country with them and would see places I might never have known under ordinary circumstances. In short, I was to get the perfect job in show biz; I was to become a designer of television special effects; which for someone who couldn't conjure was pretty good. Considering there were only two such jobs in the whole world it was a miracle. But before then we were all caught up in the war and even after it finished it would be seven years before I could convince the BBC that I was ideal material for television.

Six of those years were spent with BBC Engineering Research and were very pleasant, so much so that I almost abandoned my quest for a job in showbiz. But in the evenings when I watched TV the yearning re-emerged and my desire to be part of it grew ever stronger. But to relate what happened I need to return to the end of hostilities and victory in Europe.

G e r m a n y

It was 1945 and I was standing in the wings of a small German theatre holding a loaded revolver. The chambers had been filled with blanks and my finger hovered nervously around the trigger. We were into our fourth performance of *I Killed the Count* and had reached the sequence where two of the principal characters were engaged in a life and death struggle during which one would shoot the other. I heard six clicks as the actor's weapon (an old and unreliable starter's pistol) repeatedly misfired, followed by the mangled cry of 'Ouch!' which was my cue to fire the 9mm service revolver in the wings. Called upon to do this at an earlier performance I'd been disappointed by the sound from my gun, the report being deadened by the surrounding drapes. Aiming to improve things I'd hit upon the idea of discharging the barrel into an empty bucket which I'd placed on its side at the edge of the curtain. I hadn't rehearsed it, because blank cartridges were scarce, but believing this would focus the sound and enhance the effect I pulled the trigger.

There was a plop.

I could have achieved a more convincing gunshot by shouting out 'Bang!' but there was worse. To my horror the not very clean bucket began to smoke. A small blue cloud picked out in the balcony spotlight drifted across the stage. Audiences are not supposed to laugh at this point in the play, but the sight of the smoke followed by my misguided attempts to blow it away from behind the curtain caused this one to titter. When I caught my foot in the bucket and kicked it onto the stage 300 airmen roared with delight stamping their feet with an enthusiasm that would have astounded a modern pop star. The performance of the unfortunate victim clutching his stomach and slumping to the floor served only to increase their merriment and it was several minutes before anyone could return to the plot.

I admit that *I Killed the Count* was not a triumphant entry into the field of special effects, but it gave me a desire to be part of show business. I wasn't smitten with the smell of the grease paint but I was definitely hooked on the lure of the footlights – and switchboards and scenery and everything that made this such a different and fascinating way of life.

At the end of the war I had moved over to Supreme Headquarters Allied Expeditionary Force and had become part of General Eisenhower's personal staff, responsible for preparing his daily statistics and intelligence reports. In his war room it was my task to keep the war maps up to date. This was undoubtedly a 'cushy number' although not without its perils. As someone able to prepare maps and write reports I was sometimes sent ahead whenever he and SHAEF headquarters moved up.

During such forays I came under roof-top sniper attack in Frankfurt and once when sent to survey an abandoned airfield near our new headquarters I found that the safe path which had been marked out by the sappers (the army mine sweepers) had had its tapes blown away. Consequently my survey was carried out on tip-toes and in a cold sweat.

But now the war had ended and such dangers, real or implied, were over, as were my days as a flight mechanic servicing bombers and recognisance aircraft. Also behind me were my nights as an auxiliary fireman, when with two colleagues I was supposed to put out any fires that might endanger the Air Ministry buildings on Kingsway. This came about because I'd had to return to 'civvy street' for six months to work on an airfield lighting project but my joy on returning home and my old job was somewhat dampened by the fact that this assignment coincided with the height of the London Blitz. Like many millions of others I had started my service career as a young lad and finished it as a mature adult. Now, here in Germany, I was a set designer, scene-painter, carpenter and stage manager in an Air Force entertainment group inaugurated by Leigh-Mallory, our air commodore, where I was enjoying a new phase of my life.

We had established our unit in Bad Eilsen a pre-war health spa where there was a marvellous hotel and a 300-seat theatre. Even better, the hotel which had previously been the headquarters of the Whermacht, had cellars full of captured liquor stacked in bottles from floor to ceiling.

What wonderful days and nights they were. But in the parlance of the old silent movies 'Came the Dawn!' After several plays, hours of happy scene painting and the dispersal of a vast quantity of the captured alcohol, my world suddenly collapsed – I was handed my discharge papers. I was to be shipped back to England and demobilised from the Royal Air Force. This was an appalling blow. While others couldn't wait to get home I wanted to stay in Germany where I was having the time of my life. My attempt to bribe the Flight-Sergeant in charge of unit movements was unsuccessful, the offer of twenty quid and my entire cigarette ration proving too small an inducement.

'Just a few more weeks, Flight' I pleaded, 'You've only got to mislay my papers or redirect them to a unit in Italy.' But it was to no avail. Convinced I was mad or that I was involved in some shady black market racket he leaned across the desk, stamped my travel documents and held them out to me. Three days later I was back in Britain.

Along with several thousand others I was sent to Bedfordshire where the huge old airship hanger at Cardington had been converted into a demobilisation centre. It was full of stalls piled high with clothing and sheets of brown paper; it looked very like an East End market. We were allowed to choose what we wanted and I selected a gravy-brown suit, a mauve overcoat and a fawn trilby hat. With these exotic garments packed in a large cardboard box tied with string I travelled to my parents' home in Surrey.

Fortunately I wouldn't have to look for employment as I was returning to my original job of engineering draughtsman at the Air Ministry. This had always been interesting work, but now, with the end of the war there was little call for new airfield lighting. I had nothing to do, a fact that did not dismay my superiors because their own status depended on the number of civil servants they controlled. Any loss of staff would have jeopardised their positions. It was a frustrating time, but with so little to occupy our days my colleagues and I spent most of our time in the pubs around Waterloo and Fleet Street. This way of life continued unchallenged for almost two years.

In those days the pubs had to close during the afternoons so when I wasn't sleeping off a boozy lunchtime across my drawing board I would wander around London's theatres hoping to get a glimpse of a real stage through an open scene dock.

Then something happened which changed everything.

The BBC's Engineering Research Department had moved from its war-time base in Oxfordshire to a redundant nunnery in Balham but this building proved too small and the Beeb had searched for a larger one. They found it in Kingswood, Surrey and this, since my family had been bombed out of London, was our new home. The BBC had chosen an old manor house called Kingswood Warren which in pre-war days had been used as a school and then later as an insurance company. Now it stood empty and the agents were anxious to sell it.

The Warren was ideal. It had large pleasant grounds, adequate laboratory and office accommodation and suitable peace and quiet in which to conduct sensitive experiments. I would have known nothing of this had I not read an article about it in my local paper. It sounded enticing and so I wrote asking for an interview.

Because I lived in Kingswood I was regarded as someone who might know his way around the district and was quickly offered a post of development draughtsman. I spent a short time in the nunnery in Balham before I was moved to the Warren where I was given a drawing board in an office overlooking immaculate lawns and Cedar trees and was also given a place to park my bike. This was much more convenient than commuting to London every day. It was a happy period of lotus eating and tranquillity and I was to enjoy it for six years. We played cricket in the lunch hour and tennis in the evenings and while, at the end of a working day my colleagues had to walk to the railway station or drive to London my journey took five minutes on two wheels.

But eventually, after six years of drawing wiring diagrams and component layouts, I grew restless. The BBC had a policy of advertising all its job vacancies internally in order that staff could move around and take advantage of fresh opportunities and in those days management kept employees informed of vacancies by pinning a list of jobs to office notice boards. At first I didn't read them as I was perfectly happy where I was, but as the years passed I began to study them with growing interest. There were vacancies in television, but as I didn't know where I would fit in I could only wait and hope that a job would turn up which I felt I could do.

In the end, enticed by the prospect of working once again in show business, I began sending off applications whenever I thought my credentials faintly matched those asked for. But I was never even selected for an interview. I grew desperate. I was so determined now to leave engineering that I treated my applications as a lottery and would send off an application form just to see if I got a response. Later in my

BBC career I would sit on interviewing boards and saw how impossible it was for an inexperienced hopeful to compete with those already doing the work.

In the end, as I collected more and more rejection slips, I started to apply for jobs that were wildly outside my experience until eventually these tactics upset my local management. I was told that my applications were regarded as frivolous and time wasting and that if I didn't stop sodding about I would be asked to seek employment elsewhere. Fortunately, however, the BBC being genuinely paternalistic decided that my keenness merited a special interview.

Told about this I was over the moon, but there was a penalty clause: should I fail to impress the examining board I had to agree to stay at Kingswood, possibly for the rest of my career. Despite this forbidding footnote it was wonderful news and I had no doubt that I could impress the examiners. I went over and over my CV. I had been responsible for 'noises off' (I called them 'sound effects') in *I Killed the Count,* I had designed and made scenery for at least four stage shows. I was the inventor of 'The Book', a unit of portable scenery used when we toured Germany – and there was so much more.

As it turned out I was extremely fortunate. Interviewed by a sympathetic and friendly board (the members of which, apparently, knew even less about television than I did), I triumphed. 'What television needs,' I remember saying, 'is a new form of back-projection.' which was a pretty smart assertion from someone who had never seen a back projection unit in his life. They liked it and wrote a report suggesting that I should be interviewed by Richard Levin, the Head of Television Design. This was the chance I'd been hoping for all along and, surely, if I'd managed to convince a board of five I could do even better with just one person. But then of course I hadn't met Richard Levin. Intoxicated with my own brilliance I dreamed away the two long weeks I was forced to wait and dying to get to my appointment. But eventually the fateful day arrived and wearing my best suit and carrying a posh leather brief case I caught a bus to Shepherds Bush.

The Interview

I had never been to Television Centre so I had no idea what it looked like or even where it was and when I looked it up in the *London A to Z* it was shown only as a large space called White City. There was a stadium nearby which I knew to be a dog track, but in 1954 the main building of Television Centre had yet to be built.

When the bus reached Shepherds Bush I got off at The Green, a triangle of grass in an otherwise unrelieved landscape of buildings and tarmac. The bus would have taken me on to White City, but because I was early I thought I'd take a look around.

The first thing I noticed were the male and female public lavatories, one double block on each corner of the triangular green. Six public toilets in such a small area seemed incredibly civilised, but apart from a super-sufficiency of loos post-war Shepherds Bush had little to recommend it. Newspapers and empty beer bottles littered the streets while the shops looked run down and in need of paint. A dingy pub which had its doors open to ventilate the previous night's fug of stale beer and tobacco smoke looked about as enticing as a redundant tram shed. This was very different from the pleasant country pubs around Kingswood Warren.

I hadn't slept well the night before because I had lain awake rehearsing my opening lines. 'Oh yes sir', I was going to say, 'I've designed dozens of stage sets – and I've painted scenery.' a great opening gambit in the small hours of the morning, but now, walking towards The Centre it sounded pathetic. What was that great introduction I'd thought of the previous evening? Oh bugger! Why hadn't I written it down? Not as sure of myself now as I had been when I'd boasted to my colleagues that I was about to join television, I felt my confidence oozing away. Slowly and thoughtfully I walked up Wood Lane.

If Shepherds Bush Green looked sordid the huge site at White City seemed even worse: it was a tip. The BBC had chosen it as an ideal location for its new television service because it was large and empty and in London but on that day no hint of what the architects had in mind was even remotely apparent to me. The thirteen acre site had remained undeveloped since the original Franco-British exhibition of 1908.

I almost walked past the entrance which, unbelievably, was under a railway arch, but by following the direction of an arrow crudely painted on a board I found a new concrete roadway. To the left was a strange elevated railway station supported on tall wooden poles and although a flight of steps led up to the platform it didn't appear to be in use. This was weird – in fact the whole place was weird, because to my right was a long facade of decaying, but still quite elegant plaster work that must have been a main entrance to the aptly named 'White City'. Behind it was a huge rubbish dump – a vast area of ground littered with old beds, motor tyres, prams and heaven knows what else. Rising above all this stood a mouldering plaster pagoda, several corrugated iron buildings in the final stages of decrepitude and a pile of wooden cable drums.

However, there was no doubt that I had come to the right place because ahead of me was a magnificent new brick building with high scenery doors, a loading bay and a temporary car park. This, I later discovered, was called the Scenery Block.

If the building was impressive the main reception certainly was not. Pushing open a teak and glass door I found myself in a tiny stair well manned by a uniformed commissionaire sitting in a cubicle the size of a small wardrobe. He leant on a counter which was just big enough to accommodate his *Daily Mirror* and a telephone. He asked my business and I told him that I had an appointment with Mr Richard Levin. He fished under the counter and brought out a ledger, then, sucking his pen he carefully entered my name and my time of arrival. He then invited me to take a seat on the settee placed with its back against the staircase.

There was already another visitor sitting there and I dropped down beside him. To my astonishment, I saw that this chap was Raymond Huntley, a well-known movie actor. I couldn't believe it; within a minute or two of arrival I was sitting next to a famous actor. He had crossed one leg over the other and I was shocked to see a large hole in the sole of his shoe; perhaps this acting lark wasn't as well paid as I'd been led to believe. Facing the settee were two very smart new Otis lifts and as one of them opened Raymond Huntley and I both looked up; it was Richard Levin's secretary who had come to take me upstairs. She was a lovely girl and just what I imagined an executive's personal assistant would look like. Ushering me into her office she offered me a chair and asked if I would like a coffee. At that moment I could have murdered a cup of coffee but I was too tense to accept. This for me was make or break time and I needed to concentrate. She went into an adjoining room and had a quiet conversation with an unseen person whom I took to be Richard Levin the legendary Head of Design but I heard only a faint mumble of sound through the communicating door; then the girl emerged and called me in.

Levin's office was large, tastefully lit and expensively furnished. In the centre was a large black leather-topped desk appointed with a gold pen set and a large executive leather bound blotter on which had been placed a green folder; there were no files, papers or in and out trays. He sat in a tall black leather swivel chair with his head tipped back and as he looked at me through his glasses I noticed that his eyes blinked continually. He didn't get up, didn't smile and, as far as I can recall didn't offer to shake hands; he merely invited me to sit facing him on the opposite side of the desk. Taking his time he opened the green folder, studied it for a minute and then came straight to the point. Still blinking he said: 'I see you want to become a set designer.'

Had he asked me that question anywhere else – say, in a tea queue or on top of the Empire State building I would have given him a confident reply, but here in his office where the walls were hung with bronze framed original costume and stage designs for the Royal Opera House, Saddlers Wells and, for all I knew, La Scala Milan I realised I'd be pushing my luck to seek work as a lavatory cleaner. He pointed to my brief case and asked, 'What examples have you brought to show me?' What examples? Oh Sweet Jesus, why had I brought the bloody brief case? Almost paralysed with embarrassment I produced my two stage designs, a couple of awful daubs entitled '*Aladdin* – the Cave Scene'. Handing them across the desk I watched the space between his eyebrows narrow in pain. He passed them back without a word. For a full minute he sat in dreadful silence, then passing his hand across his forehead as if to expunge the memory, he asked me about my work in the Research Department. This was a subject I'd hoped to avoid, not because I wasn't a competent engineer, but because all my hopes were pinned on getting into showbiz and miles away from nuts and bolts. But he pressed me. 'Do you know anything about fibre glass?'

In 1954 fibre glass was in its early stages of development and was being used mainly in the construction of hand-built car bodies. Few people knew anything about it – and I knew less than few people. Nevertheless I realised that at all costs I must prolong the interview and to have admitted ignorance would have brought our meeting to a close – so naturally I said 'Yes'.

When I say I knew nothing about fibre glass I had once read a magazine article in a barber's shop which briefly outlined the technology. Now I struggled to recall what it had said. Strangely, however, Levin didn't question me. He simply said, 'Good, I've got a representative from a plastics company coming here this afternoon and I'd like you to meet him. Be here at two o'clock please'.

Dismissed, I found myself in the corridor clutching a briefcase and wondering what the hell I'd done. I just couldn't believe I'd been so stupid. My first thought was to flee leaving a message to say I'd been taken ill, but then I reconsidered. It was just possible that even with my minuscule knowledge I might still be able to handle the situation. Could I contact anyone who knew anything about fibre glass? I had less than two hours to affect a miracle. And then I remembered the library. On my way through Hammersmith Broadway I'd seen a building with a stone lintel over the entrance incised with the words 'Hammersmith Public Library' – surely there they would have books about fibre glass. I ran downstairs and caught a bus to the Broadway.

The librarian was extremely helpful and produced a pile of books on modern plastics which he laid out on a table. Opening them one after another I found to my delight that fibre glass had been well covered in two of them. There were detailed descriptions of its composition, its moulding techniques and even a range of applications – exactly what I wanted. Taking a sheet of paper from my briefcase I made notes. My strategy was to memorise certain key phrases and technical terms which I could trot out in conversation. Even a superficial understanding of the process would do because, armed with a little knowledge, I felt sure I could bluff my way through the meeting. I jotted down terms like 'reduced setting times', 'preferred ambient temperatures' and 'single application, multi-purpose, release agents'. I listed materials which sounded important, such as 'woven strands', 'chopped mat' and 'random lay' until my paper (which I noticed with little regret, was the back of '*Aladdin* – the cave scene') was full.

At two o'clock I was back in the secretary's office prepared to meet the sales rep. Although Richard Levin hadn't told me why he was so interested in fibre glass he explained his purpose to the salesman. His intention was to investigate the possibility of using fibre glass for the production of lightweight scenery. Television designers at that time were forced to use film studio techniques in which three dimensional scenic items and large props were constructed of timber and plaster, which made them extremely heavy. This was fine in a film studio where sets are semi-permanent, but in the TV studio where sometimes items had to be moved in and out during a live performance anything heavy was a blinding encumbrance. Levin had realised the need for lightweight items which could be moved quickly and quietly, an inspiration which was to prove almost revolutionary.

The sales rep, who was very anxious to clinch a deal with the BBC, set out to explain everything in detail, but because Levin had introduced me as 'our expert' the man knew I was the one to impress. Suddenly I was no longer the unspeakable painter of dog's excrement, but a powerful player in an important game. Nodding sagely I let him run on about his company's products until I judged it right to intervene; I shot a question: 'What are the gelling characteristics?' He responded quickly with a technical reply that I didn't understand (I didn't even understand the question) so I cut in again. 'Yes I know that would affect the working times' (whoops, Wilkie! Don't overplay your hand.) 'And what release agents would you recommend for untreated plaster moulds?' This was getting better and better. I was now totally in command. It was a confidence trick that amazed even me. Levin was certainly impressed because he'd stopped blinking.

An hour later and after the ecstatic salesman had left with an order for a substantial trial batch Levin became more confidential: 'Look', he said, 'If you agree, I'd like to arrange for you to come here on a three month special attachment. I need someone to set up an experimental fibre glass workshop. Would you be willing to do that?'
Would I be willing to do that? I nearly leapt across the desk and kissed him. That afternoon I floated home on the bus, my head full of wonderful dreams. I knew Research wouldn't block my attachment

because it came from the top. But I couldn't believe my incredible luck. I'd gone to Television Centre hoping to get a job as a junior scenic design assistant third class and I was going home with a special assignment to set up a whole new department. This wasn't a bus – it was The Orient Express and from its windows I could see that Shepherds Bush looked quite beautiful.

J o i n i n g   T e l e v i s i o n

Dreaming the final days away at Kingswood Warren, my new department at Television Centre had grown in my imagination to such an extent that by the time I bought my colleagues a farewell drink the fibre glass section had become a suite of workshops and offices. Levin had implied that he wanted me to create a fibre glass unit and that was what I was going to do. But I would need a free hand of course. I was looking forward to our next meeting at which I would outline my plans. He would send for coffee and nice little biscuits and we would discuss the future. Dreams fade in the morning light but mine grew stronger and so, dressed again in my best suit, I made the journey to the Centre. This time I knew where I was going and although I was early I went straight to reception.

There was a different chap on the desk but it didn't matter. I told him who I was and explained that I wanted to see Richard Levin. 'I'm going to work here.' I explained. He didn't comment but brought out the ledger and ran his finger down the page. Then he looked at the previous page and the one before that but my name didn't appear anywhere. He asked me to wait a moment while he phoned someone who might know something. However, after several phone calls, each producing a negative response, he was no wiser and his brow was looking decidedly furrowed. I began to wonder if I'd got the right day. In the end I decided to go up to Levin's office and sort things out myself; the commissionaire seemed relieved and went back to his newspaper.

I knocked on the door of the outer office but the secretary with the dazzling smile wasn't there; instead there was a different girl who asked me what I wanted. Only slightly nonplussed I explained who I was and said that I wanted to see Richard Levin. 'He's not here.' she said: 'He's on holiday and I'm only a temp. I'm afraid I don't know much of what's going on – my job is to answer the phone and take messages. Do you know where you have to report?' I didn't. She looked concerned. 'Oh dear. Do you think you could wander around and try and find someone? Most of the designers are on this floor, perhaps one of them can help.'

From being slightly nonplussed I was now very nonplussed. My earlier self-confidence befitting the head of a new department had evaporated and my managerial swagger had become an apologetic limp. Wandering along a corridor I found several people who, when I'd explained my predicament, did their best to help but unfortunately all they could do was to pass me on to somebody else who turned out to know less than they did. Worse still was when they suggested that I go to a certain office where 'someone there would be sure to know' because when I did manage to find the place the 'someone' didn't have a clue or the office turned out to be a store room. I must have heard the word 'sorry' a thousand times.

Totally deflated now, I decided to take a break and seeing a lady wheeling a refreshment trolley I bought a coffee and a cheese roll. Balancing the plate on a radiator I was forced to eat the cheese roll with one hand while holding the china cup in the other. It was all very undignified and people looked at me as they went back and forth along the corridor. Having consumed the roll and coffee I felt better. Hiding the empty cup and plate behind a door I went back to reception. I remembered that somewhere on the ground floor I'd seen an entrance which led to the workshops – perhaps I'd have better luck there.

I found it without difficulty because on the double doors it had a large sign which bore the stern warning 'Workshop Area. No access to unauthorised persons' so I went in. Beyond the door was the carpenters' shop, (well, it wasn't so much a shop as a sizable factory). I was immediately on familiar ground, reunited with the magical sounds and smells of the scenic workshop in Germany. I paused and looked around savouring the heady aroma of fresh sawdust, glue, size and paint. I heard the friendly sounds of circular saws and routing machines – and men whistling as they went about their work. But I'd been spotted lurking by the door and an irate workshop manager came across and wanted to know what I was doing there. This area was subject to a strict 'No visitors' rule, he told me, because of the dangerous machinery; he wanted to know why I had just walked through a door clearly marked 'No Entry to Unauthorised Persons'. I apologised and told him my story. To my amazement he knew all about me.

'Ah, you must be the chap who's going to work with Alfie Hilburn. We've put your stuff in there.' He led me to a room at the far end of the workshop where he showed me my grand new department – a wooden bench in one corner of the plaster shop. I couldn't believe it; Good God! Was this it, was this my new department?

The workshop manager, misinterpreting my impersonation of a poleaxed cow, assumed my look to be one of professional appraisal and introduced me to a little man in a brown dust-coat. This was Alfie Hilburn who I was told was the Master Plasterer. I didn't know what a master plasterer should look like but Alfie was small, bespectacled with thinning hair brushed straight back and in his brown work coat he looked more like a clerk in a railway parcel office. Although at the time he was just another face among the many I'd seen that morning, Alfie was later to become a true friend and one of the nicest men I've known. He had spent a lifetime in the film industry and was an expert in every form of plaster work, something that I was going to be very, very grateful for in the months ahead. From the start he treated me not as an unwanted intruder in his domain, but as a person with whom he would be pleased to share his working days – and he was already taking care of me.

The various tins and boxes that had been delivered by the plastics company had been neatly stacked below the bench and to these Alfie had added some useful items from his own supply. Foreseeing my need for disposable paper cups and rubber buckets which could be cleansed of even solid materials, he'd placed these alongside a small pile of clean rags, a couple of paint brushes and some old newspapers. The workshop manager left after telling me that Alfie would show me where things were. When he'd gone I explained to Alfie that Richard Levin had asked me to create a fibre glass unit and told him what I was hoping to achieve – although it didn't sound so grand now. I thanked him for his kindness in providing a space for me and the newspapers and things but this, I explained loftily, was only temporary because when Levin returned the whole thing would be sorted out.

Still trying to maintain the demeanour of an expert I selected a few tins and bottles at random and unwrapped them on the bench. To my relief I noticed that while none of them carried instructions they did give tables of measurements and quantities for mixing, which was all I needed to know: I was ready to experiment. Borrowing a screwdriver from Alfie I prised the lid from a large canister of resin and reaching across to lay the lid on the bench promptly resined the sleeve of my best suit. Sympathetically Alfie helped me scrape the sticky mess from the fabric, but it would need more than that. He asked what we should use as a solvent. I hadn't a bloody clue. Alfie saw through my posturing at that moment and going to a metal cupboard produced several cans of fluid which we tried in turn.

My best suit had clearly become my worst suit but this being my first day in television I'd worn it because I wanted to look like a manager. Alfie took a much laundered brown dust-coat from his cupboard and suggested that from then on I should wear it whenever I was working. He was right of course, but wearing it made me feel awful. The white coats worn by the scientists and engineers at Kingswood Warren showed their superior status – brown coats were for people who swept floors and cleaned sinks. I vowed that before the month was out I would buy myself a white coat.

A   T r o u b l e s o m e   C o l u m n

Although he must have known I was working downstairs Richard Levin didn't visit me for three weeks. By now I had learned to mix epoxy resin without smearing it all over my clothes and had successfully reproduced items from Alfie's plaster moulds. These moulds were intended primarily for papier mâché, a material then widely used for making scenic items such as rock-faces, brickwork and tiled roofs. But when used for papier mâché their surfaces had to be smeared liberally with Vaseline, a substance that fiercely rejected the release agents I needed for fibre glass. Alfie cleansed them with turps and handed me pristine moulds that I could work with. I think he saw that the new technology would inevitably replace his own but was willing to make sacrifices in the cause of progress. Nevertheless his unselfish attitude was quite unusual and I certainly had cause to appreciate it.

By then I had produced a number of lightweight items to order including a couple of decorative panels for a set designer who became my first customer and the one responsible for my work being seen for the first time on television. My conceit must have been insufferable in those days. I spent hours in the local pub trying to steer the conversation round to yesterday's television and the opportunity to mention, quite by way of chance you understand, that I had made those two large panels that so enhanced the set. Unfortunately it was an afternoon programme and nobody had seen it.

These tentative explorations into the theory and practice of fibre glass lay-ups did not impress Richard Levin because when he eventually deigned to see me I asked him if he had seen the schools set which featured my two panels. He didn't answer, presumably expecting an explanation. I hurried to tell him that I had made the two fibre glass panels that had been attached to the flats. He looked at me as if I'd accused him of walking through Shepherds Bush with his flies open so I changed tack. I showed him other things I'd made, little things that were my early test pieces but he dismissed them out of hand. 'I want you to make an eight foot column.' he told me – and went away. I could see I was going to have to get used to this man. In the Research Department I was accustomed to having long discussions before embarking on a project, but here things were obviously different. Levin's instant requirements had to be met with instant fulfilment.

Production of a mould for an eight foot column was quite beyond me. For starters where would I find an eight foot column from which I could take a mould? Fortunately Alfie came to my rescue yet again. Explaining a technique used in the film industry he showed me how we could make a plaster of Paris column by turning it on a length of heavy steel pipe in the fashion of a lathe. This would produce a master complete with capitol and base in plaster. From this we would then be able to make a two piece mould in which we could reproduce a shell copy of the column in fibre glass. I could see what he meant but I was worried that this process would be terribly slow. Plaster takes a long time to dry and in this instance looked as if it would need about a year, give or take a long hot summer and I sensed that Richard Levin would not be pleased. Small items can be dried in a hot oven, but eight feet of something we weren't even going to be able to lift off the bench would have to dry naturally in its own sweet time.

Two days later Levin came again. He wanted to know when he could expect his column. My explanations were accepted but not sympathetically. Frowning and blinking he went away again.

During the next days I too fumed and fretted suggesting to Alfie all manner of absurd ways in which we could speed up the evaporation including, I seem to remember, lighting a fire underneath and turning the column like a carcase on a spit. Countless buckets of water had been used to create that master and all those buckets of water weren't going to evaporate overnight. With nothing practical to do I made a few more small objects but with little enthusiasm. Until that wretched column was dry and a two-piece mould made (more hours of drying) I felt useless.

To pass the time I experimented with the materials, mixing different compounds of chemical accelerator with different grades of resin. At one time I must have overdone it because the contents of a rubber bucket suddenly became dangerously hot. Choking white fumes floating around the workshop alerted me to the fact that I should dispose of this stuff without delay. Grabbing the bucket handle I ran coughing to the ring road where I emptied a chunk of smoking plastic onto the concrete roadway. It crackled and fumed and smoking bits flew off in all directions. Because the weather was mild the tall outer doors of the main workshop had been folded back allowing the carpenters and painters to have a glimpse of the world outside. These chaps were able to watch my antics as I pranced around kicking the pieces into the gutter. And that was how I first met Jack Kine.

Jack was a scenic artist and that afternoon was applying some exotic finishing touches to one of the sets. It wasn't often that the scenic artists had to work directly on the flats, but they were brought in whenever the work required a certain level of skill. Normally the painting of sets was the responsibility of the scene painters, but their work was limited to simple applications of paint and minor ancillary treatments. But let me explain the system of scenic production from raw timber to the finished set:

First of all the various scenic flats were constructed from drawings – this was the work of the machinists and carpenters. When the flats were finished they were numbered on the back, labelled with the name of the programme and studio for which they were intended and put on trolleys. The next step was to wheel them across the workshop to the setting floor where they would be erected and assembled in the arrangement they would take in the studio. Here the painters would work on them, papering, graining, varnishing and, if required, ageing them or dirtying them. Finally such things as door furniture, cornices and papier mâché panelling were added. But when special art work was required it was the task of the scenic artists to add the finishing touches.

That afternoon Jack, perched on the top rungs of some aluminium steps, was working on a painted tapestry. From his position above the top of the flats he was able to see my flight from the plaster shop and my futile attempts to disperse the smoking resin. He climbed down and came outside to take a closer look. I don't know what he said, but he helped me kick the pieces into the gutter. He discovered, as I had done, that hot epoxy resin sticks to leather shoes and if you attempt to remove it while it is active your fingers get burnt. I said I was sorry and went back to the plaster shop. He returned to his ladder, sucking his thumb and looking ruefully at his shoes.

From then on whenever we met we would chat briefly, passing the time of day and commenting on the weather. On one occasion while we waited for the tea trolley he showed me a photograph of a model ship he'd built and I saw what a superb craftsman he was. I told him so, adding that it was a beautiful model – and I meant it.

Every morning when I arrived in the plaster shop I would feel the column. I felt it on top and underneath and I probed the inside and tested it with tissue paper – but it was always damp. Then, one morning, after what seemed a million years it was dry enough to absorb a coat of sealant. Alfie had already felt it and agreed with me that it was dry enough to work on and so, fired with anticipation, we prepared to make the two female moulds.

I hadn't worked on anything this big before, but it was small beer to Alfie who had made things much, much bigger in his film studio days.

He took on the responsibility of making the two-piece mould, which fortunately ensured its success. I admired his expertise although I was chafing at the time it all took. Once again we had to endure several days of 'drying time'. The final replica of the column didn't need to dry out as fibre glass cures itself in a matter of hours. All I had to do now was to fasten the two halves together and sandpaper the seams so that they didn't show up as flash marks. Finally we gave the finished column a coat of stone-coloured paint.

There was no point now in trying to hurry things, but it took almost another two days before the sanding, filling and painting was finished and the eight foot column stood dry and erect on the workshop floor. I could see now that with the seams carefully sanded and the whole thing resplendent in its final coat of paint it looked good. Tapering slightly towards the top and fitted with its capitol and base it was a column to be proud of and I knew that Alfie felt as pleased as I did. We had, after all, created something unique – the first ever item of lightweight scenery for television. I phoned Levin.

Seconds later he swept through the door. He had few words for me, however his eyes went straight to the column. He walked forward, gave it a tentative fireman's lift and nearly fell over backwards. If I was delighted, he was ecstatic. He stood beaming at it with an expression that could only be described as besotted. This was the fibre glass scenery he'd been hoping for and with this single item scenery production had taken a huge leap into the future.

Eventually he was prepared to talk. He wanted to know how the two halves had been welded together without showing the join and how long it would take to produce more of the same – and so on. He told me that he intended to show it firstly to his designers and then to the heads of other departments. I think he saw himself performing a weight-lifting act in front of the Director General. I assumed he meant to display it in the workshop but not a bit of it. This column was Levin's baby and he wasn't going to be parted from it. Swinging it onto his shoulder like the bloke with the iron girder in the old Guinness advert he ordered Alfie to hold the door open, then beaming with delight he carried it upstairs to his office. For days afterwards he could be seen carrying it everywhere, even, I was told, into the loo.

My reputation restored I was once again the blue-eyed boy, but my three months attachment was coming to an end and I was desperate to prolong it. The idea of returning to Kingswood Warren was unthinkable but clearly my usefulness to Richard Levin had declined and now that I'd made the column what more could I do, except produce more of the same? I considered turning out other items of scenery, but this would have been merely a variation on a theme; that column looked like finishing my TV career. It had taken Levin no time at all to convince everyone that fibre glass was the 'new material' and that the Design Department should now set up a full production unit. I was the obvious candidate to run it but, desperate as I was to remain at Television Centre, I saw that this would be a politically fatal move. A permanent post it might be and a most inviting foot in the door, but I didn't see myself as a workshop foreman. I wanted the footlights and the chance to meet actors. I asked Levin if I might have another meeting with him, suggesting that I had 'some new ideas'. I had judged it well; Levin loved new ideas and seemed intrigued by the possibility that I might have other tricks up my sleeve. Agreeing to my request he arranged to see me the following week.

This gave me the opportunity to come up with something new. Fibre glass would be a hard act to follow, but I had to think of something. For hours I thought and thought – something must come to me before I turned up in his office. But what I didn't know was that Richard Levin was already making plans for my future. Meanwhile I desperately continued racking my brains.

A Visit to Lime Grove

With nothing constructive to do now that the fibre glass column was finished I thought I'd take a look around Lime Grove. It seems strange, but in the weeks I'd been working at Television Centre I had not once set foot in a TV studio. Now I would visit The Grove and see for myself the place where the programmes were made and routed to the transmitters. With a feeling of anticipation bordering on excitement I set off for the studios. Television Centre and Lime Grove Studios were just over a quarter of a mile apart and although the route was bisected by the busy Uxbridge Road it was an easy walk from one to the other. In those days I used to go to the the White Horse for lunch, a large and pleasant pub near the market which served good beer, sandwiches and pies. Leaning on the bar and listening to the conversation of people around me I realised that other members of BBC Television went there too, but I was too much of a new boy to recognise any of them.

As a member of staff I was permitted to enter BBC premises anywhere in the country and during my six years in engineering I had already visited Broadcasting House, The Langham Hotel, Bush House and several of the transmitter sites around the country; now I was about to add Lime Grove to the list. I knew what the building looked like because pictures of the main entrance were screened night after night on the box as viewers were shown famous people going in and out and celebrities with shiny limousines being greeted by commissionaires in smart uniforms. The Grove was the nearest thing to Hollywood that Britain possessed and although it lacked the searchlights and the police holding back the crowds I felt proud that it belonged to the BBC.

Lime Grove, once the home of Gainsborough Pictures, had produced movies every bit as celebrated as those made by other famous British studios such as Ealing, Pinewood and Elstree – and now I was going to see it for myself. I was about to enter the studios where so many of the films my boyhood chums and I had paid sixpence to see (one shilling and sixpence and a bar of chocolate if any of us were trying to impress a new girlfriend). I walked down Lime Grove and there it was! A huge building in a street of suburban houses. I could see the line of shiny cars parked alongside the kerb and there was the commissionaire moving to and fro outside. I slowed my pace wanting to take it all in, then, not wishing to appear like some gawping peasant I got to the entrance doors and swept inside.

The reception area was far bigger and posher than the one in Television Centre and it had a much grander reception desk. Instead of a solitary commissionaire and his *Daily Mirror* there were three beautiful girls who could have come straight out of *Cosmopolitan* or *Harper's Bazaar*. At that moment they were all engaged in telephone conversations and with beautifully manicured hands they wrote in smart appointment books. Occasionally one would call across to the people sitting in the chairs around the walls with such messages as: 'Mr Onasis would you please go to the press suite', 'Your Grace, they're waiting for you in make-up'. It was the 'busy scene' from a thousand Hollywood movies. As one phone was replaced on its cradle another would be picked up. Standing at the desk I tried to look important and glanced at my watch, but it made no difference; their experience enabled them to judge a person at a glance and my plum coloured fifty shilling suit obviously put me at the lower end of the scale – if not off it altogether.

Eventually, two of the phones stayed silent long enough for one of the girls to notice me. With a voice straight from the deep-freeze she asked me what I wanted. I said I wanted to look around. Bateman with his cartoons of 'The man who sat in the oldest member's chair at The Carlton Club' could not have captured the look on that girl's face – all of their faces in fact, because they all seemed to hear my response. My girl looked at the other two in disbelief. 'You want to look around?' she asked incredulously. Her voice had changed from cut glass to Dame Edith Evans in *The Importance of Being Earnest*. 'You want to look around?!' By now even those sitting in the chairs behind me were beginning to take an interest. They sensed that they were about to witness someone being dragged away by the police. As the commissionaire moved across to cut off my retreat I explained that I had just started work in Design Department and because I needed to know the layout of the studios 'and I, er, wanted to look around please'. She waved me to an empty chair and, after a fiercely whispered conversation with the other girls, telephoned someone. These were the days before we were issued with identity cards and the only way she could confirm my story was for her to phone someone in authority. At that time Lime Grove was constantly under siege. Reporters hoping to get celebrity interviews, agents trying to promote their clients, lunatics intent upon destroying this instrument of the devil and viewers who had written plays or wanted to submit their ideas jostled for space on the pavement outside with bus-loads of autograph hunters. And all these had to be recognised and separated from the politicians, actors and celebrities who came to appear in programmes. Until that moment, I gathered, the receptionists had never encountered anyone who wanted to 'look around'.

Eventually I was summoned back to the desk and told that I *could* go into the building but that I must *not* enter any of the studios, nor any of the other areas that I was hoping to see. I must not approach actors or impede anyone working anywhere, but I was free to use the canteen. The direction of its location and the rules for using it were spelled out to me and, watched by the people in the chairs, I slunk off. Going through the opening by the reception desk I turned right but a commissionaire stepped in front of me. 'Not that way. That's the Hexecutive Suite!' he bellowed in a voice that could be heard in the street outside and I saw flecks of saliva around his mouth. Like a character in a Whitehall farce, I walked backwards swivelling clumsily and exiting down the other corridor.

Lime Grove was always a dark place. Subterranean corridors sparsely illuminated by naked bulbs or inadequate and dirty fluorescent tubes were occasionally lit by thin shafts of daylight filtering down the iron staircases that served as fire escapes from the studios above. No one down below was able to tell whether it was cloudy or sunny but you did know when it was raining because everything in the basement dripped, even the light fittings. Conditions in that corridor seemed more akin to those of a Victorian prison than the centre of electronic entertainment and yet this was the main thoroughfare to some of the offices and ancillary buildings. I'm convinced there were places in that corridor that had never been seen by human eye, but this was the way to the canteen so I followed the instructions I had been given. Above head height, but only just, were pipes, tubes and conduits that would have made the Pompidou Centre look like a billiard table. Of every diameter and description they hung from the ceiling on dusty iron supports. I could see daylight at the end of the corridor but before I'd gone that far I came across a lift which, from its location, I assumed was the one that passed through reception. I'd seen its doors open and close a dozen times while I had been waiting and I'd noticed that while the outer door and facia were relatively modern, the lift was antique with folding lattice doors and big brass press buttons for up and down. I decided to forego the gastronomic delights in the canteen and go on a tour of the building – after all, that's what I'd come for. I pressed the button on the wall, but then I remembered that the lift was controlled by an attendant and not wanting to meet up with anyone in authority I dived up the staircase that surrounded it.

In its heyday Lime Grove was the film studio where my favourite comedian, Will Hay had made all those wonderful comedies – or so I believed at the time. Later I found out that he'd also made films at Islington and Ealing, but now, as I climbed the stairs I gently caressed the handrail wondering if traces of his fingerprints survived somewhere along its length. Will Hay died from cancer in 1949 but I like to think that had he lived he might have appeared on television – and I might have met him.

I went to the top floor intending to work my way downwards, but not far from the lift I found two studios, one of which, despite having all the lights on and its scene doors wide open was obviously empty. Looking round to see if anyone had spotted me I went in. It was magic. Not since my days in the German theatre at Bad Eilsen had I felt like this. Multiple banks of lights hung from the ceiling while around the walls were neatly stacked bunches of scene braces and stage weights. This was Studio E and I couldn't foresee the future where this was the studio I would spend hours and hours of my future working life. At the far end of the studio I noticed the control room. It was a very modest affair raised just a few feet above the level of the studio floor, but I'd never seen a control room before and it looked very grand and highly technical. The multi-coloured pilot lights showed that the equipment was switched on and I could see the monitors behind the huge sheet of plate glass that looked across the studio floor; it seemed to me like the bridge of a ship. Concerned that someone might come in and ask me what I was doing I left and went back to the stairs. Opposite Studio E was Studio D but the doors were shut and the iron levers on the outside (which sealed the studio against noise) were firmly in the closed position. I carried on down. On the way I passed Studio G which was also closed and a red light outside was on – which I assumed meant they were recording a programme. I tiptoed back to the Victorian prison and found my way to the canteen. It had been an exciting introduction to the hub of the industry and, despite the fact that the only studio I had been in had been bare, I was more determined than ever to get a permanent job in television. I wanted to walk into those studios unafraid and unchallenged – to be accepted as part of the establishment and to be on first name terms with those gorgeous girls in reception.

C o m i n g   T o g e t h e r

For once ideas did not come and with only a couple of days to go I was still desperately trying to think of a scheme to impress Richard Levin. A great deal of my inspirational thinking was done on the Green Line coach because these new vehicles with their improved design were meant to give passengers a quiet, comfortable environment markedly different from a London bus. The trouble was that the cloistered comfort would send me to sleep and I would awake somewhere in the Tooting area (where I had to change to the bus) with my notebook unused, my pen on the floor and dribble down my coat.

But not now. With only forty eight hours left time was too short. I sucked my pen and stared out of the window – and then something came to me! It came with such a blinding flash of clarity that I almost leapt from my seat shouting 'Eureka!' Of course! Television needed its own special effects designer, a designer with an open brief and the imagination to tackle any problem! With all humility I can claim to be capable of coming up with unusual ideas – I've seen eyes light up when I've outlined some of my schemes. However, I do have a tendency to see the potential of an idea without fully considering the problems. If something looks good I become so enthusiastic that I launch into it without troubling to examine the small print. But for once I sensed that I'd hit upon a winner. Nevertheless I might have asked myself which programmes would need special effects. Conditioned by the many movies I'd seen I visualised myself directing battle scenes, fire sequences and sinking ships.

Unfortunately Television wasn't yet operating at that level, it was a small medium with modest aspirations. Would Andy Pandy have benefited from an exploding wicker basket? ('Bye bye, boys and girls' Kerboooom!) and was it likely that *The Grove Family* could be sent on a fateful voyage across the Atlantic? However, my enthusiasm remained undiminished and as the bus approached Shepherds Bush I began work on the details. I knew that Richard Levin would be disinterested in a proposition with a general brief – he would require something more specific to enthuse him; I would have to come up with an example. It must have been a good morning for thinking because once again I saw what I could do.

Television captions and graphics were ripe for development because they were still years behind the cinema. While even the poorest B-movies opened with swirling drapes or animated lettering, television showed only static opening titles that were at best hand-painted by the designers, or at worst block letters impressed on paper by a machine kept in the caption artists' room. There was a standard size for captions which was seven inches by five. End captions were nearly always machine-printed and the number of credits was strictly limited. The cards were set up on two caption easels in the studio and shown in sequence by switching between cameras.

I felt that I could improve upon this method. Simple though it was the business of swapping from one caption to the following one called for precise coordination between the people in the control room and the scene boys who had the job of snatching the cards from the rack between switch-overs. The sight of a shaking hand coming into view or a card being dropped was an agreeable part of the evening's entertainment but it didn't enhance television's reputation. So how would I replace this system? On the end of Alfie's bench I sketched furiously, covering sheets of paper which I spread out for evaluation. Some I redrew, others I screwed up and threw away. My final design was an esoteric device consisting of two slide projectors and a screen on which the projected pictures could be dissolved from one to the other giving the traditional cinematic cross fade. It was a novel concept but expensive and although it had the virtue of employing only a single camera, had it been built it would have consumed more time and money and been far less easy to operate than the simple method of placing cards on easels. However, I hoped that Richard Levin would see it as 'forward thinking'.

But all this mental thrashing about was to count for nothing – events would render my brainchild stillborn. On the day of the meeting I wore my ex-best suit, hoping that if I kept one arm by my side Levin would never notice the fact that the material was strangely rigid. I'd scrounged a folder from Alfie and had filled it with my doodles and specifications which, to bulk them out and make them seem more important, I interleaved with sheets of green paper. Then I went to the great man's office. His secretary having invited me in apologised for not being able to give me the visitor's chair – Jack Kine was sitting in it. I acknowledged him briefly, wondering what the hell he was doing there. It was time for *my* meeting and I was annoyed that it might be cut short in order that Jack Kine could talk to Levin about something else. If he was going in first, I hoped whatever it was it wouldn't take long because I wanted plenty of time to explain my great new invention. It was a bad start and I was irritated.

The secretary kept going in and out of Levin's office as if some great constitutional crisis had arisen. She took papers in and brought papers out and seemed incredibly busy. This was not at all – the atmosphere of calm and tranquillity I needed to explain the benefits of my caption scanner was being shattered by all this bustle. Eventually she put her head round the door and said 'Will you come in please?' We both got up, Jack from the chair and me from the top of the two drawer filing cabinet. Neither of us knew which of us she wanted. She added 'Both of you please.' Both of us? What on earth was going on? I followed Jack into the inner office.

Levin, seemingly unaware that we had already met, introduced us to each other and invited us to sit down – and then turning to me gave the reason for our both being there. Jack Kine, he explained, blinking through his glasses, had come up with a brilliant idea – the creation of a special effects section. My lower jaw must have crashed to the floor. What *was* this silly man talking about? It was *my* brilliant idea! How could it have come from Jack Kine? But then I saw something I hadn't noticed when I'd entered the room. On Levin's blotter were Jack's boat photographs. Levin, who never wasted time discussing minor details, went on 'I want you two to set up a Visual Effects unit and we'll see if it works'. Then twitching his eyes at me he added 'I'll ask Kingswood to release you from the end of the month and you'll be transferred to television. You'll both keep your present salaries and you'll be classified as design assistants. I'll find you a place to work, but in the meantime carry on with what you're doing until Mr Buchinger sends for you. He will be your manager and will tell you what to do'. He waved us to the door and we were dismissed.

With my mouth still looking like a broken rat trap I tottered into the corridor and searched feverishly for a cigarette. He hadn't even looked at my folder. I saw Jack Kine light a cigarette and noticed that his hands were shaking. For a few moments I could say nothing – I didn't trust myself to talk without exploding. There were so many unanswered questions and while I realised that I wouldn't have to go back to Kingswood, I didn't feel like celebrating. My wonderful brain child had been mugged in the maternity ward. Huffily I suggested that we go somewhere and talk. Jack looked at his watch. He said he was working on a backcloth which was needed that evening and time was short. I told him I'd wait in the plaster shop – after which we'd go to the White Horse. It was plain that neither of us relished the prospect of working with the other; we didn't see ourselves as partners.

Jack came to the plaster shop at lunch time and we went straight to the White Horse. Neither of us said very much on the way there but after a pint and a sandwich we started to relax. Grudgingly we admitted it was a wonderful opportunity and discussed how it might work to our advantage. Another pint and the prospect of working together didn't seem quite as daunting. We tried to recall what Levin had said about our responsibilities, but neither of us had taken it in. We remembered that he'd said we would be working under Buchinger, an administrator in the Design Department, and we weren't happy about this. If we were to work together then we would want to do it in our own fashion without supervision or restriction. We knew Buchinger to be a nice man and fair minded, but one who would be unlikely to share our belief in the unorthodox.

Two more pints cleared our vision perfectly and much happier we went on to talk about various effects; it was then I learned that Jack had already serviced some of the programmes. At that time it was customary for designers to produce working drawings of everything they required, but without being able to specify the means or methods by which their ideas for special effects could be achieved they were at a loss. They had an ally in Bill King, the helpful and resourceful property master, but as he had only limited manufacturing facilities the need for a special section able to supply items that no other section could or would provide had become apparent. But until such a unit was formed Jack had been on hand to offer his services – an offer eagerly accepted by designers who recognised his expertise.

This situation demonstrates the unregulated state of early television which was run by two groups of people. One was the autocratic BBC administration under the control of Broadcasting House and the other comprised the free-wheeling, show business arty types under the control of Richard Levin. The unions had not yet started to exercise their muscle and so 'ad hoc' solutions in which a scenic artist doubled as a provider of special effects went unchallenged. Fortunately for us we had come upon the scene at the right time and thanks to Richard Levin were now to form the sort of section that the service needed. The more we looked at things the better they seemed. Perhaps we could even develop my caption machine. Always the opportunist I suggested that we have one more drink, but Jack reminded me of the unfinished backcloth and so we arranged to continue our discussions the following day. Solemnly we shook hands.

Life, we felt, was likely to be full of opportunity and now that we knew each other slightly better we were able to come to terms with the arrangement. This was television and we were on our way – Buchinger didn't stand a chance.

We   are   Given   an   Office

Later that week we decided to go to Buchinger's office to sort things out. Buck had been schooled in BBC protocol and had been taught to play everything by the book. It was known that he disapproved of Richard Levin's 'wild schemes' but as he was subordinate to the Head of Design he could only grind his teeth. It was likely that he would see us as another example of Levin's determination to arrange things himself without bothering to go through the proper channels. And he was right. Levin had no time for what he regarded as outmoded bureaucracy and was determined to cut the ties with Broadcasting House and create a new order for television. He didn't always get his way; the Mafia of old boys was a powerful one, but by constantly waiving the rules he accomplished a great deal. In his stand against the old order he had the overwhelming support of his own designers and the other craft units and, furthermore, he had the backing of the directors and producers. With such forces arraigned against them the administrators daren't openly oppose him. Television owes much to Richard Levin.

The meeting with Buchinger was short and to the point; he was in charge of the Design Department's administration and we had better not forget it. He told us that Levin had already selected the office in which we were to work and from the look on his face I wondered who'd been evicted. Being in favour with the head of one's department doesn't mean you don't have enemies. Told that our office was on the second floor we went to inspect it. It was the same size as most of the other rooms in that corridor, but it was next door to the gent's toilet, an ideal location because, apart from the obvious saving on time, shoe leather and bladder strain it would provide us with water, an essential ingredient in the production of special effects. With water one can wash dirty coffee mugs, clean up spilled chemicals and put out small fires before they become big fires.

The room had been furnished with a worn oak table, two chairs, a battered steel cupboard with a twisted key that was firmly stuck in the lock and a bent wood hat rack.
'What the hell's that?' asked Jack
'A bent wood hat rack'
'I know what it is, but what good is it to us. Is this all we've got to produce Visual Effects?'
The trouble was that we were outside the norm. Designers, and that's what we were, designed things and had them made in the workshops. Buchinger was willing to give us all the pencils and paper we needed, but he had no means to finance a workshop.
'You got any spare tools at home?' I asked.
'A few. You?'
And that's how we started. The tools may have been bought in Woolworths or even handed down to us by our fathers, but we managed to scrape together a basic kit. Polishing and de-rusting them we laid them out on a shelf in the cupboard.

I was the first to take up residence because Jack had to continue working until a replacement scenic artist could be found. For nearly a month he haunted the office, bringing with him sundry bits of scrap metal or wood that he found in the workshops and asking over and over again if I'd heard anything. Then one day he rushed upstairs to tell me that a new scenic artist had been recruited and that arrangements were being made for him to join me on the following Monday.

I had learned a lot about Jack's past by that time. He had started work at Alexandra Palace in 1937, but when it ceased transmitting in 1939 he was told to go home and await events. His weekly salary of 2 pounds 10 shillings was sent to him by post, but his father, morally offended by such decadence, made him go to Broadcasting House to enquire how long this lotus-eating was likely to continue. Jack was interviewed and passed to Mr Tugsbury the BBC's chief architect who, faced with the prospect of losing most of his young male staff to the armed forces, was delighted to find a spare pair of hands. He suggested that Jack could be of use and passed him on to a third interviewer who assigned him to the stores of the carpenters' workshop. This was housed in an 19th Century building, with, unbelievably, a private coach house in a narrow street at the back of Broadcasting House. The coach house had become the carpenters' workshop which valued today, Jack reckons, would be 'worth a bit'. His immediate gaffer was a chap not much older than himself by the name of Charlie Denman who was also awaiting his call-up. Jack and Charlie became great mates and they divided the task of clearing and reorganising the stores with Jack doing the sorting and Charlie attending to the paper work. Jack found the task quite pleasant and soon had the locks, hinges and knobs graded and assigned to their correct metal trays but the smaller items took several days to sort out. Mixed together were hundreds of screws – roundhead brass, countersunk ditto, cheese head and mushroom head – long, medium and short. There were nails oval, nails wire and nails small panel. But to his satisfaction he eventually had everything sorted and in good order.

Bombs had started to fall on London and the two lads were detailed to take regular night duties on fire watch. They were given a stirrup pump, two water buckets and a third containing sand. One night when they heard bombs falling closer and closer they dived under one of the benches. It was a wise move because the final terrific bang demolished the building and brought everything down around them. Uninjured, but covered in plaster dust and severely shaken they managed to free themselves and to make their way over the debris to Broadcasting House reception where they were given hot drinks and made to lie on camp beds. Jack returned to work two days later and although much of the heavy rubble had been pushed back from the streets he saw the evidence of his labours. Scattered amongst the bricks and shards of glass in Portland Place and Regents Street were screws roundhead brass, countersunk ditto, cheese head and mushroom head, long medium and short. And there were nails oval, nails wire and nails small panel – and there was Jack, vowing that if he ever got his hands on that bastard Adolf Hitler he would make him sort screws and nails (red hot of course) for the rest of his something life.

Now that Jack and I were together we took stock. Our main requirement was for a work top on which to make props and set out studio plans – and so we built our first bench. It was a conversion of something that Jack had found in the basement (he was very good at finding things and in the following weeks equipped the room almost exclusively with bits and pieces that he'd discovered laying around unsupervised.) But the bench had been much used and didn't look posh, so using our own money we bought a tin of maroon paint from a stall in Shepherds Bush market. Jack had no difficulty in finding a paint brush and we gave our bench a smart appearance – in fact we gave it two coats of smart appearance.

Unfortunately the paint we'd bought never dried. Presumably concocted by one of the local back street enterprises it remained permanently tacky. For weeks, despite our attempts to cure it, it never changed. Whenever we put a sheet of paper on the top of the bench we would have to peel it off to remove it. One day David Attenborough came to the office (he wanted to know if could make a photographic reflector that he could take on safari) and with boyish enthusiasm, leapt onto our bench and sat on the fatal area. It was terrible. Too late to warn him that our maroon paint had a wanton affection for warm clothing we listened to him in glassy eyed silence. When he got down there was a faint ripping sound that seemed to take him by surprise. Apparently the African jungle hadn't prepared him for predatory sticky benches. Fortunately the paint that had entrapped everything from a fourteen inch monkey wrench to a glass ash tray had not affected his trousers and no damage was apparent. But more of David's request later.

Within two or three weeks we had a passable workshop and designers and directors were coming in to find out what we could provide. Word had gone out that we were 'Design Department's Visual Effects Unit' – a concept so novel and so ambiguous that it attracted people from all over the building. After David's experience we decided we really must cure the tackiness of the bench top because, short of surrounding it with barbed wire, we had no means of warning visitors that it was lethal. We started by dusting it with talcum powder, but gave it up when the smell of cheap baby powder became nauseating. Next we attempted to remove the paint with thinners, but the smell of acetone upset everyone in the surrounding offices. Later we tried to dry it out with a blowlamp and again upset our neighbours who objected even more to the smell of burning paint than they had the fumes of thinners. What sort of Special Effects men were we when we couldn't even dry paint? In the end we gave up and covered the top with a sheet of hardboard.

I originally entitled this book 'Why didn't it work?' because things frequently went wrong; perhaps our bench was an omen, a forewarning that we should have heeded. A tin of paint, for example, might not be a tin of paint at all – it could be a tin of maroon coloured fly paper adhesive.

Eventually we received our first official commission. Richard Levin had been invited to appear in the studio as the commentator and interviewer for a short programme on art and design called *Mobiles*. The set, as I remember it, was a simple arrangement of drapes with a couple of cloth covered rostra on which to display the various items. But as head of design Levin would need to show his team of designers that he could come up with original ideas and so to close the show he'd devised a clever, albeit hideously tricky method of presenting the end credits. Names were to be displayed on a spiral of paper which would revolve slowly in front of a camera while the lens moved downwards following the text.

As his newly appointed visual effects designers it was our responsibility to provide him with the finished article. Our reaction when he gave us the specifications was one of airy dismissal. 'A revolving spiral? – knock it out in an hour, Guv. Any difficult jobs for us?' It was only when we thought about it that the problem became obvious. At that stage we had no special effects equipment or materials whatever – we had only the few tools we'd brought from our homes. Looking round our room, we saw the truth. There were the few ancient screwdrivers, two saws, one hammer, half a tin of non-drying maroon paint and a bent wood hatstand – it didn't look promising. But Jack thought he had the answer. Stored in his attic at home was a disused electric gramophone. This, if it worked, could be our salvation. He thought that when he'd put it up there it was okay but couldn't be sure. He decided to go immediately to his house and collect it leaving me to make the paper spiral and some sort of device from which to suspend it.

By the time Jack returned carrying a brown paper parcel, I had built a base, a small cycloramic background and a four foot gallows from which I thought we could hang the paper strip. But now our attention was focussed on the electric gramophone. The elderly mauve and hairy twin flex had an equally elderly two pin plug – which we removed and replaced with a 13 amp three pin plug. To our relief the turntable spun into life. But could it be slowed to a suitable speed? It couldn't. However much we adjusted the speed control the motor revolved much too fast for the spiral caption to be read by the viewers. However we were employed as special effects designers and it was up to us to think of a way of slowing that motor down.

Fortunately it didn't prove too difficult. By hideously distorting the governors (three brass weights riveted to steel springs) and adding a small piece of card to act as an air brake we reduced the rotation to a crawl. Now it remained only to assemble the various items and try it out. We didn't give it much of a test – just long enough to be sure that it ran satisfactorily; we didn't want to tempt fate or over strain the buckled springs.

The next day we took it over to Lime Grove where, satisfied that we'd done a good job we set it up in the studio. The electricians, who had never heard of us, were minded to summon their shop steward but they weren't sure of their ground. They examined our electrics and replaced the hairy lead. They also exchanged our new three pin plug for an identical one and connected it to a studio power output. Finding nothing else to investigate they switched it on – and it ran perfectly.

Buttonholing the head cameraman we explained the operation and how the spiral should be scanned and found him cheerfully co-operative. He tried it a couple of times and pronounced it satisfactory; then he trundled his camera away and concentrated on other matters. Deciding to watch the programme in our own homes (we wanted to show our loved ones something we'd made.) we gave the caption one last check over – and left.

It was on the Green Line coach nearing the end of my journey that an awful thought occurred to me. Happy that we'd given Levin what he'd asked for we'd overlooked the frailty of the all-important top bearing. Concerned with the method of turning the spiral we had rather glossed over the means of support. I'd hung the top of the spiral on three inches of cotton thread, adequate for a short run in the studio but bloody useless for a prolonged one! Suppose someone switched it on and left it running? I froze in my seat. We hadn't warned them! I could see it all too plainly. Kept running the thread would wind itself up, turning into a chain of knots which would become double knots and then triple knots – and then it would break or tear itself from the paper spiral. And this, our very first job, was for Richard Levin, the head of our department and a man not given to accepting excuses or explanations. This was live television and the awful consequences of making him look foolish in front of half a million viewers and the laughing stock of his own designers turned me to jelly. There was a phone box at the end of my lane; even at this late stage I might be able to avert disaster by contacting the studio. But the Green Line was still two miles away from my destination, a journey that took a nightmarishly long time.

When it reached my stop I leapt from the exit doors and ran to the phone box. Fortunately it was unoccupied and scrabbling for loose change I phoned Lime Grove.

'Studio D' I yelled – 'Urgent!'

I was put through without delay, but was told that the studio had broken for a tea-break and there was no one there to accept my call. I sweated; I had to establish contact with someone. In those days one could actually speak to the operators and be sure of getting a response. I was transferred to the control room where an engineer was tuning the monitors. I asked him to get the floor manager.

'Hang on' he said.

And I did hang on – and on and on. Eventually there was the *brrrrr* of disconnection and my coins, the only ones I had, dropped into the metal box below.

I went to my mother's house where my wife was waiting for me. None of us had telephones in our homes so I was unable to make any further contact with Lime Grove. Anyway it was too late to do anything now. I knew they would be on the final countdown to transmission. I sank into an armchair and looked at the screen. On it came – the first production in which I would see something that Jack and I had designed and made – and I was paralysed with fear. After the opening announcement appeared a small black and white Levin, blinking in the studio lights. I was too distraught to talk. I simply stared at the image. Oh please God, dear, dear God don't let it happen. He must have taken pity, because everything ran smoothly and the show finished, as it was intended to do, with a spiral caption revolving slowly while a descending camera followed the names.

A thin broken voice I didn't recognise as my own said. 'Jack and I made that'.

A   S o r t   o f   E x p l o s i o n

To say that we were elated by the success of our spiral caption would be wrong. We had shown, if only to ourselves, that we could triumph in the cruel face of adversity but we also knew that on our very first assignment we'd come within a hair's breadth of calamity. We were sensible enough to see that we must never have any doubts about anything we made for a programme or hide any misgivings from each other. We would thoroughly test everything, we told ourselves, and we would agree that what we were providing was the best possible solution. Even at this early stage we knew that our credibility would depend upon us always presenting a common point of view. And now we awaited our next job.

But the days passed and nothing came in; it seemed that no one wanted us. With so much time on our hands we fussed around the office. We had acquired a small box of drain testers from a chap in props and amongst them was a small cylinder of cardboard containing about an egg-cupful of mealed gunpowder. Its primary purpose was to create the sound of an explosion on stage and was known unsurprisingly as a stage maroon. The cardboard case was double wound with thick string and then dipped in glue. Finally it had been given a coat of orange paint and furnished with an instruction label warning users that it should be fired only in an open metal dustbin.

But what intrigued us was the fact that it was initiated by a four and a half volt torch battery. This was something new; until then we had been familiar only with fireworks of the 'light the blue touch paper and retire immediately' variety so we did what any seriously minded researchers would have done when confronted by something new – we took a hacksaw and cut it in half. Inside, as well as the gunpowder was a thing we were later to know very well. It was a pyrofuse, a small electric initiator less than an inch long. We put the components of the maroon safely in the cupboard intending to experiment with them later. We returned to our life of boredom.

There is only so much one can do to establish an office and we'd done the lot. A calendar, a work chart and a table of timber sizes had been hung on the wall and the ash tray had been emptied and wiped clean for the second time that day. And then one of us had an idea. We would make an advertising gimmick, something animated and intriguing – something that would capture the imagination of those who saw it and show our versatility as effects designers. It was a childish idea, but we couldn't just sit around smoking all day long and as we hadn't enough money for both cigarettes *and* beer, the smoking was limited.

We sketched our idea on a memo pad and went down to the carpenters' shop to scrounge some wood. Childish or not, at last we had something to do. The 'something' was a two foot long display panel containing six windows of Perspex and tracing paper. Each was illuminated from behind by a torch bulb, and in front of the display, we placed a single press button. We set it up on the bench and went back to our table and smoked two relit cigarettes. The first (and as it turned out, the only person) to experience our novel advertising gimmick was Stephen Taylor, one of Levin's most talented production designers. He wandered into our workshop to find out how things were going and we showed him our device, the first window of which was already illuminated showing the word PRESS.

'May I press it?' he asked

'Of course'

He pushed the button firmly causing the first window to go out and the second window to light up. It said 'Do you want to go on?' Stephen pressed again following the instructions given in each window. The last window said something like 'If you press again you'll get a surprise!' A slightly wary Stephen stood back from the bench expecting a squirt of water or something similar and pressed the button for the final time.

There was an explosion that rocked the room.

We had used some of the gunpowder from the maroon to make what we thought was a small banger and had wrapped it in several layers of stiff paper and sticky tape. Stephen, unprepared for this assault on his ear drums, was visibly shocked. Jack and I, who thought we knew what was coming, were even more shocked. On a large stage such as the one at The Royal Opera House this bang would have rocked every seat in the auditorium. In a small office it was the equivalent of firing a six inch naval gun in a bathroom. As the smoke cleared, we stared at each other in disbelief. I saw Jack mouthing the invocation which starts with a four letter word and is followed by 'me!', but I couldn't hear him because I'd gone stone deaf. Our work-chart had fallen from the wall and various other items that had been dislodged in the blast lay on the floor.

Our neighbours reacted in a predictable fashion. For several seconds they probably stood or sat absolutely still – stone figures transfixed in time – then, as their senses returned they tumbled out of their offices and hurried along the corridor to our room. Opening the door they expected to find us dead, but instead saw us trying to tidy up. According to their viewpoint there was indignation and disappointment in equal measures. In no time at all they were knocking on the door of Ian Beynon Lewis's office demanding that our reproductive organs be nailed to a board. That afternoon we were sent for and given a first class telling off. We were asked to consider what effect our thoughtless action might have had on members of staff with dodgy hearts or weak bladders. We agreed to scrap our advertising gimmick – but in a single performance it had achieved its objective; people were talking about us.

The discovery that we could ignite pyrotechnic devices with wires and batteries was to provide us with a leap into the future. We contacted the pyrotechnic makers and discovered that they sold a whole range of explosive devices for stage and film production. The most important single item for us, however, was the pyrofuse, obtainable from Strand Electric the London based theatrical suppliers. These tiny cardboard cylinders were fitted with something like a match head which ignited fiercely when its two wires were connected to a battery. With these we could do many things. We could safely set fire to piles of material doused with petrol without singeing our eyebrows, blow up 'booby-trapped' cars and ignite or explode things situated a long way from the cameras. We found too that we could drop objects from the studio gantry by hanging them on nylon fish line and, on cue, burning through the line with a pyrofuse. This proved particularly useful for falling beams and ceilings that had to crash from above in fire sequences.

Throughout our career we were constantly discovering interesting techniques – a fact that made special effects design a very exciting field. Using pyrofuses, we later built an armoury of stock effects that could be employed in a variety of places and all actuated by remote control. There were arrows that could be made to fire themselves into scenery, bullet holes in almost anything, blood that erupted from bullet torn clothing and mirrors that would shatter at the press of a button. Later, when we discovered plastic detonators, we were able to improve these effects because detonators, unlike the pyrofuses, packed substantial explosive power. Now we could shatter bottles and vases, blow holes in wooden doors and simulate machine gun fire across a battlefield.

These discoveries didn't all materialise at once of course, but came to us over a decade or so, a period in which we were called upon to produce myriad visual effects and special props. It was a period in which we learnt our craft, honed our skills – and still made a mess of things. A decade after our first ill-judged explosion in the office we were guilty of doing it again, but this time it was a miscalculation. We had been asked to film a period gas balloon and basket which would be brought down by musket fire – and the director wanted it to be dramatic. No mere hiss of escaping gas and a limp return to the ground – our brief was to construct a model balloon that would sail aloft and, on cue, burst into flames and plummet to earth.

Earlier, for another programme, we had recorded a similar sequence in which we'd used a giant six foot diameter weather balloon inflated with hydrogen. It had considerable lifting power and when released shot into the air carrying a slow burning fuse attached to the underside. The effect was both startling and satisfying. The fuse ignited a small incendiary charge taped to the rubber neck which quickly set fire to the hydrogen producing a huge ball of flames which twisted and cavorted high above our heads. The smoking remains of the envelope fell gently and were almost entirely consumed by the time they reached the ground. Because of the size of the balloon we had carried out our test in a field, but now that we were working to a smaller scale we confidently tried it out on the roof of Television Centre.

We selected an appropriately sized party balloon, inflated it with hydrogen and took it onto the Design Block fire escape. Up there we fastened a small length of slow fuse to the neck and let it go. But it didn't rise. Driven by the wind it sailed horizontally across the roof and was immediately sucked down into the open well opposite the reference library. We were horrified – we had fully expected it to go up – not along! There was another surprise. What we didn't know was that hydrogen in large amounts burns fiercely; in small amounts and under compression it explodes violently. Expecting to see flames rise out of the void we were shocked by the bang. Our balloon exploded like a hand grenade. The bang echoed round and round the building, bouncing from wall to wall. It was followed by a silence which was broken only by the sounds of running feet as we fled back to the office.

Strangely, nothing was ever said about this incident. No complaints were made and in subsequent visits to the library in which we tried to find out what had happened it seemed our balloon had never existed.

Perhaps the girls were trying to protect us from the wrath of management. To Irene Thornley and her girls I tend our belated but deeply grateful thanks. Had they complained we would almost certainly have been transferred to other work – or even given the sack.

We Launch Morecambe and Wise

After the episode of the balloon we decided that all testing should be carried out on the waste ground outside. It was muddy and dirty and probably riddled with typhoid, botulism and beriberi but it offered privacy. From then on, weather permitting, we would work out there, and as long as we remembered to have all the inoculations and not to lick our fingers we should stay out of hospital.

It was a strange place. Several of the original White City Exhibition buildings remained, including an oriental pagoda made of wood and plaster. There were also the iron skeletons and corrugated sheeting of several other buildings and large parts of the ornamental boating lake still faced with thousands of the original imported tiles. It was also a repository for all the unwanted items which over the years had been heaved over the wall by the residents of Shepherds Bush.

One day we used the remaining part of the boating lake to test-fire a ground maroon which we had acquired as a sample from Brocks. It was a fine morning and on our way to the derelict lake we passed the lads from the Buying Department who loved to spend their lunch hour kicking a football around. Not wanting to interfere with their game we decided to go as far away from them as possible, setting up our maroon at the extreme end of the pool. We wired it up, moved back a bit and pressed the firing button. The effect, seen from our position was amazing. The entire group of footballers leapt into the air before looking around in confusion. Ordinarily the sound from such a pyrotechnic explosion would have dissipated in the open air, floating away as a mere 'crack' and from where we were standing it sounded no more than a moderately loud bang. What we hadn't realised was that we had placed the maroon at the centre of a semi-circular tiled wall which had acted as a directional sound reflector. The bang therefore appeared to come from under the footballer's feet, hence the bewilderment. Bill Eldridge, the unfortunate chap who'd kicked the ball as the ground exploded had to spend quite a long time sitting on a wall. The sight of a small plume of blue smoke rising from the far end of the boating lake led the lads to put two and two together and they were far from pleased. I think we were lucky not to have been hung from the pagoda.

Everyone involved in television production in those days was looking for a new show or a new idea and the set designers finding themselves in this novel and exciting medium responded with enthusiasm. The design block at Television Centre became a power house of creativity while at Lime Grove scenery and props were being ferried in and out in a never ending stream. The dark green vans and scenery lorries travelling around the streets of Shepherds Bush became almost as familiar as London buses. It would have been impossible to work in television at that time without feeling the buzz of excitement that permeated the entire organisation.

Ronnie Waldman, the head of light entertainment, had his office at Lime Grove and one afternoon he asked us to meet him there. He didn't waste time but took us to the restaurant where he bought us tea and buns and told us that he wanted to discuss a brand new comedy series he'd commissioned. He told us that it was to be called *Running Wild* and would feature two relatively unknown comedians called Eric Morecambe and Ernie Wise, supported by Alma Cogan and several others. The shows would be staged at the Shepherds Bush Empire which, unlike the Lime Grove studios, was able to seat a large audience – and Ronnie knew that a live audience would be essential to create the right atmosphere for a show of this kind.

Later, the BBC would adapt this theatre as a fully equipped television studio, but at that period it was just as it had been before the war, a theatre for the presentation of variety shows. Despite its suitability for audience shows its raked stage and restricted camera access meant that several rows of seating had to be ripped out and replaced with a wooden floor to accommodate the camera dollies and their unwieldy cables. The zoom lens was yet to be invented and going from close up to long shot entailed changing lenses by using a sort of turnkey which passed right through the body of the camera and rotated the lens turret on the front. It also meant that the camera had to track nearer or further from the subject. Lens changes were carried out while the camera was 'switched off and another was taking the picture. Manhandling the heavy wheeled base back and forth was tricky enough but the operators had to ensure that they didn't run over their own cables or those of their colleagues, which meant that the moves had to be plotted in advance. Up in the gallery these manoeuvres were shown on a diagram so that the production staff knew where each camera was and what it was going to do. Snarl ups didn't often happen, but when they did everything descended into chaos. This was live television and once the show was on the air there was no going back.

However, these were problems to be sorted out by engineers; for Jack and me this great theatre was ours for the evening. On stage we would rig our effects and props and operate them in front of an audience. We were performers. If this was new to us it was also new to the press and they were quick to see its potential. We were photographed and written about and our props were afforded the coverage that sometimes rivalled the publicity given to the stars. Ronnie Waldman had given us draft scripts and that evening as we read through them we saw that they were stuffed with gags and comedy sequences requiring our participation. *Running Wild* during its six weeks in the theatre would employ us full time, which was wonderful. We made many of the props at home enlisting the help of our wives when we required cloth, needles, sewing machines or things to be patiently held while the glue dried.

The viewers did not take to Eric and Ernie which is strange when one knows how they were to dominate television comedy and were loved by both BBC and, later, ITV audiences. Even now they are gone, their recordings are still screened and they still figure high in the ratings. But in *Running Wild* they didn't score or amuse; in fact the critics were damningly hostile. Here are some of the cuttings I pasted into my scrap book at the time.

SORRY TO RUB IT IN MR WALDMAN
Television's new Wednesday series 'Running Wild' ran completely off the rails last night. It looks as if it has been financed out of the poor box and written by somebody who has annexed the gags from a troupe of gloomy, down trodden Pierrots. Morecambe and Wise are not top-flight national stars and they are positive heroes to tackle a TV comedy series

RUNNING WILD IS ABOUT RIGHT
A fair sample of the humour dished up.
First Comic: 'I've got a fear of being locked up. I think it's a complex'.
Second Comic; 'The Magistrate calls it six months!'

NOW I'M WILD TOO.
Mr Morecambe and Mr Wise, two comparative youngsters in show business started their own series on TV last night why on earth viewers had to be given this stuff I really don't know.

I particularly treasure the reference to 'First Comic' and 'Second Comic' but in fairness the critics could not all have been wrong. Perhaps neither they nor the viewers were ready for this style of humour. There is no doubt that the pair relied more on props and gimmicks than oh the slick stand-up humour they developed later, but as TV is a visual medium we'd all felt we should use plenty of visual humour. As the criticisms grew in vehemence so Eric and Ernie became unsure of themselves, turning quite frequently to Jack and me for comments and suggestions. 'Should this sketch be shorter, should that gag be replaced by something else, could the audience actually see what was going on?' Knowing that we were looking at the show from the stage they assumed we had an ideal vantage point from which to assess their performances. We tried to be helpful, but didn't make reliable sounding boards. Knowing that some of our own work might be cut we assured the two that this was okay or that was fine, when in fact we were far from impartial. Every gag that didn't get an immediate laugh eroded their confidence and they became more and more depressed. They assured us on more than one occasion that at the end of the series they would never set foot in a television studio again. Eric and Ernie were popular in later years because viewers got to know them and to enjoy their style of humour. Ernie's play writing, Eric's face slapping and the gags about wigs and short, fat, hairy legs were used over and over again. However this repetition did nothing to lessen their appeal and eventually the popularity of the Eric and Ernie show enabled them to invite other celebrities to appear in their programmes. The chosen stars were delighted to become the recipients of the boys' special brand of gentle humiliation. Victims such as André Previn, Des O'Connor and Peter Cushing were among my own particular favourites.

While in later years they appeared confident and self-assured, in *Running Wild* they were anything but. At that time they were new and performing before an audience that preferred its established favourites from radio and the cinema. As each episode was panned the two of them cast around for scapegoats. The director Bryan Sears came in for much backstage mumbling which he didn't deserve. 'Did we know him well?' they asked us, 'was he the best director for the job? Was there someone who would be more in tune with their style of humour?'

Towards the end they even started to question each other's contributions. I remember on one occasion as Jack and Eric left the stage Ernie, finishing a discussion said to me 'Well, you know what Eric's like!'

Their material in *Running Wild* was mildly funny, but often lacked a pay-off. A sketch may contain many laughs, but if its ending is limp the applause is almost certain to be equally half-hearted. They weren't helped by the fact that 'canned' laughter couldn't be added afterwards because there wasn't an afterwards. Without a practical method of recording we too were on edge and prone to fluff things. On one occasion we had provided a crystal ball into which Ernie, as a costumed fortune teller was supposed to gaze, explaining that this was a fool proof method of forecasting the weather. The pay-off involved Ernie seeing an approaching rainstorm and getting a jet of water full in the face. This jet, which came from the base of the crystal ball, was operated by Ernie himself pressing a small button on the table.

To achieve this we'd installed a soda water syphon below the table with a connecting rod from the syphon to the button which Ernie covered with his hand. In rehearsal it worked without a hitch, but during the dinner break someone decided that the tablecloth should be replaced by something more ornate and had made the change, cutting a small slit to accommodate our operating knob. Came the moment when Ernie delivered his final line and aligned his face a few inches from the jet. With half closed eyes he pressed the button. Nothing happened! He repeated the line and pressed harder – nothing! His eyes were now wide open in panic. Grey faced, frozen in their chairs they tried to ad lib, praying that the stage would open and drop them from sight. I was standing close by and had no idea why the knob hadn't worked. I grabbed a fire bucket, hurled myself up a short flight of stairs to a stage-side box and flung the contents over Ernie's head. What it looked like I shall never know, but it was the only thing I could think of.

When we examined the table afterwards we found that the new cover was much thicker than the original and had become trapped between the press button and the table top preventing the lever of the syphon from being fully depressed. It was my fault; I should have operated the soda syphon from behind the table and not bothered with all that clever stuff of knobs and levers. Another lesson learned.

Whether the old theatre had a malevolent TV-hating ghost, I don't know but in a later sketch Eric and Ernie, dressed as Mexican gipsies, were supposed to enter from the wings. Ernie would be playing an electric guitar and Eric carrying a large amplifier. While Ernie strummed the guitar and sang Eric should have put down the amplifier and, clapping his hands performed a wild 'ole' dance – at which point the amplifier was to blow up. Jack, who was operating this prop, was relying on a visual cue from the floor manager which would be the signal to press the firing button. With his eyes fixed firmly on the floor manager's arm he couldn't see the technician walking across the stage who was about to obscure his sight line but the floor manager could – and he did the natural thing – he waved the bloke out of the way! Unfortunately, Jack took this for the signal to fire.

Eric and Ernie standing by the curtains were taken completely by surprise – especially Eric who was holding the amplifier. They staggered onto the stage wondering what the hell they were going to do, but somehow saved the day by ad-libbing furiously. The audience in the theatre saw the whole thing and roared with laughter but the viewers at home heard only the applause. They saw a smoking comedian come on dressed as a Mexican Gipsy carrying some singed and buckled cardboard who appeared to say a few words and go off. Up in the control room Bryan Sears, the director, was as mystified by the whole thing as the viewers; he stared at the transmission monitor in disbelief. I think that when he saw his two singed comedians in the wreckage of their best sketch he came very near to tearing up his contract and walking out.

N i n e t e e n   E i g h t y - F o u r

Jack and I were given the responsibility of designing and making the special props needed for a new production of George Orwell's *Nineteen Eighty-Four*. The production would rock the nation.

The props required included the Speakwrite, the Pornowrite and the frightening Telescreens with their proving cameras. Today, such a task would prove no problem, but in 1954 television design was restriction by primitive resources and miniscule budgets. There were no electronic effects and precious few optical ones, and innovation came from the imaginative use of plywood and Seccotine.

Despite these limitations, *Nineteen Eighty-Four* because the most powerful play ever transmitted forcing the national press to cover the story for seven consecutive days. It was transmitted live which meant there could be no editing and no retakes, because on those days television plays had to be performed as they would have been in the theatre: sequentially, but without an interval.

Live transmissions were regarded by some as a challenge and by others as a nightmare. But whatever the opinion, the strain of working without a safety net affected everyone involved. It was worse for the actors, particularly the nervous ones who, despite their theatrical training, were worried they might 'dry' in front of the cameras. The technicians were also affected when things went wrong.

Because the play had several, vital working props which Jack and I had to operate in the studio, we were beginning to experience 'butterflies'. True, everything had been rehearsed during the day and had gone well, but now it was time to transmit and Mr Sod and his well-known law were waiting the wings.

As the minutes ticked away, my attention centred on the studio clock and as I watched the ascending hand my mouth went dry. Everyone had taken up their positions in the studio adopting such static postures that they seemed to have turned to stone. If you'd dropped a pin at that moment it would've clanged like a bell.

The floor manager, the much-loved Paddy Russell, wished us luck and called down the remaining seconds in a calm and reassuring voice. But it was she who needed good luck, because from the moment it started it would be her responsibility to carry the whole show.

The red light on the wall flashed three times and then stayed on – while my butterflies grew into vampire bats. We were on air.

On a studio monitor I watched the opening sequence, a montage of London scenes devastated by war and pestilence. I heard again the words that were designed to set the mood of hopelessness that would persist through the play.

There are few dramas that can so effectively depress the human mind than *Nineteen Eighty-Four*; in the cinema it would have created a major furore. But this evening it was being fed into people's homes where, in darkened living rooms, viewers watched their screens with mounting disbelief, shutting their eyes to the horror, but unable to switch it off.

In the studio the mood was electric; the whole had suddenly become transformed. The plays, reacting to the heightened tension, had turned *Nineteen Eighty-Four* from a television drama into real life.

Jack and I although no less affected than anyone else, were forced to remember that we had things to do. First there was the Speakwrite, the machine supposedly able to translate spoken text into printed words. Peter Cushing, a news writer, sat in front of it, tapping buttons and speaking quietly into a microphone while checking the printed strip. Squatting on the floor by his right knee I had to control the motor that drove the roll of paper from a slot in the top of the machine. When he dictated into a microphone I had to switch it off. Designed by Jack, the Speakwrite had an outer case that looked modern and expensive, but inside, a short length of paper roll was being transported on some rather dodgy Meccano gears. I glanced at Jack who appeared to have his fingers crossed – not a good omen.

My main concern was to eject enough paper for the strip to be visible on camera, but not so much that it would run out before the end of the scene. In hindsight I realise we could have fitted the mechanism, and a much bigger paper roll, under the desk. We could then feed the strip up through a dummy machine, but these were early days and we haven't yet appreciated the fact we could determine specifications of the things we made. On this occasion we'd produced what we'd been asked for – a futuristic typewriter to spool out paper on a desk – and that's what we'd built.

As well as being the days of live performances, these were also the days of miserable budgets. Television had been allocated only a small part of the licence fee and had to operate almost solely on inspiration and enthusiasm. Even the actors were paid only nominal fees. Because of these cash restrictions, Jack and I had become adept at creating props from scrap materials and household utensils (a tradition that exists today) and collected everything we thought might come in useful.

The most important prop in *Nineteen Eighty-Four* was the Telescreen. This was Orwell's famous spy device supposedly installed in every home, office and public building. It comprised a TV screen (which we decided to make daringly circular) and a speaker which churned out non-stop propaganda. The important part however, was the surveillance camera situated below the screen. This all-probing, all-seeing eye was supposed to trap the unwary and seek out dissidents.

The fact that the studio equipment was basic and offered none of today's sophisticated inlay devices meant that the pictures on the Telescreens were simply 35mm slides projected onto screens of tracing paper; the projectors being hired from a shop in Shepherds Bush market. But the spy cameras had to appear to be working and in order to create the effect of constant surveillance we designed units consisting of big glass lenses (salvaged from scrapped roadside oil lamps) with rotating lights behind them. *Nineteen Eighty-Four,* it must be remembered, was still in the future and this is how Jack and I saw modern video cameras.

The revolving lights were small pocket torches strapped to the spindles of old-fashioned, spring-wound gramophone motors which were slowed down to a suitable speed. Full wound, the motors would turn the small circles of light for about ten minutes, after which they would to be re-wound. We'd made three of these Telescreens which, in the studio, were located in different rooms – in fact I seem to recall that one had to be taken down and quietly repositioned during the performance because we needed four. The working parts were mounted behind the flats where we could easily get at them, but were, nevertheless, situated some distance apart. To keep them working, Jack and I took it in turns to walk around behind the sets, winding them in sequence.

Everything went swimmingly until about half way through the play we discovered that we'd mislaid the winding handle – the one and only winding handle! We had overlooked Sod's Law. Somewhere in the studio one of us had put it down and forgotten where we'd left it.

There are three degrees of panic – mild, frightening and absolutely terrifying. Ours went off the scale. Without that handle, all three Telescreens would come to a stop – including the vital one that had to be revealed during one of the most dramatic sequences in the plot. For a split second he and I stared at each other in disbelief, then we took off! Heedless of the need for silence, we ran around the studio like charging bulls, thrusting aside actors awaiting their cues and tossing costumes, props and equipment into the air. I remember scrabbling around Peter Cushing's feet while he was actually delivering his lines. Being a true professional he showed no surprise – not even glancing down. But it was a rotten thing to do to an actor in full flow.

We found it in the nick of time, nestling on a ledge at the back of a flat. From then on it was tied to Jack's belt by a length of string.

Although impractical to break the action during this live transmission, we had brought it to a halt many times during rehearsals. This is normal practice as rehearsals are designed for getting things right, but not the dress rehearsal. This final run-through is meant to simulate the actual performance and must be treated like one. Timings, lighting, cues, must have all been established. But it was during the final run-through that Jack brought everything to a shuddering halt.

We'd designed and built a large machine which Orwell dubbed the Pornowrite. Its function was to create and print pornographic novels for the masses – the unspeakable Proles. It was an impressive looking prop with control knobs and levers and with a large revolving print roller mounted on the top. Yvonne Mitchell, who had to operate this machine, was supposed to look round in an unguarded moment and get her and trapped in the works.

The roller, being merely a large cardboard tube painted silver, meant that she was never in any danger. But it didn't seem that way to Jack. He was controlling the machine off-stage and had to kill the switch the moment Yvonne became trapped. Arriving at that scene in the final rehearsal, she thrust her arm deep into the casing and *screamed*. Jack froze. In that instance he'd seen the awful consequences of not shielding the electric motor. Yvonne had obviously come into contract with live terminals and had been electrocuted. With a face the colour of paper he leapt up, caught his foot in a heavy camera cable and went across the set like a bent penguin. He reached the scene, miraculously still on his feet, and grabbed her arm, pulling it free. 'Are you alright?' he gasped. The astonished actress, who knew nothing of hidden electric motors, was dumbfounded. 'What the **** are you doing, Jack?' she hissed, 'Can't you see I'm acting?'

Towards the end of the play there was that well-remembered scene played with such poignant drama by Peter Cushing and Andre Morrel. It was the famous rat scene in which Peter was supposed to lose his mind. This took place in the infamous Room 101, the torture chamber in which dissidents were forced to confront their worst nightmares. In his role of Winston Smith, Cushing was supposed to be terrified of rats and so his personal torture was to have a cage containing two of them strapped to his face. A sliding shutter kept the rats at bay, but once this was withdrawn the starving animals would be free to enter his face mask. Small wonder the concept was frightening.

I've watched that scene again since its original transmission – fortunately *Nineteen Eighty-Four* was recorded on film, the only method by which classics could be preserved for posterity. But I shudder when I look at our primitive rat cage made from plastic and plywood. If it convinced viewers that this really was 1984, years ahead, then credit must be given to Peter Cushing and Andre Morrel for their superlative performances which transcended the crudity of our prop.

But the problem of making the animals seem ferocious was one that almost beat us. Two slavering sewer rats had been procured for the job, but refused to act. The poor things, intimidated by the studio lights and the transparent cage, cowered against each other fearing their last moments had come. Gentle probing with sticks only confirmed their fears and they lay on the bottom of the cage, shivering like jellies. They were returned to their keeper and two tame rats were hurriedly procured from a local pet shop.

Unfortunately these rats were white and would have to be coloured brown, so Jack went to the make-up room to beg some Leichner powder. Colleagues back stage are invariably good friends, but there is a firm understanding that no one encroaches on another person's preserves. The girls were adamant; if make-up was required it was *their* responsibility to provide it. Jack when back to the studio and returned carrying the two white rats – to find himself suddenly alone in an empty room.

The replacement rats performed energetically, but not in the way we'd hoped. Fed be well-meaning studio staff who kept poking bits of sandwich through the bars of their cage, they'd eaten and slept throughout the afternoon. However, once stuffed into the torture mask the warmth of the studio and perfume of their make-up woke them up and encouraged them to copulate with unrestrained vigour.

We did eventually get the shot, but how Peter Cushing and Andre Morrel didn't collapse with laughter I shall never know. It can't be easy to act out naked fear while peering at two gay rats having it away like knives.

One distressing occurrence was the theft of a major and nearly irreplaceable prop. It was one of those liquid filled glass domes you shake and make snowflakes swirl around a small model. In the story, Peter Cushing was supposed to find this in an antique shop and buy it as a present for Yvonne Mitchell. It was a particularly nice example and been chosen with considerable care. Unfortunately it was left lying on the shop counter at the end of the final run-through and someone had taken it.

Despite Rudolph Cartier's impassioned plea for its return it was never found, and the unfortunate property man had to find another. This was one occasion when Shepherds Bush market failed to come up with the goods, but someone had one at home and offered to fetch it – a frantic journey to bring it to the studio in time. It arrived with only a short time to spare.

Viewers are sometimes unimpressed when told about the stress of working in show business, but *Nineteen Eighty-Four* provided it in spades.

D r y   I c e

After *Nineteen Eighty-Four* we lived for several weeks on our sudden elevation to fame. The end credits had clearly shown our names in big letters as being responsible for the effects and suddenly our friends were lining up to buy us drinks and wanting to talk about the programme. They wanted to know if Peter Cushing really was afraid of rats? Who was Big Brother? (He was in fact Roy Oxley, the programme's designer and a pre-war colleague of mine at the Air Ministry.) Strangers were introduced to us and were told that we were the chaps who'd made the Telescreens and the Torture Room 101 and we'd been interviewed in the press and had our photographs taken. The awe in which television was held in those days was amazing. We walked on air, but eventually came back to Earth when the publicity and excitement died down.

But by then we were left awaiting our next job. Unfortunately it didn't come. Perhaps the programme organisers had been so astounded by the controversy whipped up by *Nineteen Eighty-Four* they were afraid to raise their heads above the parapet. We felt let down and unwanted and, with nothing to do spent more time in the White Horse than was good for us. And now with no shows to concentrate on we decided to make some much needed special effects equipment.

Our designs were purely hypothetical because we had little idea what we would be called upon to provide, but we did know that we wanted to get rid of the tin bath. Not that we really owned it; it was kept in a property store room at Lime Grove but it had become our responsibility to use it. At that time the chaps in props didn't like us. Not only had we begun to ape the militant trade unionists we so despised but we were 'giving ourselves airs.' This was naughty, but with all the publicity we had acquired it was perhaps understandable. Given the authority to undertake all special effects we protected our rights as fiercely as the other sections safeguarded theirs and while I don't think we were ever guilty of saying 'Don't touch that – that's my job!' we came shamefully close to it. But about the bath; it was one of those long galvanised steel things known colloquially as a tin bath. It featured in fireside scenes in miner's hovels where it would be set up in front of the grate so that the coal dust produced by honest toil and sweat could be sluiced from the honest miners's body. It usually featured the honest wife scrubbing the man's back or hovering nearby with an enamel jug of hot water and a threadbare towel until the miner, suitably cleansed, could drag himself to the table and wolf down the meat and two veg before going to the pub and spending the entire evening with his mates – but you recognise the scenario.

The tin bath, when not used in plays, was employed as a dry ice generator. It was kept by props and until we came upon the scene had been operated by the prop men to create dream sequences and mist effects. But now Jack and I, 'Levin's bloody newcomers', were to take this fun work away leaving them to supply mundane things like the furniture and cutlery – small wonder that they were incensed. To add to their discomfort the Property Master, their own boss, ordered them to turn over to us the special effects equipment held in Props, which wasn't much, but it diminished their status.

The technique they used for dream sequences was to set the bath on four piles of bricks and to heat the water by placing a large cast iron gas burner underneath. The operator would bring the water to scalding and then chuck in some broken dry ice, avoiding, if possible, the hot splashes that shot up. Despite its crude technology it worked and the effect was immediate. Copious clouds of dry ice mist would pour over the edge of the bath covering the studio floor in a layer of white clouds. Unfortunately it couldn't be turned off, unless of course one waited for the water to cool or were sufficiently brave to thrust a hand into very hot water and fish out the bigger lumps of dry ice.

And now this was our responsibility. It is possible that the burner the lads turned over to us was not the one they themselves had used (perish the thought), because the tap was small and incredibly stiff and the rubber hose which connected the burner to the studio gas supply was scorched and cracked. The first time we used the bath we learnt the truth – the CO_2 released along with the water vapour displaced the oxygen around the bath and extinguished the gas flames. The smell of gas alerted us to the fact that the tap must be turned off but under the clouds of vapour it was impossible to see anything and the tap could only be found by groping around under the bath. Inevitably our probing fingers came into contact with the red hot burner before we were able to locate the tap, a painful experience that caused us to leap about like silent Morris Dancers.

At the end of the programme we had the exasperating job of emptying the bath. This couldn't be done by lifting and carrying it so we had to remove the water a bucketful at a time, emptying them down the urinal in the gent's loo – something which we discovered had to done slowly if one was to avoid a back flow of water soaking one's shoes. The smug satisfaction of the prop staff, who had learnt how to deal with these problems was intolerable – until we found that if we tipped the water slowly down the fire escape the people using the subterranean corridor would think it was raining.

The necessity to protect our hands from burns and our shoes and socks from being deluged made us determined to devise a practical dry ice generator – and we came up with 'the dustbin'. This was an ordinary galvanised dustbin with another drum inside. It was heated by a thermostatically controlled immersion heater and the space between the inner and outer drums was insulated with expanded polystyrene which muffled the sound and cut down the heat loss. It worked incredibly well and following a short testing of the prototype we built two more. These gave greater control and enabled us to disperse the three generators around the studio. Plugged into the studio sockets they could be left to look after themselves freeing us from the need to check on gas taps or water temperature. To create a dream sequence all we had to do was to put the dry ice into the hot water. This we did by filling a plastic bucket drilled with several large holes with broken pieces of dry ice and lowering it into the hot water. When we wanted the effect to stop all we had to do was to lift the bucket out.

In a later modification we provided a tap to drain the water, but even without this innovation it was possible for two men to lift the generator and carry it to the loo, or if were anxious to get to the White Horse, out to the fire escape. With some justification we congratulated ourselves on our design because it seemed so modern. It meant that directors wanting misty vapour for studio riverbank scenes, bogs or graveyards could have it in any configuration. They were delighted that we were able to supply equipment which was demonstrably not a tin bath. Furthermore our generators were quiet. Dry ice tipped into hot water bubbles noisily, prompting the boom operators to complain. Now, with lids on the dustbins the sound of boiling caldrons was barely noticeable.

Unfortunately, we became the victims of our success. The property men would have nothing to do with our dustbins and we had to store them in the workshop. Although by now we had been relocated to a bigger room on the second floor the three dustbins took up a great deal of precious space. Management eventually gave us a store room in the basement which solved the problem and allowed us to house our collection of stock effects away from the workshop. But it wasn't just the storage, the dustbins proved a nuisance to us in other ways. Now valuable days had to be spent in the studio hanging around waiting to lower a bucket of dry ice into hot water. We tried to co-opt the scene crew in the operation, explaining how simple it was, but spurning 'the crumbs from the rich man's table' they would have none of it. Eventually the situation resolved itself when an industrial engineering company produced a really sophisticated dry ice machine; it had fans and lightweight ducting to squirt the vapour in different directions (including upwards and downwards, something our devices weren't able to do). Furthermore this company arranged to hire the equipment and the operators to tend it in the studio. At last we were free of all dry ice commitments.

Movie makers had been using dry ice for dream sequences long before Jack and I came upon the scene and had, presumably, overcome the problems that in the beginning confronted us. However, unlike film studios, television studios have pristine floors that are painted with water-soluble paint and because dry ice clouds are composed of water vapour, things in the studio get very damp – including the floor, a fact that came to our attention during a ballet scene. The development of washable floor paint was a boon for television designers because where there are a number of different scenes, every set will demand a different floor treatment. In the studio the sets are positioned and dovetailed into a pattern which is designed to make the best use of space and so the floor will have a number of different finishes. Parquet tiles, flag-stones, dirty concrete, polished marble and so on. Every sort of floor can be reproduced in paint. Some are applied by hand using long brushes while others are printed using rubber rollers. At the end of transmission the scenery is struck and the linoleum floor is mechanically washed. It is this which makes the TV studio different from the film studio where the floors, which are made of wood, can be rough and full of holes.

Our Archimedean discovery was that removable floor paint becomes sticky when subjected to prolonged immersion in dry ice mist. The ballet sequence which brought this home to us was set in a long leafy dell with exotic trees and plants. It looked splendid. The dry ice covered the entire studio and gave a truly magical dream-like quality which impressed the director no end. However, we got a forewarning of impending disaster when one of the ballerinas appeared to stumble. Knowing the floor was free of all cables and similar impedimenta I put it down to a chance mishap. But there were some unexplained clicking noises as the girls twirled around the floor and I swear I saw a silver shoe leap from the mist and fall back again without containing a foot.

The true catastrophe happened when the male dancer, who had to run the length of the glade and finished with a gazelle-like leap into the air never made it. About half way along he slipped in the goo and almost disappeared from sight. His progress was seen only as a feathery bow wave as, flat on the floor he hurtled towards the bank of shrubs at the end. Two shrubs toppled over and fell against the cyclorama bringing the dancer to a halt. Shocked silence was followed by a groan as he slowly got to his feet and we saw that his immaculate ballet tights resembled overalls worn by painters or young children in finger painting classes. Rehearsals were delayed as the floor was scrubbed clean and the sticky shoes and ruined tights were taken back to a distraught wardrobe mistress. It took a lot of explaining at the inquiry which followed and at which Jack and I were curtly told by management to 'investigate' the problem. Neither of us could see how we would be able to solve it and eventually it was filed away under 'must look into this'.

We were to learn that water vapour can affect things other than painted floors because dry ice was responsible for another fiasco. It concerned an orchestra which the designer had arranged to perform below a dry ice waterfall. Seated on chairs and dressed in tails, white shirts and bow ties they made a lovely picture and during rehearsals made equally lovely music. Unfortunately on the final run-through when the director called for the waterfall effect their rendition underwent a profound change. About half way through the piece the conductor's trained ear detected that someone was playing flat. Within a minute no one needed a trained ear to hear that the entire string section was performing below the woodwind. Musician stared at musician, but even with the music now sounding decidedly off-key they played on until the part where the timpani came in. These large copper drums are tuned to produce a clear sharp sound, but the tops, being natural skins (not the plastic tops in use today), gave the sound of rubber hammers belabouring wet washing – which was not an effect a composer would normally call for.

We should have explained to the director that certain materials (of which cat gut and animal skins are two) are anhydrous, absorbing moisture and going limp. The conductor waved his baton above his head bringing the rehearsal to a close. We got around the problem by reducing the amount of cloud while the designer put the musicians on rostra placed well forward of the waterfall and about eighteen inches above the floor. The effect was somewhat short of the original conception – in fact the waterfall looked more like a white shroud being waggled in the background but we all learned another valuable lesson.

T h e   R e a l   J a c k   K i n e

Although still in our first year Jack and I had begun to adapt to each other and to our new life. Everything was exciting. Time away from work was spent thinking about work. We arrived in the office early in the morning and often left long after the official leaving time and, if there was an opportunity to work at weekends, we grabbed it. In 1954 we worked during every public holiday including part of Christmas. Perhaps subconsciously we felt it was all too good to be true and that like the perfect dream it would vanish and we would be told that our section was to be reorganised or amalgamated or something equally hideous. The principle of letting two men run a section, making their own decisions and handling every programme without supervision seemed so far removed from the BBC policy that we both felt it couldn't last. And one day our fears were confirmed. About three years into our partnership when we were firmly established and well able to deal with any requirements the axe fell. Richard Levin had been using a redundant BBC engineer to develop an experimental project in which, by an arrangement of spray guns connected to electronic circuitry it would reproduce a fully coloured backcloth from a scanned coloured photograph. These days with modern technology it would be possible but in the fifties it was little more than an impossible ambition. Levin was aiming at another coup – another fibre glass column to show the world that he was in the vanguard of innovation. But the machine wouldn't work. Week after week the problems multiplied – and so did the costs. Eventually Levin bowed to the inevitable and scrapped the whole project.

But what to do with the engineer? Now even more redundant than before? Unfortunately Richard Levin had widely publicised his intention to automate scene painting and now he was forced to admit that his dream-scheme couldn't be realised. In a moment of pique and without considering the implications he decided to put this chap in charge of the two of us. He considered that this introduction of new blood and new thinking would improve our output. Ian Beynon Lewis warned him that it would lead to trouble but Levin, smarting from his disappointment steamrollered it through. It was a ridiculous idea and unfair – not only to us, but to this poor sod who probably hated the assignment as much as we did. But he couldn't show it. He had been put in charge and he was determined to take his responsibility seriously. He was an organiser and had decided that from now on Jack and I must be prepared to do things by the book. He would accept all briefs and allocate them to us as he saw fit.

At first Jack and I were too shell-shocked to take it in. We were the experts in the field and this bloke, who had seemingly never created a special effect of any kind in his life, was going to tell us what to do and, god save us, how to do it. We retaliated. We said he could screw himself and from then on ignored him. It was a rotten thing to do, but we were fighting for our very existence – our lives. I think it was no more than two weeks before Ian Beynon Lewis sent for us and told us that things weren't working out as Richard Levin had hoped – as if we didn't know – and that arrangements would be made to return us to our former autonomy the following Monday. Jack and I celebrated in the White Horse. 'Can you imagine coming here and drinking with the bugger?' asked Jack.

The reason we had become such a successful duo was that although thinking alike and reacting alike, we had different talents. Jack had qualities that I didn't possess. He was an accomplished artist trained at the Slade and a craftsman of extraordinary ability. He was able to create tiny working models and do all those fiddly things I could only strive at. But the skill I most admired was his ability to concentrate on whatever he was doing. In this he was quite single minded. I, on the other hand, would be working on one thing, worrying about another and trying to solve the problems of a third. Nevertheless he was prepared to tolerate my shortcomings because from time to time I had ideas and was, he admitted, useful around the workshop. Above all else I appreciated his unique sense of humour. Jack seldom repeated jokes he'd been told in the pub but was able to recount his own experiences in a fashion that made even the most mundane activity seem hilariously funny. His sense of humour lightened the intervals between takes and did much to smooth out those nervy occasions when things were not going well. His sense of humour and his ability to tell a good story was still evident in later years when he told me about his eye operation.

He was in his seventies when his sight began to fail. Eventually he became to all intents and purposes, blind. But then a new form of corneal surgery gave him the hope that he might have at least part of his sight restored. It was recommended that he should have a consultation with a specialist at The Radcliffe hospital in Oxford and arrangements were made for him to undergo the operation on just one of his eyes. It involved seven hours of patient work by skilled surgeons and covered a range of technological advances from laser mapping of the cornea to freezing of the eye and the use of sound waves to break up the clouded lens. Squeamish readers may not wish to be given precise details of the surgery involved so I won't continue but the thought of having eight stitches in the eye ball still causes me to wince. After leaving hospital he phoned to tell me about it, dwelling at length on those first moments when he realised he could see. 'I looked at my hands' he said'. And they were *claws*!' The disgust in his voice was obvious. 'And my arms – all scrawny!' He was telling me about one of the most incredible events in his life and it was coming out as a comedy sketch. As he explained it, without his sight he lived inside his head unable to read or paint and with the only visible signs of anything around him being a series of shifting grey and black patches. Then this miracle occurred. In the preliminary discussions at the hospital the surgeons explained that the treatment, if successful, (and that gave him food for thought) would enable the light falling on the still functioning cones around the periphery of the retina to be focussed in such a way as to make it appear that the whole eye was working. Naturally, with so great a depletion of the retina the operation would be capable of producing only a partial image – dead cones cannot yet be restored to life – but for someone unable to see anything but blurred shapes, this promised a lifeline. He was told that he would gain enough of his sight to be able to move around freely and to enjoy once again the scenes of everyday life, an enhancement that to most of us would rank above winning the lottery. Who could fail to appreciate his feelings at the time? 'When it was all over I sat up in bed', he told me. 'dying to raise the bandages, but afraid that if I did I'd ruin everything. But I just had to find out whether the operation had been a success or a failure. The surgeons had told me the bandages must remain in place for at least a day, or until the eye had recovered from the trauma of being jabbed with a needle, cut, stitched and welded'.

'The day dragged by' he went on 'and I realised I was pressing the knob on my talking watch a hundred times an hour. Even the radio failed to interest me, and you know what that has always meant to me. Eventually, I could stand it no longer so lifting a small corner of the bandage I slowly opened my eyes. The world was still black. Of course I was looking (if I could look) at the inside of the bindings. Even more slowly, not knowing what to expect, I looked down. It was amazing; I could see the sheets and the world beyond the foot of the bed. Then I lifted a hand and attempted to focus on it – my god! It was a shrivelled claw!' This made me realise how anyone deprived of sight for any length of time relies on memory and the sense of touch – and how distorted a mental image can become. Naturally I was delighted for him – so much so that I didn't tell him that his bony hands had always looked like claws, but when you've spent many years holding bits of wood while your partner glues or paints them you notice such things.

Jack had started work in television long before I did, having joined the staff at Alexandra Palace in 1937. However he was given full employment status only after a years' probation and so didn't officially join the BBC until 1938 when he was classified as a draughtsman and scenic artist. Life at Ally Pally, according to him, was fun but somewhat humdrum and he and his colleagues took every opportunity to brighten things up by playing jokes on each other – or on the management. Once when a party of Bishops was being given a guided tour of the studios someone got the idea that Jack and his mates should dress up as parsons. They rolled their trousers above their knees and wore cartridge paper clerical collars pinned around their necks. Circles of black paper on their heads simulated what they thought was religious headgear. Knowing that the visitors wouldn't be brought to their dusty and dirty part of the building one of the chaps suggested they arrange their own delegation by holding a mock fashion parade on the stage of the old theatre. The theatre, which had lost its audience seating, still had the stage and front tabs, and with only minor additions had become their scene painting workshop. Turning the handle they closed the dusty curtains and carefully grouping themselves around the stage they sang a comic song accompanied by an erotic dance. Slowly they cranked the wheel and reopened the curtains. So intent were they on their performance that they didn't see their audience, but when they did they froze. Standing out front was the party of Bishops. Normally such behaviour would have called for a severe reprimand if not instant dismissal, but as the Bishops had so hugely enjoyed the joke no mention was made of it.

Jack had originally trained as a model maker at a time when most of the work was created by hand and the level of skill required was phenomenally high. These skills enabled him not only to make any model we were asked to provide, but to assess the time it would take and the materials we should use. And this period provided one of his most famous anecdotes.

While working as a young apprentice for the famous architectural firm of J. Thorpe in London he was told that he must always look smart. His mother conscious of the fact that his socks always seemed to be hanging over his shoes made him wear sock suspenders to keep them up. These hallmarks of sartorial elegance, popular before the invention of self-supporting hosiery, comprised an elastic strap that went around the calf from which hung adjustable elastic with a clip to support the sock. Jack's suspenders were new, bright red and to him, utterly repellent. They were also unreliable. One morning on his way to work by Underground one of the suspenders unclipped and fell around his ankle. Had he noticed it this would have been embarrassing to the young boy, but what neither he nor the chap sitting next to him realised was that the clip had neatly hooked itself into the man's trouser turn-up. It might have fallen out again, but at the next station the luckless chap got up, folded his newspaper, took his umbrella from the rack and made his way to the exit doors. Unfortunately, when he tried to alight he found that something was holding him back. That something was a bright red umbilical cord connecting him to Jack's sock.

We shall never know whether it was the sight of this long red thing or the realisation that on the end of it there was a young lad with his leg in the air who was gripping the arm rests to prevent himself being dragged along the aisle, or whether it was the fact that he was about to be carried on to the next station that caused the man to panic, but what we do know is that he became frantic to free himself from the bond and for a brief moment indulged in a balletic tug of war while standing on one leg. Eventually the metal clip bent and the man, free of encumbrance, leapt through the closing doors. Jack looked at the suspender which, still attached to his sock, had flown back to him like a homing pigeon. But it was now four feet long – and thin. His sock had also suffered a lethal enlargement and was hanging over his foot like an empty coal sack. Quickly he reeled in the dead elastic, stuffed it into his pocket and with a scarlet face dashed away to another carriage.

D a v i d   A t t e n b o r o u g h

Jack and I made many good friends during our career, but such friendships are not uncommon when people work closely together. Showbiz, because of its high level of excitement and publicity, creates a particular type of camaraderie. Unfortunately the media often gives the public a wrong impression, promoting the view that showbiz friendships are shallow and affected – a view fostered by the effusive tributes and emotional speeches trotted out at award ceremonies. But these public displays have little to do with the genuine friendships that develop between performers and those behind the scenes.

Because he came upon the scene at the same time as we, did Cliff Michelmore became a friend. Furthermore for many years he and Jean lived in Reigate, not far from Kingswood and during the Suez petrol crisis he would often give me a lift home. Cliff interviewed Jack and I on our first television appearance. Featured as the two men who were responsible for all the special effects, we demonstrated, among other things the magic effect of putting dry ice into hot water. I became so carried away by the occasion that I held onto a piece while I answered Cliff's questions and was alerted to the fact that I was clutching something that was burning my hand only a split second before it would have been too late to let go. 'Look at this children, how to get frostbite and lose all your fingers – it's a great party trick.'

Another friend from the same era is Sir David Attenborough, well known for his splendid animal programmes although probably less well remembered as a one-time controller of BBC2. In that role he would routinely summon his managers to the executive dining room on the sixth floor of Television Centre for a working lunch. These were always well-attended because he was able to give us an overview of BBC plans and programme scheduling – and a cracking good lunch.

There are several memories of Sir David that come to mind, one is the occasion of the sticky bench I mentioned earlier, but what followed remains fixed in my memory and shows our naivety in those days. David came to our office at Television Centre to ask whether we could possibly design a lightweight reflector that he could take with him into the jungle. Reflectors are used to direct sunlight into dark areas under trees and is an essential item where there is no form of ancillary lighting. A reflector needs to be lightweight, easily portable and sufficiently robust to survive the rigours of transportation.

After he'd gone Jack and I considered the problem. The material would need to be both reflective and lightweight. Perhaps our scribbles in the White Horse generated an unwarranted optimism – or clouded our vision, because shiny and light meant only one thing – so we chose aluminium. Today there are many excellent lightweight reflectors on the market. Made from metallised fabric they are stretched tightly over circular 'clock' springs and can be reduced in size by twisting the spring into a figure eight and then, by folding the top half over the bottom reduced even further. So why didn't we think of that – or anything even remotely practical? The fact remains that we chose aluminium.

We left the White Horse and walked to a metal shop in the Uxbridge Road where we bought two large sheets of thin aluminium and then, bursting with enthusiasm, carried them back to the Centre. It never occurred to either of us as we frequently paused to take a rest – that this lightweight aluminium was bleeding heavy. We'd decided to make our reflector in the shape of a circular lady's fan and thinking this was a clever idea, we marked out the sheets in segments tapering from eight inches wide to one inch. Each was three feet long making the final reflector a respectable six feet in diameter. We drove a rivet through the centre and threaded strong tape through holes in the blades to space them the right distance apart, then we phoned David to tell him that his reflector was ready for collection.

Was the optimism beginning to wear off or were we having second thoughts about our design? Jack didn't appear to be as enthusiastic as he had been when we made our preliminary sketches. When David arrived we tried to rekindle our enthusiasm and, having agreed to demonstrate its merits, I opened it with the flourish of a conjurer producing a bunch of flowers. I noticed that Jack was standing back as if he were merely an interested spectator. I demonstrated the fact that it opened out to a six foot circle but our trumpery catch failed to locate and the blades collapsed. Jack rallied sufficiently to help me fix it and, concentrating on bending it into shape, neither of us saw David's face. I wish I had. It must have shown strong emotions. When we'd levered the clip back into shape he told us that it was just what he wanted. We belted the catch with a hammer a couple more times and showed him how to repair it in the jungle. Short of hanging a pair of pliers on it and, perhaps a tin of Brasso to buff up the aluminium I don't think we could have done much more to convince him what utter prats we were. He heaved it onto his shoulder, thanked us again, staggering off down the corridor.

I have often wondered where he disposed of it because ten tons of sheet aluminium cannot easily be abandoned in the street or thrown over a wall. It calls for ingenuity to get rid of something that cumbersome. We did fulfil one of the specifications; it was certainly 'sufficiently robust to survive the rigours of transportation' – it was so robust that in hostile territory it could have been used as a bullet proof shield.

Yellow   Phosphorous

Now that we were in our first effects workshop we kept it as tidy as possible, but as the requests for our services began to increase, the working space got smaller and we were forced to saw wood balanced on chairs and paint things propped against the steel cupboard, and even to assemble props and models on the floor; it was time for a re-think. We couldn't increase the room space and so we had to devise a method of using it more economically. This led to us spending a weekend installing a new bench and a set of cupboards. The bench ran the length of one wall and the underside was fitted with three twin-door compartments. By some administrative jiggery-pokery (would you believe it?) this bench had been constructed in the carpenters' workshop as scenery but the quality was first class and the cupboards below the worktop would have graced any kitchen. They were fitted with the appropriate hinges and catches so all we had to do was to cart the various components upstairs and fix them in place. When it was finished it looked enormous; it offered not only a much grander bench and working space but lots and lots of useful cupboard storage as well. We took the old bench downstairs and set fire to it near the Pagoda. The bits that were painted maroon burnt with a strange light and sizzled ominously.

Having learned not to paint a bench top we booked out three sheets of hardboard and tacked them down, reasoning, as previously, that when they got dirty and spattered with glue, oil and paint we had only to replace them with clean sheets. We were forced to leave a gap between the bench and the wall because the only two power points in the room were lower than our worktop and would have been inaccessible had we not left a space for leads and connectors. To prevent pencils and screws rolling down behind the bench we nailed a thin strip of wood along the back.

And so the months passed until early one evening we encountered a problem. For some reason we were working with yellow phosphorous. Phosphorus has the habit of combusting spontaneously when exposed to air and so it is stored in bottles of water. Carefully we removed a piece from the brown glass bottle, placed it on a sheet of paper on the bench and holding it firmly with forceps chopped off a tiny piece with a knife. The knife blade came down and the piece of phosphorus shot across the bench, leapt over the strip of wood and disappeared down the back.

We looked at each other in horror. Behind that bench there was detritus resulting from months of labour. I pictured it. There would be wood shavings, sawdust, the odd sandwich wrapper, sheets of script, Perspex swarf and much, much more. All these inflammable materials had inadvertently gone down that slot when we'd been clearing up. And now in this perfect bed of tinder a small piece of yellow phosphorus was slowly drying out before bursting into flames.

Two things occurred to us. One was that when building a bench against a wall it's a good idea to cover the space between them even if the cover is removable. The other thing that occurred to us at that moment was that we were about to go home and the offices around us had already been vacated for the night. There was nothing for it but to dismantle the bench. The alternative, to spend the night in the workshop hugging a fire extinguisher, did not appeal. Clearing a space in the middle of the floor we opened the cupboard doors and started to remove the contents.

Straight away we saw that when we'd assembled the bench we hadn't filled in the backs of the cupboards and so were now looking at the wall. Splendid. We had only to remove a few of the items stored in the central cupboard and hook out the litter that had collected there, sift through it carefully until we found the phosphorus and then, thankfully, we could go home.

Jack laid a sheet of caption card on the floor while I held our desk lamp so that he could see what he was doing. He got to his knees and peered inside. His part in the operation was to carefully pull out the mess and lay it out on the cardboard while I scanned through it for the phosphorous. He looked round at me and whispered 'I can see it! Pass me the long-nosed pliers.' He'd seen the phosphorus on a section of metal trunking. He didn't want to risk losing it again and so was ultra-careful in handling it. I took the cap off the bottle of water and held it out, but he ignored the bottle and laid the tiny yellow chip on the cardboard sheet. I think he wanted to make sure that it was the phosphorus and not a piece of cheese.

We had half-expected the chip to burst into flames between the jaws of the pliers but nothing had happened. Now with our gaze fixed on the sheet of cardboard we waited and waited and still nothing happened. Were all these alarming stories about spontaneous combustion really just schoolboy folklore? We sat around smoking and looking at our watches – nothing! We returned the dormant piece to the water and went home.

Later that month, anxious to find out if phosphorous did ignite spontaneously we took the bottle with us when we were working on a firing range. Selecting a remote spot we carefully emptied the sticks of phosphorus onto the ground. Again nothing happened. No sudden explosion, no searing heat. Although free of water and clearly drying out they lay there, inert, harmless, benign. Eventually they reluctantly agreed to smoke themselves to extinction, but never once did we see any flames. Taking the bottle of phosphorus to an open firing range exemplified our determination to be cautious whenever there was a possible risk. Neither of us regret our semi-paranoia because although it did occasionally cause us to underplay a scene we knew that to injure anyone in the course of our work would have had had dreadful repercussions. Accidents will always happen and mistakes are inevitable, one of mine shows what I mean.

I was booked to talk to an engineering society and had taken with me several action props and devices, one of which was a Thermos flask. This was not your common or garden boring old lunch box thing, but simply the glass interior set in a short length of cardboard tube mounted on a circular base. It is important when giving a practical lecture of this type to dress up even the most mundane of things so that they are presented excitingly. The black base and the shiny silver glass container gave my dry ice demonstration an added mystery, but in fact the Thermos container was used only to get a few pieces of dry ice to the lecture venue without it melting into gas. It now stood on the table along with the latex hand, the blood knife and the breakable bottles.

Like all vessels containing frozen gasses the flask had to be left open at the top to prevent a build-up of pressure. For my demonstration I intended to show how dry ice can be used to produce a drinkable witch's brew and so I tipped out a few knobs from the flask and dropped them into a glass of warm water. The dry ice immediately erupted in clouds of white vapour. I drank some (it is simply the carbonic element of fizzy drinks) and not wanting to take any dry ice back with me I poured more hot water into the Thermos which also produced a grand display of vapour.

I was half way through my next demonstration when there was a loud bang, followed by a moment's stunned silence and then laughter accompanied by a generous round of applause. I hope it didn't show that I'd gone into shock because I had to continue as if nothing had happened. Modestly acknowledging the ovation I noticed that people in the first row were brushing small flecks of silver glitter from their clothing. Of my Thermos flask nothing remained. When I'd poured in the water it had cooled and then frozen, forming a plug in the neck. The evaporating gasses being trapped caused a pressure build up which eventually blew the flask to pieces. A small piece of that razor sharp glass in someone's eye could have finished my career.

Whole studios have been destroyed by someone being careless or making a mistake. One, in Italy, was sufficiently spectacular to be reported in our own national dailies while another, this time in the UK, destroyed most of a very large and expensive sound stage. Both, I believe were caused by unattended smoke guns setting fire to inflammable props. Obviously the people responsible did not expect this to happen; if they had done they would have filled their studios with firemen. At the Beeb we were very careful about hazards of this sort and although from time to time the strictness of the firemen irritated us, we eventually finished our television careers without a stain on our characters.

We had the responsibility for artiste's safety while they were taking part in stunts or being subjected to potentially dangerous effects while the firemen were responsible for ensuring that they didn't catch fire. Between the two of us we tried to make sure that the studios, scenery and props weren't incinerated during a lunch break or that our dash to the canteen didn't lead to slipshod behaviour.

Q u a t e r m a s s *I I*

Quatermass II was another six-part science fiction drama which had an extraordinary impact on the viewers. Written by Nigel Kneale and produced and directed by Rudoph Cartier it was a wonderful showcase for our new visual effects unit and provided ample opportunity to demonstrate what the pair of us could do. However, in creating a rocket take-off we were attempting the impossible – it was a challenge for which we were pathetically unprepared. How were we going to produce that searing jet of flaming gas that blasted from the bottom of a space rocket? In 1955 rocket take-offs were yet to become commonplace and apart from the V2s that rained down on London during the last phase of the war few people had even the faintest knowledge of what rocket propulsion was all about.

Jack had designed and made the rocket, a sleek model twenty four inches long and spray painted in matt silver. It stood on three fins and had a long tapering nose – it was the space rocket of schoolboys' dreams.

To create the thrust we considered various trick shots and superimpositions but were unable to see how we could combine these with a shot of a rocket lifting from its launch pad. After a long discussion we could think of nothing better than to try a pyrotechnic. Foolishly we chose one that would fit the hole in Jack's rocket – a fearsome monster that turned out to be one of the biggest in the Brocks catalogue. It contained an awesome amount of propellant and a final display (which we intended to remove) of 'brilliant blue stars'. We bought four, one to try, one for the take and two for retakes.

Our intention was to test it on the waste ground outside which, apart from a newly built brick wall defining the boundary with Wood Lane, still contained all the rubbish that had been dumped there over the years. Taking with us some wire, adhesive tape and a few tools we walked to the far end of the site where, we hoped, we could fasten the rocket to something solid. This would enable us to observe and time its duration. Near the pagoda we found an old wooden cartwheel that was both big and heavy and would do perfectly as an anchor. Although the spokes had seen better days it was encased in a rusty iron band which was as firm as the day the wheel had been made. Cutting a length of wire we fastened the rocket case securely to the rim and laid it on a flat patch of concrete. Then, using my wristwatch to time it we lit the blue touch paper and started the countdown.

For a moment the fuse smouldered and sparked – and then there was a short fizz. We moved closer to assess the picture the camera would see; we made viewing tubes with our hands. There followed an almighty blast of flame and smoke that rocked us back in surprise. Everything in the path of that searing jet was swept away. Paper, dust and even empty beer bottles were hurled across the concrete and the wheel began to turn. Those who have fired even a medium sized rocket will know the acceleration that rockets can achieve. In an instant they hurtle miles into the sky where they explode to gasps of Oooohs and Ahhhhhhs. But speed denotes power and we had, strapped to our wheel, a veritable tiger-by-the-tail sort of power. Our rocket, stick-less and bound hand and foot, struggled to free itself while Jack and I realising the enormous forces we had unleashed retreated to the Pagoda where we peered nervously from either side. The wheel was now spinning vigorously on its hub. Then, like the Great Panjandrum of war time fame, it spun upright and ran across the ground. Flames and smoke belched from its rim as it gathered speed. Near the perimeter wall it ran into an obstruction and came to a dead stop – but the rocket didn't. Slipping from its bonds it carried on, clearing the wall by inches and flying down Wood Lane at head height. Jack and I, petrified with fear, could only stand and watch. A sudden shower of bright blue stars in the vicinity of White City Underground Station told us where it had finished up. Speechless and shaking, we returned to the workshop. Supposing, just supposing, our rocket had caused an accident. Everything else was forgotten. Timing the duration was forgotten: spacecraft and their means of propulsion were forgotten and the excitement of working on another *Quatermass* serial was forgotten; instead we listened at the open window for bells, the chromium plated bells carried by police cars and ambulances in those days. Mercifully Wood Lane, apart from the noise of moving traffic (yes, moving thank God.) was apparently normal. We might have thanked our lucky stars except that stars seemed inappropriate.

The next day was spent in dread. Would we be summoned to an office upstairs and asked the terrible question: 'Do you know anything about a rocket apparently fired from the grounds outside?' Would there be several policemen waiting for us to accompany them to the station? But as the morning passed and there was no summons to go upstairs we ceased to fear the worst and were able to return to the problem of jet propulsion. We walked to the White Horse where two pints of beer soothed our tattered nerves and allowed us to concentrate on the problem of creating the take-off thrust. Once again we sat round the table with paper and pencils but this time pyrotechnics no longer figured in our calculations. Instead we concentrated on simulation. We needed some method of producing a visual blast but a method we could control. We knew what it should look like – by God didn't we just – and in the end we came up with a plan to lift the model from the launch pad on a six foot length of tube. This tube would also be used to feed smoke and compressed air to the rocket base and would carry leads to a powerful car headlight bulb which, tucked up inside the body of the rocket we hoped would light the smoke and make it look like flame.

All this demanded a highly complicated arrangement of pipes, reservoirs for the smoke, compressed air bottles, gimbals and heaven knows what else. And that's how it finished up. The tube was fitted behind the model where it would not be seen by the camera. We'd made sure of this in various tests we'd carried out and were satisfied that the illuminated blast looked powerfully convincing. But we'd made the mistake of carrying out our tests in daylight and now we were faced with the requirements of the lighting cameraman. Trying every combination possible there was no way in which that model could be back lit without producing a shadow of the tube in the smoke. And so the tube which was hidden from view produced a perfect replica of itself for all to see. Of course, we might have suggested that the back light should be switched off but you don't tell a lighting cameraman how to light a model; not even Rudolph Cartier would have dared to do that.

As well as being asked to provide the rocket we were also asked to design and make the space suits that would be worn by Professor Quatermass and his fellow astronaut. Jack designed these, again on the lines of the 'futuristic' images conjured up by the space fiction writers and illustrators of boy's comics. It was a powerful design but the only method of making the suits was to have them moulded in heavy latex from a plaster sculpture. It worked well in that they looked good and were obviously pressure suits that could have been worn in zero atmosphere, but looking good was what it was all about. The fact that they were cast in aqueous latex meant they were very heavy and extremely inflexible, factors which were responsible for us making our acting debuts on TV. Because this was live television and there was no opportunity to break transmission Jack and I were cast as white-coated laboratory technicians with the responsibility of getting the two men into their space suits. This had to be done quickly and in time for their next scene – the interior of the rocket which was a small set on the opposite side of the studio. John Robinson as Quatermass was able to get there under his own steam but poor Hugh Griffiths, a small man, was quite unable to dash across the studio clad in the heavy space suit. We solved this by picking him up and, out of view of the cameras, rushing him over to the other set and strapping him into his seat in front of the control panel. However, what we didn't know (not that we could have done anything about it) was that in the process of moulding the lower half of the space suits an amount of hard rubber had formed in the crotch of the trousers. In hoisting poor Hugh so that he was clear of the floor his body weight was supported entirely on his private parts. Fortunately his agonised cries, muffled by the helmet, were not picked up by the boom operators. His condition was not improved when Jack and I, intent upon getting him there on time, dumped him down in his seat. This time his scream was horribly audible.

The development of telecine meant that Rudy Cartier could now use filmed inserts and because the model of the rocket take-off was safely in the can this sequence needed only to be slotted into the programme during transmission. Thanks to this innovation, instead of trying to do the impossible we could relax with only the spot effects (those done in the studio) to be dealt with. We were particularly grateful for this technology when it came to the monster in the tank because this too, being pre-filmed, was safely laced up on the telecine machine and meant that there was no frantic rushing around in the studio. But the monster in the tank was to prove even more of a problem than the rocket take-off.

H a n d   i n   G l o v e

Rudy Cartier had chosen to use the boiler house at Television Centre to film the interior of the 'secret laboratory' in which the alien monsters were being cultivated. The boiler house had been built in advance of the main White City complex and was incorporated in the Design Block; it had recently been equipped with its full complement of massive oil fired boilers which at the time stood unused and sparkling new. They were ideal because they had large inspection ports which would permit Professor Quatermass to open the door of one and peer inside. The studio electrician had managed to put a light behind the door so that when Quatermass, seen from the side, slowly opens it he is dramatically lit from within. He then has to recoil in horror at what he sees and in the next shot we are shown what he is looking at. The sight, which so greatly disturbs him – and the viewers – is a writhing monster in a tank of boiling acid.

This sequence was our responsibility and we had constructed a model of the inside of the tank and the monster. We had it all ready including two four foot rostra on which to film it but we hadn't assembled the components because Rudy needed the area to film Professor Quatermass entering the secret laboratory. Impatiently we stood around as the cameraman arranged his lights and fussed over his camera.

After what seemed hours Rudy had finished this sequence and was ready for us. He knew that he had taken longer over some of the shots than any of us had allowed for and now, slightly apologetically, he reminded us that we were limited for time. Glad to get going we assured him that it would take only a minute or two to have everything ready and dragging the two rostra into the middle of the floor and leaving a six inch gap between them we unpacked the component parts of the model.

The monster was a rubber glove filched from a bucket in the cleaner's cupboard which we had dressed with pieces of torn rubber. These nasty-looking fronds were stuck to the individual fingers with a powerful adhesive. The monster was to be operated from below by Jack who, with his hand inside and sitting under one of the rostra, would animate it as a scary glove puppet. Because it was meant to be in 'boiling acid' we were going to cement the wrist of the glove into a hole that we'd cut in a tin bowl. This bowl would then be half-filled with hot water into which we would toss a few chunks of dry ice at the last moment. This would produce white clouds of vapour which would look suitably dramatic. Relatively new to the viewing audience dry ice had become our stock answer to any request for fuming chemicals and now it was to imply boiling acid.

Laying out our bits and pieces I think we both wished we'd done a bit more work on the model instead of telling each other how good dry ice would look. Not to worry, we'd soon have it ready and unlike the rocket take off this had no hidden snags. We set the bowl on top of the rostra, unpacked the dry ice, stood the curved miniature wall at the back and, lastly, took out the glove which we had carefully wrapped in tissue paper. But something was wrong. Our monster which had looked so good with its frightening arrangement of fronds and tentacles when we'd packed it away now looked like a rotting lavatory brush. We examined it in disbelief. We'd wrapped it carefully and put it with the other things in a cardboard box but it was plain to see that the adhesive and the fronds had amalgamated in an intimate bond. This monster would never writhe and squirm or wave its tentacles. It might have served as an embalmed monkey or a frightening example of what can happen if you mistake battery acid for shampoo but there was no hope of it frightening people. Too late we realised that the special glue we'd used simply loves glue of the same type – it's used in the construction of aircraft and spaceships and they are not meant to fall apart. Now in intimate contact with each other the fingers of that glove had welded together side by side in a solid lump. We tried to prize them apart using a penknife but we succeeded only in slicing through the rubber glove. We changed tools and using a blunt piece of wood we somehow managed to separate the individual fingers. Telling the horrified Rudy who'd watch us unpack that it would take us only a few moments to put things right we suggested he should send the crew off for a smoke while we went back to the workshop. Worriedly Cartier reminded us again that time was running out, but unheeding we shot off, carrying with us an embalmed monkey and a tin bowl with a hole in it.

Upstairs we didn't say much to each other, we knew exactly what we had to do and we were far more worried than Cartier. Having more or less separated the fingers we tried to improve their appearance. Next came the most difficult part of the job and one which we should have undertaken when we had plenty of time – cementing the glove to the inside, of the metal bowl. This task was made more difficult by our earlier use of the penknife which had left a one inch slit in the wrist. We carried out a quick repair with sticky tape and praying to whatever god (if any) looks after special effects designers that it would hold long enough to get the shot in the can. We rushed back to the boiler house.

To prevent a repetition of finger-mating we'd showered the glove with talcum powder – which now made it look like iced seaweed and we had to wash it with water; it was all taking time. We were using a fast setting compound to cement the wrist of the glove to the bowl but for once this highly dependable adhesive remained obstinately soft. We endeavoured to speed up its action by using a hair drier but this only caused it to blister; it needed time to set – not heat. Eventually, having done as much as we could, we stood back, crossed our fingers and let the camera man light the scene. Then we got ready for a take.

Jack squeezed himself into a space below the left hand rostrum and stuck his hand into the glove. Too late he remembered that the glove was a left one and in his efforts to insert his right hand he had undone a lot of our work; we had to squeeze more sealant into the bowl. Having fetched a bucket of hot water I told everyone that I wasn't going to pour it into the model until I was assured that everyone was absolutely ready. 'Hot water with dry ice cools rapidly', I explained unnecessarily. The traditional call for red light and bell was given (although we had neither in the boiler house) and Rudy gave his command to stand by. I suppose we should have realised that when a person is sitting below a rostrum with his hand up a monster's bum it is sensible to provide said person with a comfortable seat but we'd overlooked that. Given that we'd overlooked so many important things – including the necessity to have everything ready and tried and tested before the filming the omission of a seat seemed almost trivial. Now, unable to sit, Jack had to squat uncomfortably across one of the angled supports. This posture seemed to affect his voice because a tortured wheeze came from below which said 'Noke oko!' I asked the wheeze to speak up.

'NOKE OKO!'

Of course – I'd forgotten the cocoa. There was a tin of the stuff in the box and I should have used it to thicken and darken the water. Grabbing the tin I emptied the contents into the water where, needless to say, they didn't mix. Now there was another worrying factor; I thought I could hear dripping. There followed a subterranean heaving as the luckless operator tried to exchange his squat for a crouch. Another strangled whisper, which I took to be 'Carry on – carry on' came from below before the bubbling of the dry ice drowned out all further communication; I moved aside to clear the shot. But why didn't Rudy give the word for action? Why was he asking the cameraman for another look through the viewfinder? If we didn't go soon we'd have an interesting sequence of a rubber glove lurching about in a tin bowl. I made a calm and dignified suggestion.

'Shoot the bloody thing for Christ's sake, it's leaking!'

I've seen that sequence again since it was first shown and it doesn't look at all bad – perhaps the interval of passing years has improved it but it hasn't blotted out the memories. I can still see Jack's tortured posture as he attempted to balance himself on a sloping brace. To millions of viewers it was a glimpse of the ultimate horror – the monster that with thousands of others were being cultivated to take over our planet. But those viewers might have been less impressed had they known that in reality the monster was merely a toilet cleaner's glove being waggled about by a bloke in a wet shirt, pissed off and smelling of cocoa.

C r a c k e r j a c k !

Looking in the index of the definitive reference book *British Television* I see that *Crackerjack,* one of the earliest and certainly one of the most popular children's programmes, first appeared in 1955 and was presented by Eamonn Andrews although I think that the following incident took place two or three years later than that. Trying to recall events I believe the victim was Leslie Crowther (although I can't be sure); I know it wasn't Peter Glaze because he took the part of the gun-slinger and when I recently asked Michael Aspel whether he was the unfortunate man he denied all knowledge of it.

The question remains – who was the actor who made television history? It's not recorded anywhere so I may never find out, but let me tell the story from the beginning: It happened during an episode in which we'd set up a sketch similar to the one performed by Dean Martin in cabaret (one of many performers and circus clowns who had used the same gag). It was the scene in a Western saloon where the gunslinger becomes embroiled in an argument with another customer and drawing his gun shoots the man six times at point blank range. Having received the entire contents of the six-shooter the man turns to the gunman and says, mockingly, 'Yah boo, didn't touch me' and picking up his beer, drains the glass, whereupon six jets of liquid spurt from his chest (they don't write 'em like that anymore).

Jack and I had cobbled up a special waistcoat which was highly decorated in order to camouflage the nozzles of the jets and the six tiny plastic tubes that fed them. At the back of the garment these tubes were joined together to a single, larger diameter tube which then joined another hidden in the man's trousers. This one emerging at the ankle was connected to a soda-syphon on the floor. The operation should have been as simple as it was effective; press the lever of the syphon and the six jets would spurt fiercely followed, we hoped, by gales of laughter from the studio audience.

Unfortunately for us however, this actor had a fussy little dresser who couldn't bear the thought of his man having to wear the nasty crinkled waistcoat that Jack and I had strapped around his middle. He pulled it about and tugged and smoothed it a dozen or more times before we went on the air.

However, what we didn't know was that his ministrations had separated the two pipes at the back of the trousers. Came the cue and I pressed the lever of the syphon – nothing! I pressed harder – still nothing. But the audience gave a gasp and then erupted in boisterous mirth. How daring of the BBC to show an actor wetting himself on television! Until the dribbling incontinence turned into a fulsome cascade neither Jack, who was standing behind me, nor I could see what was happening. In the control room the producer was completely mystified because he saw only the close-up shot of the actor's face and upper torso on his transmission monitor and, like the millions of viewers he couldn't understand why the studio audience was convulsed with laughter: all he knew was that the effect hadn't worked and he would have to cut quickly to the next sequence The inquest would come later, but for me the highlight of the show was the actor's face as two pints of cold soda-water surged around his loins. Sickly smiles I have seen, but this one, a mixture of shock and dismay was something I shall always treasure. It's a great pity that while I can still see his expression I've forgotten who it was. An event like that these days would figure in one of the many programmes devoted to bloomers or cock-ups, but when things went wrong for us we preferred to cover them up and carry on as if nothing had happened.

M o r e   S n o w

Back at the centre Jack and I went through the mail. Usually anything that turned up in the In Tray was simply confirmation of something we already knew about, but this was different. It was a marked up script from a director who wanted snow. Our spirits sank. Snow – that *bête noire* of television designers. As a child I loved snow. You could jump in it, slide through it and even mould it into missiles to fling at unsuspecting school-mates. In winter it transformed the dreariest landscape into a wonderland of whiteness and purity, but later, as a driver trying to get two young boys to school I found it far from endearing. Between my house and the village school is a steep hill which in winter becomes a bloody snow covered steep hill – and to add to the difficulty there is a blind right-angled bend at the bottom. Now I have to admit that under those conditions I cannot handle a car. While other drivers sail up it reading a newspaper I slide around and tippy-toes sideways into the hedge. I have owned many cars including a powerful 7.5 litre sports-car. I have had Land Rovers, front and rear wheel drives saloons and automatics – and I have never once after a snowfall, managed to climb that hill. The trouble for me has always been the bend. It's the sort of bend that demands a special skill in clutch and brake control – which I don't possess (a rotten conjurer *and* a pathetic driver?) While other cars go past me I sit and fume with my wheels churning impotently.

There were times however, when I appreciated the snow. In earlier years, before gritting techniques were established depressions in my lane filled with drifting snow, closing the road and confining us to our homes. Milk was delivered in crates to the local pub where, before hauling the bottles back on a sledge and distributing them at points along the lane where my neighbours could collect them, I enjoyed a wee warming dram.

The worst snow fall I ever encountered was in Lincolnshire when during the war blizzards swept across the open countryside and covered our airfield with a thick blanket. Operations had to be suspended and because the roads were blocked delivery of food supplies were cut off; we had to send foot patrols to Gainsborough to get bread. If we weren't all to starve it was essential to open the roads and I was assigned to snow clearance. This meant shovelling the stuff manually into open trucks (which had to do half the journey in reverse because it was impossible to turn round) and was damned hard work for the shovellers. I remember uncovering a bus stop sign, which I suppose was about eight or nine feet tall and showed just how snow can drift into depressions. To keep us at it we were supplied with navy rum of legendary strength, but surprisingly, there were some sad men who didn't like it and offered theirs to anyone prepared to swap cigarettes for a tin mug half-full of pure Jamaican crystal spirit; suddenly snow clearance didn't seem so arduous. The worst job was clearing the air-raid shelters. They were open at both ends and quickly filled with wind-blown snow which rendered them useless. Digging them out was a thankless task because the next snow blast filled them up again.

Our squadron of Hampden bombers parked along the dispersal roads had to be swept free of snow and manhandled into the hangars where they would not be seen by enemy aircraft. Of course the hangers, which did not in the least resemble country cottages could be recognised from a distance of twenty miles, but apart from scrawling 'Not here, we're away bombing Bremen' in the snow there was little we could do to protect them from German bombs. The airfield, set among smaller fields, stood out clearly in virgin whiteness. To a trained German reconnaissance crew cruising miles away it would have told them that they had found just what they were looking for. However the C.O. had an idea and instructed us to collect ash from the stoves and boilers and lay it in lines to simulate hedgerows. In different circumstances he might have made a brilliant special effects man.

But all that was in the past. Now in television, faced with different problems, I regarded snow as the most hateful stuff in the universe. On location directors would call for it to be spread over fields, around buildings, on the branches of trees and piled against windows and doors. We began to dread scripts which read 'The two men are seen staggering across the Arctic wastes, their eyes shut against the blinding snow.' Why couldn't the author have written 'a few snowflakes on the wind warn the men that there might be trouble ahead'? Even viewers who demand every penny's worth from their licence fee must feel compassion for people like Jack and me faced with the task of creating a Siberian landscape on the Yorkshire Moors in summer. When a director such as our dear friend Rudolph Cartier called for 'More snow boys – I must have more snow', our hearts would plummet. A timid suggestion that by moving his camera he could avoid showing the bare patches usually met with a withering look that sent us scurrying to find 'more snow'. In the studio we used sawdust covered with powdered chalk to simulate snow on the floor (agricultural salt was forbidden because it corroded the aluminium wheels of the camera dollies) but sawdust and chalk were later superseded by expanded polystyrene granules which looked fairly realistic and was easier to handle. Furthermore it could be swept up and re-bagged for further use.

Outdoors, fire-fighting foam, which could be sprayed over grass and vegetation by powerful pumps, became our mainstay with materials such as flour, talc and white scene paint being used to create local effects. Jack and I, as the new *wunderkind*, were determined to provide everything we were asked for, but we were lamentably short on experience. Had we studied the techniques of the movie makers who had, after all, been creating special effects for years we would have learned that as far back as the silent era movie makers had faced similar problems and had solved them. Of course, their equipment and techniques were primitive but ours were nearly non-existent. While we pompously avoided asking others for advice we did read books and our bibles were Brock's original manual on *Pyrotechnics* and Hoffman's encyclopaedic works, *Magic* and *More Magic*. The former gave us the recipes, materials and methods of manufacture of fireworks while the two massive volumes of Hoffman provided us 'with the secrets of conjuring tricks and stage illusions. In earlier times these books could be found in public libraries, but now modern tastes dictate that library shelves be stocked with books about pop stars and footballers. However neither of these works revealed the secret of dressing large areas with artificial snow.

Falling snow in the studio presented problems of a different kind. We first experimented with a sophisticated technique known as lobbing handfuls of torn paper over the top of the scenery, but launching it as high as we could it invariably coalesced into lumps which fell to the studio floor like suet dumplings. We then tried spreading it on a sheet of hardboard balanced on the top of the scenery from which, by mounting a high step ladder, we attempted to blow it evenly onto the set using an electric fan. This was not a good idea because it either fell spasmodically or went all over the cameramen. Fortunately neither of these experiments where ever tried in productions – the sight of an unexplained sheet of hardboard falling into shot followed by an electric fan either dangling on a flex or hitting the floor in a shower of sparks might have required explanation.

I can't recall who told of us of the method supposedly used at the Royal Opera House but it opened our eyes to a whole new world of practical effects. For falling snow, the clever stage hands at 'the Garden', we were told, used an assembly of two wooden battens fastened to a sheet of scene cloth. The cloth, slit in several places, formed a trough which could be filled with paper snow. The technique was to gently lift and lower the battens on either side of the canvas allowing some of the paper flakes to escape through the slits and float to the floor below. Suet dumplings were trapped because the slits were too small for them to pass through.

This type of gentle snowfall was known as 'Christmas card' and, having learned about it we made a prototype consisting of a sheet of scene cloth nailed to two wooden battens and took it to Ealing Studios to experiment with. It was obvious that we couldn't operate it in the way it was supposedly used at Covent Garden by raising and lowering each batten alternately – our arms weren't long enough to hold it out from the gantry, but we reasoned that if we hung it underneath we could work the battens from either side. Trouble was that we couldn't figure out how to pass one of the battens underneath the swaying walkway (which was forty feet up in the air and beyond the reach of step ladders) and then fill the scene cloth with confetti. We managed it after passing a ball of string from one side to the other, an operation accomplished by poking our fingers between the wooden slats. To the string we tied some sash cord and we were home and dry. However, when we operated the battens the effect was disappointing. We took it down again and made more slits in the cloth – which produced slightly better results, but was still far from the effect we wanted. Was the person who told us about Covent Garden deliberately pulling our legs?

Sometime later we were told that confetti wouldn't work, we apparently needed special paper which we could get from a company called Packman Research. We got in touch with them and learned that they not only supplied the special paper, but hired out machines for producing gentle snow falls. These, they told us, were hung above the set and operated electronically! Upon hearing this we scrapped our primitive device and gave the unused packets of confetti to a secretary who was getting married.

Thinking about it afterwards we realised that by using the services of an outside contractor it would be an easy matter for scenic designers to simply order the equipment and operators for themselves, thus bypassing our Visual Effects section and although this would rob us of prestige it would also free us from the manual labour involved. Rigging snow droppers in the flies, carrying bags of snow material up vertical steel ladders and clearing large areas of studio floor afterwards would now be someone else's responsibility. We agreed that prestige wasn't everything and turned our thoughts to other things.

G h o s t s   a t
E a l i n g   S t u d i o s

And now, for the reasons I pointed out in the introduction I must go back a bit. Although we worked in Shepherds Bush and knew the shopping areas of both the Bush and Ealing well, we had never been to Ealing Studios; to us 'Ealing Studios' was merely a symbol that appeared on the cinema screen promising an hour or more of comedy or an exciting war film. Ealing, built in 1931, was one of several British studios that for different reasons had ceased to make films (Lime Grove, the home of Gainsborough and The Rank Organisation was, of course, another.) In Ealing's case it became necessary to sell up when Stephen Courtauld, who was largely responsible for the financial arrangements, decided to retire. A decision was made to dispose of the property and to transfer production to Pinewood. Ealing Studios came on the market and in 1955 the BBC was able to buy it, lock stock and property barrels so to speak for £350,000.

The demise of the film industry seemed inevitable to Jack and me; we were in television and felt little sympathy for a business which we regarded as outmoded and a dying form of entertainment. We had long held the belief that the cinema must eventually give way to the small screen. We could have been forgiven for such presumption because as our audiences grew, so cinema queues diminished and we confidently predicted the end of the movies in fewer than five years. We knew that TV audiences were reaching peaks measured in millions and assumed that one day people would give up going to the cinema and stay in their own homes where all the entertainment they could possibly wish for was available.

As subsequent events have shown, we were wrong – or half wrong. The film industry has survived, defying our prediction and is currently making millions for its investors: Nevertheless this has not been without a radical overhaul of the industry. Now films are projected onto screens not much bigger than bed sheets and shown in tiny auditoriums only slightly bigger than our own living rooms. Despite their lack of size, they offer a wider variety of films than we were able to enjoy in our smoky flea pits with their weekly change of programme. But now Ealing was extinct, an empty shell. Its name still represented the big screen and the magic of the large cinema, but to Jack and me in 1956 it proved our contention that the film industry was finished.

Our dismissive attitude was to change, when one afternoon we were summoned to Richard Levin's office and told that we were to go to Ealing Studios and make a list of the assets most likely to interest designers. We'd heard rumours that the BBC was taking over the premises and that it was proposing to use them for filmed inserts, but we had also heard that it was to be used as a scenic workshop and store. Another rumour had it that it was to become a staff training centre. Now we had the truth from the horse's mouth: it was to become the BBC's film unit and it was our task to go there and judge what facilities would be of use to Design Department.

The following day, remembering to take a notebook we caught the bus to Ealing Broadway. Laughable now but we had to ask someone where the studios were. When we found them they seemed less impressive than we had imagined but like Doctor Who's TARDIS Ealing Studios was much bigger on the inside than the entrance building suggested. Set back from the road, the gates were manned by two BBC commissionaires who had been put in charge and who had comfortably installed themselves in reception. They had equipped themselves with such vital necessities as a radio, an electric kettle, a large tea pot and a number of china mugs. Glad of company they quickly organised a fresh brew and gave us two steaming mugs and a couple of biscuits from their hospitality tin. They told us proudly that they were the sole occupants of the studios and described the place as spooky – 'just like a ghost town'. So strong was this impression that they were convinced that the empty stages were haunted by dead film actors. They said we were sure to meet them in some dark recess, or if we didn't actually see them we could feel their presence by a sudden drop in temperature. This had us wondering why Levin had chosen us for the job. However, when we began our tour all thoughts of ghostly apparitions disappeared – suddenly we were the kids who had been given the keys to the sweet shop.

Our short career in television had not prepared us for anything like this; this was the real thing and suddenly we saw what movie making was all about. The bulk of the props had gone but in a store room we found a hoard of miniature trains and railway equipment. There were carriages, railway stations, signals and track by the yard. But these were not the sort of model trains that one can buy in toy shops but were made to scale with every detail a perfect replica of their full-sized counterparts. Furthermore there were several different sizes of rolling stock. Jack and I were entranced. Searching around we found several packing cases that contained scale model ships and submarines and on racks, covered by dust sheets there were fully rigged galleons with miniature cannon and plaster seamen. We uncovered model street facades which were so real that by closing one eye we could see how they would have appeared to the camera; the detail was amazing but, of course, with the resultant image enlarged on the cinema screen many hundreds of times such attention to detail was essential. Suddenly our own efforts seemed pathetically tawdry.

In the plaster shop, which like the other workshops, seemed to have been vacated at the end of a normal working day we found evidence of half-finished jobs and sacks of unused plaster. Standing around were moulds of huge bells, and wrought iron balustrades, and there were knockers and door handles of every description. There were even moulds for tiny telephone boxes and miniature lamp posts that were perfect in every detail. Wondering how we could make use of so much wonderful treasure we left the plaster shop and went outside, our minds in a whirl.

Continuing our exploration we came to 'the Lot'. In size, the lot at Ealing was a mere postage stamp compared to those of Denham or Pinewood but at that time neither of us had been to an operational film studio and so the minuscule space allocated to outdoor filming at Ealing didn't seem at all small. We came to it on our way to the main stages and saw that it comprised two streets at right angles. On the corner where they joined was the famous pub that we'd seen a dozen times in the cinema and, opposite it, the police station that had featured in the film *The Blue Lamp*. The right-hand street had a row of shops along one side and houses on the other. The houses were fronted by iron railings and flights of stone steps leading up to the front doors. They differed from television where the majority of sets were simply painted canvas or hardboard flats cleated together with sash line in the style of theatre scenery. At Ealing the buildings were solid and the studio craftsmen had painstakingly created three-dimensional realism right down to the iron coal-hole covers in the pavement. I describe them as streets because that is how they would have appeared on the screen but in reality they were quite short and comprised only a few buildings – six or seven at the most. No doubt some of the roads around the stages and office buildings would have been incorporated to give extra length and variety. Furthermore it would have been possible to use large painted backdrops to add increased perspective to the ends of the streets. Jack and I wandered around peering in shop windows and looking into the dummy houses. We must have used the phrase 'Hey, look at this!' a dozen times as we discovered new forms of artifice.

But it felt all wrong – we were the only people there. This was unnerving because at Lime Grove we'd been accustomed to strict rules governing where one could go and which places were out of bounds. Here, at Ealing Studios, we were in a place that would have been familiar to millions of cinemagoers and yet we were free to wander anywhere and look at anything we liked. The term 'ghost town' used by the lads on the front gate seemed very appropriate at that moment.

Leaving the lot we went into the complex that housed the main stages. Entering from the daylight we had difficulty in adjusting to the gloom but we could dimly make out a long corridor leading to glazed doors at the far end. We knew the studios were on our right so we looked – or rather groped around for – a door. And there was one. It was heavily padded and had the usual iron lever to seal it tightly. Opening it we found a small L-shaped space that was presumably a sound lock with a further padded door that opened onto a large film stage. This was sparsely illuminated by a few naked bulbs housed in dusty enamelled shades hanging on long leads from the overhead gantries. These, we assumed, would be the working lights similar to the ones we had in the studios at Lime Grove, but whereas ours were bright and plentiful, these were sparse and served only to emphasise the darkness of the place. Still trying to adjust to the semi-darkness we trod carefully between these pools of light ready to get out quickly if we felt a sudden drop in temperature. Had we known it we could have raised the studio doors and let in the daylight but it was all foreign territory to us at that time and we were wary of touching anything for fear of causing irreparable damage. In the following years we would raise and lower those massive sound-proofed doors hundreds of times, sometimes to clear the smoke or fog that we ourselves had created and, at other times, to wheel in our props and effects equipment. People even raised them a few feet during a break in filming to enable their colleagues to scramble underneath and have a quick smoke in the road outside. The doors were powered by electric motors but this was one operation the electricians couldn't get their hands on because, we and others, had got there first and had clearly established a precedent.

But on this day we were having our first experience of a real film studio and everything felt strange. We were in a huge dark cavern of indeterminable height, its walls clad with dusty sound-proofing material held in position by wire netting – and there were iron ladders leading to mysterious gantries beyond the lights suspended high above the floor. Cautiously we climbed one of the iron ladders ascending into the darkness overhead. There was nothing to save anyone unlucky enough to miss a handhold (or to get ones fingers trampled on by the bloke in front) from toppling to the floor below – with predictable results. Naturally Jack and I considered ourselves capable of doing anything connected with our job but even so I let him climb ahead before I followed. When we reached the lower set of gantries we moved across and walked to the middle of the stage. We saw that these walkways still had some of the lights and cables that, presumably, had been rigged on the last occasion the stage had been used. The cables had been neatly coiled and were tied to the handrail. The gantry swayed slightly as we walked along and I noticed that it felt cold. Did the ghosts of dead electricians also come back to haunt the place? We saw that there were other gantries higher up but decided that exploration of these would yield nothing of interest and went back to the floor.

Next we went on a tour of the corridors and cutting rooms – and discovered the rushes theatre (where later we would view our own efforts and endure the witty comments of our colleagues.) We both had to admit that we were impressed and for the first time felt very much like poor relations.

The next day we listed the assets making sure that the model trains and ships featured prominently as 'being of great interest to the Design Department'. Next we listed the tank, although this had to be done by guesswork. We knew this to be below the floor of Stage 2 because the chaps on the gate had shown us a set of plans of the entire complex marked in red with hydrants and fire points.

In our imagination we could see a use for everything so our assessment of the facilities at Ealing may have been only marginally useful; we visualised the wonderful opportunities for special effects that Ealing offered and couldn't see much beyond our own ambitions. Jack did some sketches showing the position and area of the tank and in glowing terms described the model trains. Of course we had nowhere at The Centre to store them, or the six foot long model battleships and submarines but hoped that management would consider leaving them at Ealing. Alas it was not to be. Following our exploration a team moved in and cleared the workshops disposing of battleships, railway trains, cathedral bells and other, to us, priceless objects. Management then spent hundreds of thousands of pounds equipping the buildings for the film unit. The four main stages were used without modification although in time the lighting and wiring would be replaced but as far as I know the stages are exactly the same today as they were before the war.

The Lot had to change when it proved too static: it had to be made flexible, adaptable for the quick turn round of television production. Don Home, one of our small band of set designers at that time was asked to devise a scheme for making the fronts of the buildings movable. He came up with the idea of separating them into units and mounting them on scaffold towers fitted with wheels. This meant that everything – shops, pubs and houses could be moved and reassembled in any order – making the Lot almost infinitely variable and making it possible to film even short sequences outdoors with only a minimum of effort. Because of the method of assembling tubular steel, the bottom scaffold pole, essential for holding the uprights together, had to be fixed as low down as possible which meant that all the shop fronts had to be entered by going up one step. However this seemed to pass without notice and the ease with which the backgrounds could be changed made it all worthwhile.

The tank was cleaned and re-waterproofed and became as useful to the Beeb as it had been to the movie makers; Jack and I used it on dozens of occasions. The tank was covered by the wooden floor which could be lifted in sections and stacked to one side using the hand operated chain hoists which traversed the width of the stage, but because of its capacity it took a day to fill, a day to heat and a day to empty. Without chemical treatment algae formed in the warm water almost within hours, which made underwater filming difficult. On the first day it would resemble thin pea soup and on the second day, thick pea soup. At first, to film underwater, we used a special periscope lowered below the water but later, one of the cameramen, Brian Trefano, was given the responsibility of using an underwater camera and lighting gear.

At the height of Ealing's output I'm told that the BBC employed as many as fifty eight film editors in the cutting rooms while the stages were booked solid every month of the year. Jack Mewett, Head of Film Production, did a truly remarkable job in creating an organisation that almost rivalled television itself. Alas, Ealing Studios at the start of the twenty-first century is no longer a part of the BBC and has an uncertain future. While the developers prowl around waiting to get their hands on the land (and what council could resist the lure of more housing and millions of pounds of additional revenue?) those of us who worked there when it was fully operational have, like the original movie makers, a genuine affection for the place and hope that it will continue to be used for some sort of film production for as long as possible.

F a b u l o u s   C a p t i o n s

Few things mark the evolution of the electronic medium more than the opening titles. Today, fashion dictates that each programme, however trivial, has to be preceded by a kaleidoscope of whirling images that seem to have nothing to do with what follows but appear to be conceived by the title designers simply to impress other title designers.

But the point I wish to make is not a philosophical one but is intended to mark the enormous progress that has been made in television technology – a technology that enables captions and titles to be created electronically using little more than the computer keyboard. No longer is it necessary for the caption artist to create typography by hand with pen and brush. All forms and shapes and sizes of letters are stored in the computer's memory and all of these can be automatically spaced, adjusted, rendered thin or thick, long or squat and coloured in any of a thousand hues. The computer offers such flexibility that it has become the virtual Pandora's Box. By manipulating keys and juggling input sources any image can be produced and so there is little point in creating them by any other means. Sitting at a computer keyboard the designer can conjure up backgrounds, foregrounds, and the bits that go in between. He or she can animate them, shade them, fade them, merge them, join them or separate them – the permutations are boundless.

Fifty years ago we had only the most basic materials and the limited facilities of a primitive technology. However, like everyone else in television we strove to improve and widen the parameters of the medium. Consequently, given an opportunity to try out new ideas we took full advantage of it.

Captions in the first years were confined to photographs or artist painted designs accompanied by printed lettering. These were produced on small cards and placed on caption stands in the studio. Our attempts to improve matters focussed, quite naturally, on animation and the first opportunity Jack and I had to experiment came with the Morecambe and Wise show, *Running Wild*. What could be more appropriate for the end credits than to feature little cartoons of the principal characters – running? But we didn't have the luxury of the computer or even film (too expensive). We did, however, have an abundance of plywood and cardboard and from these we created the 'slider'.

Jack designed and painted seven cartoon images on caption cards about fifteen inches by ten and to make the characters run we copied an idea from a children's toy. It was the duck on the end of a stick that had a single wooden wheel on which were painted three duck's legs. When pushed along, the duck appeared to run. The upshot of this was that we were forced to make our caption nearly nine feet long because each character had a separate wheel on which we painted the character's legs. The slider ran in a frame mounted on a stand, and Jack and I supporting it at either end had to manoeuvre it through the frame stopping at each picture long enough for it to be read. We would then move on to the next one. The trouble was that from where we stood at either end we couldn't see if the caption was squarely located in the centre of the frame and we had to lean outwards at an impossible angle to make sure we'd got it right. I seem to recall that our little characters were occasionally called upon to backtrack in a hesitant manner, but our contortions sustained the audience's applause as we operated the final credits at the end of the show.

Another opportunity to make an animated caption came about a year later. It happened at a time when we were sitting around with nothing to do. It was a period when we were so slack that we sat in the office wondering if television had moved to another location and nobody had told us; only once before had we experienced a similar period of inactivity. Naturally enough programme schedules didn't always dovetail with our availability and there were bound to be peaks and troughs, but, in recent years, we'd never gone for so long without anything listed on our wall chart. We had cleaned and tided and organised the tools and equipment until the place resembled an industrial museum but we were the only people there to appreciate it. In consequence we'd spent more money and time in the White Horse than was good for us and the tendency to nod off during the afternoon was irresistible. We took to walking around the offices and corridors to keep ourselves awake and demonstrate to our colleagues that we were frenetically busy. But to no avail – work had dried up. We sat in our chairs filling the ash trays with expensive grey dust and eating fattening cheese rolls. But then, one afternoon, there was a knock on the door and someone asked if he could come in. It was Graeme Muir, a lovely man and most importantly, a light entertainment producer. We offered him a chair, wiping it clean of breadcrumbs, and opened a window; he seemed grateful (you could have smoked kippers in our room in those days). He told us that he wanted a special caption for a new show he was producing; could we design and make it? Could we make him a caption? We would have performed an illegal operation just to have some form of gainful employment. He said he knew that we were likely to be busy but if we could fit it in he would be most grateful. We tried to divert his attention from our work chart on the wall which looked like a freshly laundered bed sheet.

Graeme wanted something three dimensional and animate and, apparently, he had a budget big enough to fund it. He described what he wanted: It had to be very glamorous with lots of glitz and sparkle and it had to be busy. He wanted the name of the show to rotate in one direction while stars and other things picked out in glitter went round behind the title in the opposite direction. He admitted that he couldn't see how it should be done but he knew that we would have ideas. He told us that he wanted it to look like a Hollywood movie, a request so outrageous that it almost amounted to heresy. How could television aspire to emulate the film makers? But this didn't faze us in the least; at last we had a job, and furthermore it was an exciting one – a challenge worthy of our ingenuity.

When Graeme had left we discussed ideas and methods and once again the room filled with smoke. The caption, we agreed, would be mounted on a wooden plinth about three foot square and four foot six inches high to bring it up to camera level. On this box would be a rotating Perspex drum emblazoned with the name of the show. It would have lots of glitter and sparkle and tiny bits of mirror glued to the surface while inside would be various stars and baubles supported on fine nylon threads and rotating in the opposite direction. Naturally, these would also be dressed in glitter and sparkle. Still in the era of black and white we knew that to make it look rich and exciting we would have to use maximum contrast and, to make it sparkle we would have to illuminate it from either side with several miniature lights (the effect used by jewellers to make the rings and brooches in their shop windows sparkle and glint).

The mechanics didn't concern us at that point because we knew that motors and gear boxes could be bought from several well-known suppliers. We would design the picture that the viewers would see and work backwards – which was a mistake and one that would prove our undoing. Unfortunately we had an Achilles Heel – we could both see the potential and tended to concentrate on the interesting bits first.

Because Graeme had come to us early we had plenty of time, but anxious to be doing something we went to the stores and drew out some timber. We measured and cut several sheets of plywood and in no time at all had constructed the plinth on which we would later mount the Perspex cylinder. We painted it a tasteful shade of light blue and fitted it with casters so that it could be moved around in an upright position. We reasoned that it might be cumbersome and we didn't want the scene crew banging it into things whilst carrying it into the studio or even dropping it down on the floor.

The following day we went round to Denny's, a small specialist firm skilled in the fabrication of acrylic shop signs and fittings. We asked Mr Denny if he could make our drum and on being told that he could and furthermore would be delighted to do so we promptly gave him an order.

But getting the main motor proved more difficult than we'd anticipated. There was nothing available which would run at the speed we required. We combed Oxford Street and Lisle Street to no avail and we phoned other suppliers that we'd heard of – with no more luck. We were told either that they didn't have anything slow enough or that they could make us one at horrendous cost and within a time scale calculated in seasons. This was a blow but after much head scratching we thought of a plan which involved mounting the Perspex drum on a wooden disc and driving it by sitting it on a rubber-tyred Meccano wheel fixed to the spindle of a low-geared motor. This sounds clumsy but in fact was the method used to drive turntable record players and if it worked for them it should work for us. The difference between theory and practice can be measured in light years. We discovered that our driving device set up vibrations which affected the baubles and stars hanging inside the drum. These were turned by a separate tiny motor mounted in the top of the machine and should have been unaffected by anything down below, but when we switched on the main motor and the drum revolved the stars and baubles jiggled like drug-crazed competitors performing a Scottish reel. We struggled for several days to iron out the trouble but with no success whatsoever. Time was now getting short and in fact, almost before we realised it, it was the day before transmission. We worked late into the night, desperately trying various remedies, but when it became obvious that we were achieving nothing we decided to go home and think about it – as if we hadn't been doing that for days. The floor manager had paid us several visits during the previous week and we had shown him the almost finished job, which looked wonderfully sparkly and impressive. We even showed him how the drum rotated and how the torch bulbs on either side caused everything to sparkle, but we didn't switch on the stars giving him some bogus reason for their inactivity. He went away impressed and must have given Graeme a glowing account of what he'd seen.

But the next day, the day of the programme, found us in the workshop at five o'clock in the morning. When he'd arrived I'd asked Jack if he'd thought of a cure, praying that he'd come up with a miracle – and when he said he thought he had I was overjoyed. I was so overjoyed that in offering him the customary cigarette I spilled the entire packet over the floor. But what did it matter – he'd had an idea! Common sense should have warned me that over the past few days we'd both had ideas, thousands of them and what had those ideas amounted to? Why should I now hope that this one would be better than all the others? He explained his theory. He suggested that if we isolated everything – every single component with shock absorbing material the vibrations wouldn't get through. It meant shock absorbing the main motor and the spindle of the drum and meant a lot of work with no guarantee of success but I was prepared to go to any lengths to solve the problem. My own thoughts the night before had produced nothing that didn't involve suicide and after a sleepless night I had little to offer but despair and hopelessness. Picking up my cigarettes we set about dismantling everything.

About ten o'clock we had a phone call from Lime Grove – they were sending a van to collect the caption. I asked them to delay it a bit and when asked what I meant by 'a bit' I felt tempted to tell them the truth, which was three months. But looked at Jack and he held up two fingers indicating two hours.
'About one hour' I answered cravenly.
When the van arrived I suggested that the driver should take a tea break (or better still, his summer holidays), but he told us that the floor

manager needed the caption for rehearsal and had insisted that he collect it and bring it to the studio.

At midday the assistant floor manager came over to find out what was holding things up. Jack told him that it would be in the studio soon after lunch; apparently we were 'wiring up a new battery'. The AFM left looking very worried. Needless to say we didn't break for lunch because the components of the caption were strewn around the workshop and we still didn't know if Jack's plan would work. We'd put it together for a rough test and although the jitters were less, they were still there. More anti-vibration material was needed.

The van driver sat in the office and we told him not to answer the phone which, after days of silence, was now ringing incessantly. We fitted the extra material, this time even around the fastening screws. The clock on the wall was whizzing round and the driver reminded us that they were now back in the studio and were nearly coming up to the run through. Frantically we reassembled everything and switched on. Neither of us breathed or moved a muscle as the drum revolved. Then we switched on the top motor. The tiny stars on their nylon threads rotated smoothly; the Highland fling had disappeared, there was not even the hint of an old maiden's waltz. At first we didn't believe it, it was a fluke – it had to be! We switched both motors on and off again several times and the stars still rotated demurely. We didn't wait to test it further; it had run perfectly for more than a minute and now we were desperate to get it into the studio. In a flurry of activity we grabbed a cardboard box, filled it with the tools and materials we would need in the studio and prepared to leave. We handed the box to the driver, asking him to hold the door open. All our gloom had gone, it was now a matter of speed. The driver stood back and we pushed our lovely, flawless caption into the corridor – or we would have done if the door opening had been wide enough. Our machine was too big to go through the door! We stared at each other in disbelief. This wasn't happening! It couldn't possibly be happening! But we had made the classic error of not measuring the doorway. Everything swam before my eyes and my throat restricted so that I couldn't speak. But Jack had another brilliant idea. 'Through the window!' he yelled.

Outside our window was a flat roof and a wide fire escape that would get us down to the ring road where the van was parked. We rushed it to the window but like the door they were exactly thirty two inches wide with heavy steel frames. What bloody mad architect had this fetish for uniform openings? I admit that I became a babbling idiot at that point. We had spent days curing the judder and now our caption was trapped inside the workshop. Jack then did the bravest thing I had ever seen a man do. He took a large saw and cut the plinth in half. With the drum removed the two halves passed through the door sideways.

We rushed the pieces to the studio where we fixed the halves together and reinstalled the drum. But it was a lengthy business and by the time we'd finished the studio was breaking for the evening meal. Graeme came to inspect it and thanked us. The perfect gentleman he made no reference to the appalling delay. We promised to tell him the full story when we'd calmed down.

The viewers saw a sparkling caption and heard the opening music. The name of the show rotated, glittering in the light from six unseen torch bulbs while the little sparkly stars and baubles rotated smoothly behind the words looking every bit like the opening to a Hollywood movie – just as it was supposed to do. But this was not the grand caption we had planned. The studio audience saw only a gruesome mess – several bits of a blue painted plywood box held together with lengths of raw timber and miles and miles of gaffer tape.

Television Centre is Born

In November 1949, the *West London Observer* announced that the BBC had bought the Rank Studios in Lime Grove and, according to the reporter, was about to convert it into a 'vast TV production centre'. Had that reporter been able to see a model of Television Centre, already more than a mere twinkle in Auntie's eye, he would have been rendered writeless; here indeed was a 'vast television production centre'.

To those of us who worked there it was incontestably the finest and most imaginative television production unit of all times and we were proud to be associated with it. Nothing had been overlooked, nothing had been skimped. Compared with the repellent and, as some think, inappropriate structures defiling our cities by the end of the twentieth century it is a benchmark of taste in industrial and aesthetic design. Television Centre was designed to fulfil the purpose for which it was commissioned. As well as being a complex of studios, workshops and offices it was at the same time a building of considerable artistic merit. Defying post-war convention it wasn't square, but designed around a central pivot point – a circular courtyard. Around this were the offices constructed in the form of a drum with the studios, scenery block and ring road continuing the circular theme. Eventually this would become a 'question mark', but the addition of the tail would have to wait until many years later.

In the centre of the courtyard stands a slender column supporting a gilded statue of Helios, the all-seeing God of Greek mythology. Unfortunately from his position in the courtyard all he can see is a few office windows, which is not much of a view for a God. At its base, a large bowl mounted on legs with arcing fountains was intended to be a water feature. Sadly this was one of the few architectural features which never lived up to its promise. Spray from the fountains was swept away from the bowl by the wind, catching unwary pedestrians trapped in the courtyard forcing them to walk close to the office walls. Furthermore the sounds of splashing water (which could hardly be described as 'tinkling') were amplified by the cylindrical construction causing them, to interfere with conversation in the offices to such an extent that in summer, windows had to be closed in order to use the telephone and, it was rumoured, staff were finding it necessary to make frequent visits to the toilet.

Television Centre was conceived in the forties and built in the fifties and we, the people installed in the already completed design block, saw every phase of its construction from the clearance of the site to the final topping-out ceremony. As the concrete hardened we were able to wander round at will, peering into every nook and cranny and gazing in awe at the girder work that soared six floors above us. We were never made to wear hard-hats or to sign indemnity forms and we were never once told to keep out. The work commenced in 1951 and was completed in 1959. It was officially opened the following year but by then a great deal of the office and workshop space had been allocated and was being used. The offices were equipped with new furniture and the corridors smelled delightfully of fresh paint and new carpet.

I have a videotape which, I believe, was made by the BBC Film Unit. It is a collection of shots taken over those eight years and shows the construction of the Centre from start to finish. It commences with the site, now partially cleared of the rubbish and the bits of old buildings that had been so useful to Jack and me and shows just how big the area was. I mocked the hard-hat philosophy when I mentioned that we were free to wander anywhere but the sight of those workmen fifty years ago and the 'industrial' clothing they wore makes one's blood run cold. Most of them favoured the cloth cap which, apparently, was considered suitable head-gear, but a number of them sported trilby hats. Whether this was a badge of office worn by foremen I wouldn't know because from the neck down it seems that anything old and worn was suitable. In the summer the workers wore as little as possible preferring to acquire a healthy tan regardless of danger. The sight of men carrying buckets of steaming tar whilst stripped to the waist would cause the average Health and Safety official to apply for early retirement. Protective footwear was, seemingly, old shoes or wellies but there were many variations in clothing including, in the case of one chap in the cab of a large crane, a smart suit, shirt and bow tie. Perhaps he had been warned that he was to be filmed and his wife had demanded that to impress the neighbours he must don his Sunday best?

But while we might deride the practices of the time it was the norm in those days. The constructors and builders were men. They didn't fly to the Health and Safety officials or seek compensation for every little wound they suffered. Perhaps they realised that they had responsibilities for their own actions – their own mistakes.

The driving of the huge steel interlocking piles was the activity most of us remember because it went on and on, thump, thump, thump, seemingly for months on end, numbing our ability to work or to think. At weekends the lorries carrying yet more of these infernal steel piles were unloaded onto the site in order that each Monday morning the racket could start up again. But other lorries also turned up at weekends. These carried the huge prefabricated girders that were to be assembled by the steel fitters and as the building grew we saw just how big it was going to be.

Because the circular pattern extended to the eight studios which were grouped in a wide arc much of the steel work had to be specially formed. Each piece was given a code number and placed on baulks of timber from which it would be selected as required. Concrete was delivered to the various locations by the slurp machine, an incredible arrangement of pipes that carried the liquid compound from the huge central mixing machine to where it was required, disgorging in regular pulsing movements (hence the term slurping). I never discovered what drove tons of liquid concrete along these pipes or how they were emptied at weekends, I wish I'd been more curious. Sir Mortimer Wheeler, an eminent Roman scholar and archaeologist who appeared in the programme *Animal, Vegetable, Mineral* was very interested in the site. The fact that it was being excavated was enough to have him down on his knees probing the earth and examining the spoil. He told us that in the eighteenth century it had been a brick-field. We worked with him on his archaeological programmes and made the demonstration models used to illustrate them. On one occasion I went with him to Maiden Castle, the ancient British fortified earthworks in Dorset where I measured (or should I say surveyed) the site preparatory to constructing a scale model. He, the producer Paul Johnstone and I stayed overnight in a hotel where the three of us spent the evening in the bar, Paul and I listening to Sir Mortimer's anecdotes. He told us of the time he took the Queen on a visit to Maiden Castle. She sat in the front of an open Land Rover and he sat behind her, but because the ground slopes and is fiercely corrugated Her Majesty was being bounced around quite unceremoniously. Without being able to grip anything for support (vehicles weren't equipped with seat belts in those days) Her Majesty appeared to be in danger of being ejected from the vehicle. Mort was faced with a dilemma. Should he put out his hands and steady her or should he do nothing and risk the fact that she would end up rolling on the grass? He decided to do nothing and for the rest of the journey sat with tightly closed eyes.

Whilst wandering around the site at Television Centre one lunch time, Jack saw a Woolworth's egg whisk embedded in the top-soil. He prised it free and without removing the clay, mounted it on a panel of art board and captioned it in the style of a museum exhibit. He attributed it to the ancient Britons and sent it to Sir Mort who was delighted with the joke.

He returned the compliment by giving us each signed copies of his book on the Roman occupation of Britain. When he died it was a sad loss – and so too was the early death of Paul Johnstone, a young director responsible for bringing many intelligent programmes to television.

White City was designed to be the home of BBC TV which we all saw as a permanent institution that would grow with time. If ever a project could be described as 'state of the art', Television Centre was surely it. Among the many innovative features there was a scenic artist's studio in which as many as eleven artists could work on backcloths (eighteen feet or more high) that could be raised and lowered through slots in the floor by electric motors operated from a console of switches in the centre of the room. This enabled each artist to set his canvas at a convenient working height.

The basement at Television Centre was allocated to the property department and consisted mostly of steel racks and metal shelves. It was below ground level and never saw daylight but it was one place to which visitors were always taken. It was a veritable Aladdin's cave containing such items as stuffed animals, clocks of every period, tapestries and carpets. There were telephones ancient and modern and sharp things ranging from kitchen knives to a French guillotine. They even had boxes of period ash trays, opera programmes and ladies' fans and, tended by the knowledgeable prop staff, aquaria of tropical fish. If a designer called for an item, the property department would supply it either from its own resources of 15,000 items or by hiring it from one of its many outside contractors. Being below ground, the trucks ferrying the props to and from the studios had to be carried up to the ring road by lift. The property department had two, one was large and the other was huge, so big in fact that it could accommodate a double-decker London bus.

Another innovation was the construction of TC1. In this studio the floor could be lowered to reveal a huge tank that could be filled with water for the staging of Hollywood type aqua shows. Sadly (or perhaps fortunately) this was another feature that never materialised. The architects had probably been influenced by those exotic movies of the time starring Esther Williams and had reasoned that the BBC could emulate them. But the public taste for exotic spectaculars of this kind was already waning and so the Beeb produced *Dixon of Dock Green* and *Z Cars* at a fraction of the cost. I wonder how the writers of the day would have dealt with a request for a script in which a girl in a bathing costume was the principal attraction. I can hear them asking the obvious question, 'But what does she do for Pete's sake?' and getting the answer, 'Well, she, er, swims – and the pool is surrounded by beautiful girls who also swim – and there is this heavenly choir singing heavenly songs in a heavenly setting of er, palm trees and a beach hut into which she and the hero retire at the end of the show. As they smile and shut the door we run the credits… well you know the sort of thing.' For someone able to write an interesting scenario for finger puppets this would have been no challenge, but a talented writer might have pleaded to be given a spell on a schools maths series instead.

One studio was very much in use – the smallest of them all. Designed for puppet shows, it staged such favourites as *Muffin the Mule*, *The Woodentops*, *Andy Pandy* and *The Flowerpot Men* until the popularity of string puppets declined. Thereafter stop motion puppets such as the delightful *Camberwick Green* and *Trumpton*, produced and directed by Gordon Murray, took over.

Eventually stop motion films (the technique of moving an object a small amount, taking one frame of film, moving the object a fraction more, taking another frame and so on to produce simulated movement) were made in specialist outside studios such as the one operated by the talented team of Bura and Hardwick. Without the demand for string puppets the Puppet Theatre became redundant. Choosing our moment, Jack and I pleaded with management to let us take it over. We desperately needed somewhere as a base for storing and working on special effects whilst operating in the studios because when anything needed modifying we either had to take it back to our workshops, which at that time were about half a mile way in Kensington House, or wait for a break in rehearsals in order that we could saw, hammer or even very quietly drill. We convinced management that it made sense for us to have a workshop and a store close to the studios and, without argument, we were given the keys to the Puppet Theatre.

This was marvellous because it meant that we no longer had to work outside in the ring-road. It also meant that we no longer had to carry all our tools, materials and equipment with us whenever we were required to work in the studios. From then on we had a well-equipped base from which to work. Joy of joys the Puppet Theatre had a large sink with big taps so we could fill and empty water containers without having to trek to the toilet, slopping water over our shoes and the corridors. Furthermore, because it was sound-proofed, we could work without interfering with rehearsals. Later it was found necessary to fit the sink with a special trap as our frequent use of plaster kept blocking the main drains.

During this period our working conditions were almost perfect – leaving us with nothing to wish for. The carpenters, metalworkers, plaster shop, painters and setting area were all on the ground floor of design block, within easy reach and we could get almost anything we needed within minutes. If things were convenient for us the same could be said for the set designers. But that is the way The Centre had been planned. Looking back it seems remarkable that the architects with only their imagination and common sense to guide them – there being no other TV organisation they could copy – managed to get it all so right. The layout of The Centre was essentially practical, housing everything under one roof. All materials necessary for the production of scenery were delivered to the workshop stores where, after the various manufacturing processes had been carried out it was erected in the studios. But the clever part was that the Centre has two perimeter roads, one outside the circular building and one, running parallel with it, on the inside, an arrangement that allowed freedom of movement for road vehicles and the smaller electric vehicles and trucks which ferry stuff to and from the studios. Even the lifts, four in the front of the circle and two at the back ensured that people didn't have to walk far to get transport from floor to floor. Realising that furniture and other items would also require transportation, two large service lifts were provided at the rear of the drum. All in all I think the architects and builders of Television Centre did a first class job.

P i l e   D r i v i n g   u s   M a d

The creation of Television Centre was, in its way, to be as significant as the building of the Franco-British Exhibition in 1907. It was a ground breaker, an entirely novel concept to fulfil a grand purpose – and a piece of ancient farmland in Shepherds Bush was home to them both. The exhibition was created to establish the friendly relations and the commercial trade between France and Britain and similarly Television Centre in some way marked the beginning of Eurovision and the interchange of French and British broadcasts. Now, when it is possible to receive television coverage of events from the remotest places on Earth and pictures from outer space, it may seem trivial to point out that the first television transmission beamed beyond our shores was to Calais – just a handful of miles across the English Channel.

Those of us employed by the BBC in the late fifties saw Television Centre built on a muddy site in Wood Lane where it became, indisputably, the most versatile TV production unit in the world. Jack and I were there from the beginning and like to think we played a small part in shaping its future although the future was to be very different from the one we saw at the time. The technical areas, make up and dressing rooms were designed to be below ground and so the excavation of soil was extensive. The purpose of the steel piles that had been delivered and now were being relentlessly hammered home were to hold back the surrounding clay and prevent the Scenery Block from ending up on its side in the excavations. It grew quickly, or so it appeared to us. A huge raft of concrete was laid in the hole and the vertical girders grew from it like trees. Cranes lifted the transverse members to the tops of these where they were bolted into position by the steel erectors who, rather than climb ladders often sat astride the girders as they were lifted up. To us it was fascinating stuff; it was Meccano on a grand scale. When the infernal racket of the pile drivers finally ceased at the end of each day all that could be heard was the distant slurping of the concrete pump and the muted banter of the workmen. We could tolerate the occasional clang of hammer on steel – in fact it reminded us that these chaps were constructing the building that some of us were going to inhabit. This grand complex would undoubtedly eclipse Lime Grove and its autocratic ethos and we would have 'Cosmopolitan' girls guarding our own portals. In fairness the erstwhile frosty-faced harpies who manned Lime Grove reception were no longer frosty-faced and in fact had become good friends of ours; we wondered why we ever doubted that underneath those immaculate costumes were wonderfully friendly and charming girls with whom we were now on first name terms. So chummy had our relations become that we were actually hoping that they would be transferred to the Centre where we would meet them every morning.

As the months passed and the building grew we took to guessing what the various rooms and areas would be used for. Reception was easy to place and the studios were rather unmissable but the rest of the structure was more difficult. How could we have guessed from the empty shell that this building would house such fascinating things as news presentation suites, film cutting rooms, telecine equipment areas, a satellite traffic terminal, videotape editing sections, international and network control rooms, music and gramophone libraries, artistes' dressing rooms, green rooms, bathrooms, hair dressing salons and make up rooms. How could we have foreseen the extent of the equipment servicing workshops or known about the wardrobe department that would store more than 25,000 finished costumes – many of them created by BBC designers and made on the premises by skilled crafts men and women?

Eventually the building gained shape, with brick walls and windows and corridors that led heaven knows where. At this stage the mosaic experts, brought over from Europe, were able to commence work. These men were specialists in the art of applying tesserae and ceramics. Looking at their work years later, it is easy to appreciate the skill with which they cemented the hundreds of thousands of pieces of mosaic around the oval columns (not round, you notice) that form the colonnade supporting the building over the front entrance.

There was still plenty of waste ground on which Jack and I could try out our effects, but we no longer fired explosives fearing that we might cause some unsuspecting workman to fall down a lift shaft or plummet from the roof.

One day we needed to experiment with a miniature hot-air balloon and the road around the new building provided just the sort of sheltered area we needed. Situated between the Scenery block and the studios it would shield our model from the wind and would continue to protect it until it reached the sky above. We made it from tissue paper segments which we glued together edge to edge to create a five foot diameter sphere. But it was no easy task. Careful as we were, the glue spread to other parts of the flimsy paper and the unsticking and tearing apart caused a certain amount of frustration and an encyclopaedic range of adjectives.

When, finally, the glue had dried and we were ready for the test we fitted the burner, a small tobacco tin which we hung underneath the paper globe on thin wires. Carefully we folded the paper neatly into a manageable package and took it to the road outside. It was a sunny afternoon with only a gentle breeze, ideal conditions for our test. We placed a small piece of cotton wool in the tin, soaked it with Methylated

Spirit, lit it and watched as the hot air filled the paper sphere. Soon it was tugging at the wires supporting the burner so we let it go. It rose at once, sailing gracefully up between the two buildings until it reached the connecting bridge between the two.

I should explain that the two bridges linking the Scenery block with the main building were totally enclosed, being no more than aerial corridors. But they were later to be glazed on both sides with windows extending from the ceiling to within eighteen inches or so of the floor. They would admit plenty of light and, until the corridors were heated, plenty of cold. However, as these were early days in the schedule of construction none of the windows had yet been fitted with glass.

Fairly quickly the balloon rose to the height of the bridge where, for a second it appeared to hesitate. Then, drawn by some capricious internal draught, it was sucked into the building through an unglazed window frame. It turned left, bobbing on the ceiling, and went into the area where many of the building materials were stored. Nothing happened for two or three seconds and then an orange glow told us that the tissue paper had caught fire. Gradually it faded and the area returned to normal. We stood in the road, two men apparently engaged in casual conversation, but in reality two very worried men wondering what the hell they'd done. We knew that the area was packed with materials of every kind and assumed that all it needed to become a raging inferno was a load of flaming tissue paper to ignite it. We stood there for a minute or two until we were fairly sure that the building was not on fire or that some angry workman with a smoking cap was not looking for the perpetrator of the outrage we made our way through the carpenters' shop and returned to our office. We decided not to investigate as this might lead to another management enquiry, and so we disassociated ourselves from the whole thing. What, we asked ourselves, could anybody deduce from some paper ashes and a blackened tobacco tin?

As the building progressed we watched every phase of its construction, spending many lunchtimes wandering around and marvelling at the skill which enabled people to create something of such complexity from the hundreds of raw materials and the thousands of items that were delivered, daily, to the site.

It was planned to clad the end wall of the reception area with a grand mural by John Piper. It was an abstract design and, continuing the mosaic theme, was painstakingly worked in tiny ceramic tiles of bright reds and blues, black and gold; they produced a stunning effect. The craftsmen worked on scaffolding shrouded in dust sheets which prevented us from seeing what they were doing. I think that the architects were determined to keep the design hidden until its official unveiling and were making sure that no one should see it until then. By the time the building was finished and we were asked to choose our accommodation (in your dreams!) we had been relocated to new premises in Kensington House on the other side of Shepherds Bush Green.

I   G e t   W h e e l s

I can't ever recall feeling fed up with my journey to work. It was
something that had to be endured if I wanted to work in town and live
in the country and I had no thoughts of abandoning either. My journey
started with a two mile cycle ride to the end of the lane where I would
leave my bike and take a short walk to the bus stop on the main road.
In 1954, this main road was a single highway and carried so little traffic
that I could saunter across it to the bus stop on the other side. The bus
stop was situated under a bank of very large beech trees, the branches
of which were home to a colony of rooks: I know that colony is not the
right collective noun for rooks so I'll rephrase it by saying that those
trees held an extensive rookery. At that time in the morning the birds
were wide awake and making a racket that was almost deafening. I
didn't mind the noise because it was part of country life but the same
cannot be said for their habit of evacuating over the unprotected bus
stop, and those who stood close to it were prime targets. It seemed
that they lined up to take turns at bombing us. Their aim can best be
described as unerring.

Alongside the bus stop was a war-time emergency water tank which
had been emptied to discourage school children from throwing each
other into the slimy water. Today, the narrow main road has been

replaced by a dual carriageway and the thundering traffic it carries produces enough poison gas to have any birds tumbling dead from their nests. But the rooks and the trees have gone and in their place is a large roundabout.

In earlier times the main road followed the contours of the land and must have dipped alarming at the junction with my lane. Presumably, with the advent of the motor car and metalled roads, the dip was filled in and levelled off but this left my lane stranded some ten or twelve feet lower than the highway. The engineers dealt with this by constructing a slope. However, being short of cash they couldn't afford to spend anything like the money it would have required to make a gentle incline onto the main road and the result, I swear, was a ramp of almost forty five degrees. It was so precipitous that even cyclists with multi-geared bikes had to climb it on foot and its toll on cigarette-smoking pedestrians arriving a few seconds before the bus was gaspingly audible.

I remember too, our poor baker who delivered his bread in an ancient Clyno van and had to deal with that slope to complete his round. Red-faced and working every control and lever within reach he would struggle to propel the vehicle onto the main road and apply the brakes before the screaming engine carried him straight across the highway and down the slope on the other side. On good days he usually managed to brake in time but on wet days he often finished up embedded in the gorse bushes on the common.

From the bus stop I travelled to Tooting Broadway where I would have to leave the comfort of the Green Line coach and board the much less splendid double-decker bus to Shepherds Bush. Being a smoker I made for the upper deck where, in a fog-laden atmosphere, I would join my fellow addicts hawking and coughing their way to work. In the summer it was tolerable because it was possible to lower the windows a fraction, but in winter any attempt to introduce fresh air brought a swift and hostile reaction from those behind.

If I didn't fall asleep, ice up or spend the entire journey cleaning bird's mess from my raincoat I was able to do some quite constructive work. With a pad on my knees I planned, sketched and calculated all sorts of wonderful devices. I would aim for a window seat where I wouldn't have to get up to let someone out, but on cold days (buses hadn't yet been fitted with heaters) it was necessary to incline oneself away from the metalwork as a precaution against frostbite. Inevitably, of course, I became a motorist.

Jack and I saved what we could from our meagre salaries and bought our first motor cars. I forget which of us pioneered this revolutionary step but the liberation was heavenly. No longer slaves, fretting and shuffling in a bus queue, we were free to go where we wanted. It was a mixed blessing however because whereas we had been able to relax on public transport, we now had to fight the traffic as drivers. And our cars, like the buses, had no heaters (I think that even some of the posh ones relied on travelling rugs to keep their owners warm). In winter we wore heavy overcoats and gloves which made driving difficult; steamed up windows required regular wiping which made our smart leather gloves go soggy. I forget what I paid for my car, but I do recall that I sold it for thirty pounds – which, I now realise, was a mistake. I was told that it was one of only six made by BSA and was a version of the classic four-wheeled model of their three-wheeled Scout. The gear lever was situated between the driver's legs (which led to many coarse jokes about teaching girls to drive) and the hand brake was by the door. Having no self-starter the engine had to be cranked into life with a starting handle.

It had other interesting eccentricities. Driven over a puddle more than one millimetre deep it would jet spouts of water through the apertures between the wooden floor-boards and around the pedals. The BSA was not a user friendly vehicle, but my wife and I loved it. Occasionally we would take it out for a weekend, but such trips were rare, weekends being devoted to de-carbonising the engine or replacing one or both of the fiendish Hardy-Spicer fabric couplings which were used to transmit power to the front wheels.

My next car was a Standard 8 purchased new, straight from the local showroom. It too lacked a heater, but it smelled of plastic and cellulose paint which was so beautiful that I tried to preserve it by keeping the windows shut.

Jack and I went through a number of vehicles over the years but with fading memory I have forgotten most of mine and all of his.

For location filming we were allowed to use our own cars, but carrying props and materials soon took its toll and our vehicles began to suffer. Manoeuvring six foot lengths of timber into a suitable place between the seats would invariably induce them to scythe through the head lining or tear off the internal driving mirror. Tins of paint were also capable of lethal tendencies. With lids hammered tight, wrapped in newspaper and placed upright in cardboard boxes they would mysteriously invert themselves and leak their contents into the space holding the spare wheel. In the end, despite the generous mileage allowances we preferred to hire vehicles and forego the cash.

When I said I can't ever remember feeling fed up with my bus and coach journeys to work, the same cannot be said for the journeys home. On dark, wet or cold nights they could be monumentally dire. Although they consisted of my morning journeys in reverse they differed in the number of passengers the vehicles carried. Firstly there was the bus ride from Shepherds Bush to Tooting Broadway where I would have to get off and join the queue for the Green Line Coach. In the mornings the coach started from a depot near my home so when it reached me there were still plenty of vacant seats. But on the return journey it was packed with passengers from London and it could be hours before one came along with sufficient space to pick up the people waiting at Tooting. There is nothing more infuriating than a conductor's arm thrust in front of you, barring entry, when you know that there won't be another Green Line for half an hour. It would have been pointless trying to bribe the arm because the service was policed by bus inspectors and the conductor would risk his job by overloading his vehicle. To add to my misery there was a pub immediately opposite the bus stop and although its windows were high one could see the shaded lights and watch the occasional lucky customer going through the door and into the comforting, warm, smoky atmosphere. Not daring to leave the queue I would pull my head further down into my raincoat and concentrate on thoughts of home and fireside.

However when I became a motorist such things as the misery of the long queue at Tooting didn't concern me. I had achieved independence. I bought the BSA from a friend of mine at Kingswood Warren who, because he was buying one of the new post-war models, was very anxious to acquire some cash. The post-war cars were spectacularly utilitarian and yet one had to put one's name on a waiting list to obtain one. Told that his new model would be available shortly he was keen for me to buy his old one. He gave me a ride to show what it could do — which was seventy miles an hour in a thirty mile limit. I was impressed, but hugely relieved when the demonstration was over and he slowed down. I had little experience of motoring and had never learned to drive while my knowledge of internal combustion engines was limited to the supercharged Rolls Royce Merlin that powered a number of wartime aircraft. But the green leather upholstery and chromium plated S-type imitation hood supports on either side of the BSA had already sold it to me and although I couldn't drive it, I bought it.

The next step was to take driving lessons and I signed up with the British School of Motoring. My first driving test, taken in a local town, resulted in failure. I thought the examiner might have forgiven my excursion onto the pavement because I had explained that the sun got in my eyes. He muttered something about that being a new one, scribbled something on a pad and handed me the top copy. Through gritted teeth I thanked him. My driving instructor was sympathetic and assured me that I would need only a couple or so more lessons and that he had already made arrangements for me to retake the driving examination. Foolishly, I had told everyone that I was taking the test and having made a right pig's ear of it, I then had to tell them that I'd failed (through no fault of my own you understand). So on the next occasion I took a test, I told no one, not even my wife.

I was booked to take the second examination in another town, one I didn't know but I soon found it to be stiff with hill climbs and packed with traffic. To make matters worse the driving school had given me a different vehicle on the day and so I was as unfamiliar with the car as I was with the town. My instructor took me over the route beforehand and then drove me to the test centre. I was briefly introduced to the examiner, a grim-faced man who looked as if he ate broken glass for breakfast. Strangely, I found myself remarkably relaxed and confident during this ride; if I failed no one would ever know. Turn left here, remember to look in the mirror, extend the right arm fully and make a circular motion with the hand and then it was over. I knew the examiner would fail me because he'd tapped his clip board menacingly and he exhibited a nervous tic. When we returned to the centre he asked me several questions about the Highway Code and then he handed me a form to sign. I was so relaxed that I took the form and signed without any comprehension of what I was doing. He told me I had passed but it meant nothing to me. I simply smiled at him like an idiot. I heard him say that I should make my signals clear in future – the driver behind would like to know if I was turning to the left or merely waving at a passer-by. And then he was gone.

My instructor drove me back to Sutton, (he wanted to get there safely) but he gratefully acknowledged my gift of two pound notes which I understood was the going rate for a pass. We shook hands and he suggested that I pay attention to my hand signals etc. I took the bus back to my village, picked up my bike and raced home. I couldn't wait to remove those hateful L-plates and take my first solo drive. It was bliss – I didn't realise it would feel so good. I drove around the empty lanes making pointless hand signals and pausing at every bend.

After a day or two I became confident enough to drive to work where, at meal times, whatever the conversation, I managed to bring up the subject of cars and how, as a seasoned driver, I negotiated such hazards as Hammersmith Broadway ('You've got to tackle it positively – force your way in front of other drivers'). One day, over lunch, a chum who was obviously fed up with my tales of heroism on the road, suggested that I might like a passenger to alleviate the tedium, a companion who would fill the miles with merry quips, witty observations and pay me half a crown a week towards my petrol. His name was Barry Lynch and, as he lived on my route, it was an entirely satisfactory arrangement. I was delighted to take his money and the quips, but the witty observations seemed to dwell on the sheer beauty of young girl's legs. Many times, when distracted by a sudden shout of 'would you look at that?' I'd experience a brush with the kerb. But by far the best part of our association was that he too liked a drop of unwinding fluid on the way home.

I have spoken fondly of the White Horse, but on most days, because of our work, Jack and I finished up without having anything more stimulating than tea or coffee. On such occasions a glass of beer on the way home with Barry was very pleasant. I continued to follow the bus route home because, it being early in my motoring career, I knew of no alternative. This meant that every evening I passed the hated bus stop in Tooting. One December night Barry and I were both looking forward to an evening tipple when I drove through Tooting Broadway and, glancing at the bus queue, saw a chap who lived in my lane. I didn't know him, but I had noticed that he arrived at the Tooting bus stop at much the same time as I did and he alighted from the Green Line coach at the same stop as I did; the one at the end of my lane. On leaving the coach he walked either in front of me or behind me down the road. I didn't pay him a great deal of attention and he seemed equally disinterested in me. I never knew where he lived because after I'd collected my bike and enjoyed a cup of tea with my mother-in-law he'd disappeared.

And there he was now, standing in line for the next coach. I saw that he was going to have a long wait because he was right at the back of the queue. Telling Barry what I was doing I pulled up and walking back to this bloke I touched him on the shoulder.

'Excuse me' I said, 'would you like a lift to Chipstead?'

He looked very surprised but said that he would. And so we drove home. But there was the matter of our drink. Barry and I were dying for a quiet, relaxing pint but the chap we'd picked up seemed strangely quiet. I looked at him from time to time in the driving mirror and he didn't appear at all like a man who would kill for a glass of beer; more like a 'let's get home and study the bible' sort of a chap, (or if not the bible he was probably dying to get back to wife and a happy evening spent rug making).

Nevertheless, I couldn't eject a thirst-wracked Barry into the cold night air and decided that the Good Samaritan stuff only went so far. If we wanted to visit the pub and the stranger didn't like it he didn't have to join us – he could jolly well sit in the car. After all, I reasoned, he'd still be home earlier than if he'd waited for the Green Line. So half way home on reaching our intended watering hole I asked him if he would mind if we just broke our journey for a minute or two while we popped into The Lord Nelson. It was astonishing. How he got out of the back seat of a small two-door car ahead of the two people sitting in the front I don't know but he was in the pub and at the counter before Barry and I could finish giving our reasons for stopping.

'What'll you have?' he asked.

Barry and I realised that we'd found the ideal person to share our journeys home. His name was Jim Humphries and he was a production engineer with Cheeseborough-Ponds. It transpired that he worked only a few miles from Shepherds Bush and so was able to meet us at Television Centre every evening. Freed from the necessity to go via that hated bus stop in Tooting, we discovered many interesting alternative routes and many fascinating places to unwind – and I made a life-long friend.

T h e   S k y   a t   N i g h t

I implied earlier that after our first major successes, few epoch-making programmes came our way. Nevertheless we had several important shows on our books and while none were of the same calibre as the Morecambe and Wise show, *Quatermass* or *Nineteen Eighty-Four* they could nevertheless be regarded as ground breakers. Between 1955 and 1956 we were involved with the original Benny Hill series (before he transferred to ITV), Tony Hancock recreating his radio series and the wonderful Jimmy Edwards, who with Arthur Marshal as his bumbling assistant, played the conniving headmaster of Chiselbury School. If I couldn't share the stage with Will Hay I was highly delighted to work with Jimmy Edwards. He had become another of my favourite comedians and I felt that to take part in a programme with him was a bonus – something to be treasured.

While acknowledging the drawing power of light entertainment the planners of that era soon discovered that factual and educational programmes could be every bit as popular. David Attenborough and Johnny Morris led the way for the hundreds of animal programmes that have followed, while Sir Mortise Wheeler – with his historical and archaeological programmes and General Sir Brian Horrocks with a series of legendary wartime stories called *Men in Battle* – did the same for ancient and modern history.

Like the other presenters, Sir Brian Horrocks was a fascinating speaker and captivated his audience by simply sitting at a small table and talking directly to the camera. He didn't need to wander through the Western desert or clamber around the fortifications in France – neither did he pose beside tanks or stand on the site of World War I trenches – he sat behind the table and told the story.

Jack and I provided the only ancillary visual elements of the programme – table top models on which he could demonstrate the significant points of his talk. Sometimes these models would be three dimensional contour maps of lands or battlefields, but as he became more confident these props became more elaborate. One model, I recall, was of a prisoner-of-war camp. Jack and I really went to town on that one, making miniature huts, barbed wire enclosures and tiny practical security lights. The General was delighted and exploited it to the full. With the studio lights dimmed and the model lights switched on, the effect was incredible and hovering over it in the shadows he made the viewers believe they were actually there. Without any animation whatsoever the viewers could *see* the escaping prisoners hiding in the darkness while searchlights supposedly probed the compound. Such was the personality of the man that working solely with these models he could hold an audience spellbound for half an hour.

In 1957 we were asked by Paul Johnstone to discuss a new programme he was considering. Paul had a production office in Lime Grove and, going there we found him talking to a man we hadn't seen before. He introduced us to this bloke who looked strangely dishevelled, wearing a badly fitting suit and with a tie which appeared to have made a journey towards the back of his neck. His name was Patrick Moore.

Paul told us that the new venture, another of his educational programmes, was to be called *The Sky at Night* and he wanted to know whether Jack and I would make some models of the planets. He had the idea that if these were 'floated' past a black backing they would appear to be in space. But time was short and they ended up as balls on black sticks with Jack and I crouching below the camera lens, waddling across the studio floor holding them aloft. During rehearsals, one of the cameramen called out in a falsetto voice 'Sister Anna will carry the banner' which completely ruined our smooth traverse and even during transmission we daren't look at each other without giggling.

After that first programme and the meeting with Patrick Moore, Jack and I discussed the programme in our office. We questioned the suitability of the seemingly odd chap who was to give his views on space and the stars. I wondered if it would stretch to six programmes whereas Jack, to his credit, thought it might run to a second series. Patrick has since become the most celebrated tele-astronomer of all time and the programme has been in the schedules ever since. These days when we meet up with him we notice that he wears very expensive looking suits which make ours seem positively shabby.

W e t   W o r k

Although working in the murky water of the Ealing tank was often exasperating, it did not compare with the problems we sometimes encountered on 'wet' locations. In our 25 years we operated in and around lochs, lakes, rivers and the open sea – on boats, in ships and occasionally, when stepping from one boat to another, below the surface.

In fairness, we usually welcomed the chance to work on or near water especially if the filming gave us the opportunity to hire a boat. I have particularly fond memories of a Scottish loch where I was to work with the programme's designer, Stuart Marshal. He and I been given the use of a hired Mini and had been booked into a splendid hotel with excellent food and a wonderful bar. It was the end of the season and we didn't have to compete with the tourists. To our delight we learned that in order to do the job the assistant producer had hired us a motor boat. Although no more than a dinghy, with a small out-board motor clamped to the transom, it nevertheless would give us the chance to take to the water and explore the loch.

Each morning we drove the seven miles from where we were staying to the fishing hotel where the boat was kept. We had only to man-handle it down a short slipway and, ensuring that we had plenty of fuel, navigate the boat seven miles to the location. The drive along the loch side in the crisp morning air was magical enough but to take to the water and sail away on an empty loch was fantastic.

On the first two mornings all went well. We left our hotel early driving along the completely deserted road to the fishing hotel where the landlord was ready for us with a bottle and two glasses – Scottish hospitality demanded that we partake of a dram to ward off the effects of the morning mist – and then we took to the open water. But before leaving we checked that we had everything on board including the painter, the pull rope, the oars, the plug spanner and a full tank of fuel. Then, after a couple of pulls on the starting rope, we cast off and sailed down the loch. On this, our third morning, we had settled into a routine; I would take the tiller on the way out, Stuart was in command on our return.

However, on this morning we had travelled only a mile or two when things started to go wrong. The dreaded Scottish mist closed in. We carried a map of the loch but even so, with little visibility we knew that all we had to do was to keep the port shore in sight and we'd get to our destination. But neither the map nor our two days' experience told us what to do when the shore was completely blotted out; we were travelling blind as the grey mist rolled across the water and blanked out every sign of land. I say 'mist', but 'impenetrable pea-souper fog' would have been a more adequate description. As it closed around us it grew dark and the putt-putt of the engine became muffled. Unfortunately, being about half a mile from the bank we lost all orientation. We tried to remember if we had passed an inlet and if so, which one. How did we know that the port shore was still on our left anyway? During those minutes of confusion we had allowed our attention to wander, and now we hadn't the faintest idea which way we were pointing. I had a splendid walking compass which would have provided a fix but it was safe and sound in my desk at home.

The mist wrapped itself around the boat and it felt chilly. We wrapped our coats more tightly under our life jackets and pondered the imponderable – how do you know which is left and which is right when you can't see a bloody thing beyond the chap sitting on a plank-seat opposite you? There was no point in going on and, equally, no point in drifting. It got colder and we huddled in our inadequate clothing while we debated the situation. The best thing, we decided, was to make a number of slow circular sweeps hoping to find the shore or the reed banks which would show us that we were in shallow water. With the throttle set on the lowest notch we cruised around peering into the murk. Suddenly we were in daylight. Just as quickly as it had appeared, the mist had gone. The sun was already warming the water and there, not more than a hundred yards away, was the bank on our left-hand side. Trusting that we hadn't crossed the water and were now following the bank on the opposite side we carried on. Fortunately even we couldn't mistake the position of the sun and knowing that we were travelling in the right direction I opened up the throttle and we putt-putted towards our destination. The hold-up meant that we were late arriving at the location and our story of the awful mist was not believed. They had seen no mist and anyway our breath smelt strongly of whisky.

Working in water has special problems because water in its natural state is seldom clear and it moves around. Inevitably, the spot chosen by the cameraman and the director is opaque, deep and affected by capricious winds and malicious currents and it is obvious that for the exacting work demanded of the special effects team this spot is entirely unsuitable. However, there is little point in trying to change their minds, it's two against one. I've noticed over the years that if a shot chosen by the director is unsuitable for the cameraman the director will back down without a word of protest. But with special effects work – well everyone knows how the effects should be achieved and they will imply that if you don't know your job you shouldn't be on the location.

In coastal waters boats drift off-station, which can lead to acrimonious confrontations between the people on shore and those at sea. These light-hearted exchanges are usually conducted by loud hailer or by shouting through cupped hands, 'The model is too far to the right. The cameraman says can you move it that way (pointing to your left) about five feet?'

'What do you mean? (shouted across the water) This is the spot he chose – he said it was okay.'

You have already spent thirty minutes anchoring the model ship or submarine to the sea bed and are now fighting its tendency to turn broadside on to the prevailing wind. But your incontrovertible statement of fact generally provokes a shouted exchange in which you try to explain that the model ship is being moved by wind and water and if the sodding cameraman feels he could do any better he is welcome to swim out here and show the effects team what to do. This will be followed by a sequence of clicks, howls and squeals as the cameraman seizes the loud hailer and fumbles with the volume control. He attempts to convey his disappointment. Why, he queries, is he being asked to film a Spanish Galleon sailing past an oil refinery?

Another thing that bedevils those working on water in a small boat is the need to constantly safeguard all tools and equipment. Drop anything over the side and it's gone forever. A carelessly handled screwdriver or the only long screw you could find to hold certain important items together will, if not looked after with considerable care, hurl itself over the side and play no further part in operations. Those accustomed to working at a bench where there is nothing more provoking than clouting one's head on a vice as one recovers an errant washer, can find that old habits die hard. A screwdriver, hammer, or saw placed carelessly on the thwarts or gunnels or whatever that narrow rim around a small boat is called will of its own accord, and with only the quietest of plops, commit suicide.

Worse than the loss of an essential tool is the dilemma facing the unfortunate effects designer, who having built an arrangement of pulleys and lines which must be lowered into the water for the purpose of controlling the movements of a floating model, finds that the lines have become snagged and cannot be freed. Then the job doesn't seem at all like 'plain sailing'.

On one occasion working at sea became rather short on job satisfaction. It should have been easy enough because it was a pleasant day although slightly overcast and two of us were sailing aboard a medium sized coastal cargo-carrier. We had been allocated two empty holds in which to set up our effects and rig our pyrotechnics and we had plenty of space and the opportunity to do a first rate job. My colleague on this job was Michaeljohn Harris and he and I had been given the task of simulating a major fire below decks. The ship was being filmed in such a way that it appeared to be miles from land ploughing its way upon the open sea. Ordinarily such a conflagration would have been child's play but this was something neither of us had attempted before – a fire at sea. Nevertheless with so much convenient space below decks we had only to ignite a few smoke pots and create some flames with bottled gas and flame forks to make it look as if the entire ship was on fire.

We'd gone aboard the day before and had been entertained in one of the most delightful bars I have ever been in. It was quite small with room for only eight or ten imbibers at the most and was situated forward of the bridge where it straddled the width of the ship. It had a bow window against which a semi-circular padded bench-seat faced the small bar which was constructed from exotic polished maple. It was charming and we were very nearly tempted to sign on for the next voyage.

Michaeljohn had confided that he was prone to seasickness but thought that sailing in the calm waters just off the coast would not be like the open sea. Never having experienced seasickness myself I felt very superior. In the worst wartime crossings of the North Sea I had never once felt the slightest unease. I assured him that if he should have any symptoms of queasiness I could handle the job alone - get the gas burners going and ignite a smoke pot or two and everything would be fine. Anyone knowing anything about ships will have spotted the trouble already. Empty holds! Normally a coastal vessel of this type would sail with its holds full; to sail with them empty would be uneconomic. Someone had asked for empty holds, and empty holds was what they had got. (I say 'they'd got' but empty holds is what *we'd* got! The ship didn't pitch or roll on its way out to sea – it travelled as smoothly as an underground train but Mike was already looking green. I gave him words of encouragement. 'I'll handle it.'

But there was a strange feeling gripping my lower anatomy. I dismissed it. I was a good sailor. Even in the notorious Catskills around the Channel Islands where the wave tops sometimes block out the sky and the ship seems to be perpetually sliding down an endless slope I never experienced even the tiniest twinge. While others collapsed around me I strode the deck like a grizzled mariner, smoking a pipe and smiling sympathetically as I passed the prostrate bodies in their puddles of vomit. But this was strange – I was experiencing a feeling I hadn't known before. Could it be? No of course not! But I was beginning to have doubts about myself. I smiled sickly at Mike and sat down heavily beside him. I was feeling distinctly unwell. To my recollection only the cameraman and the director among our unit remained untroubled. I'm sure that the reason for this was that the crafty blighters knew that while we sailed within the three mile limit the bar would be closed – subject to the licensing laws that pertained on shore. I'm convinced that they'd stashed a bottle of whisky in the camera bag and were suitably fortified against whatever the sea would throw at us.

Mike and I got through the day and neither of us was actually sick but I shall never forget that horrible feeling of wanting to die. Since then I no longer boast that I never get sea sick – in fact I avoid the subject altogether.

A   L o t   o f   F i s h

Now that the Beeb had acquired the studios at Ealing everyone was eager to use them and very soon they were fully-booked. Ealing provided a new environment for television production. It had floors that you could nail things to, it had stages which you could fill with smoke without fear of ruining highly sensitive electronic equipment and it had the tank.

The first occasion that Jack and I worked there was for an opera directed by Rudolph Cartier called *Tobias and the Angel*. Among other things we had to make a big fish. It was approximately six feet long, very fat and with bulbous eyes; it wasn't so much a big fish as an enormous fish and because it had to appear from below the surface of a lake we would have to test it in a suitable depth of water. Fortunately we could do that without having to fill the tank at Ealing.

Opposite Lime Grove Studios were the Lime Grove Baths, a well-known training venue for competition swimmers and a hall for boxing matches. Jack and I had got to know the superintendent and, once the baths had closed for the evening, this accommodating chap was prepared to let us use the main pool for our tests and experiments. Such was the glamour of television in those days that for anyone to have a link with the programmes or the programme makers gave him or her special status. We didn't often need to use this facility but when we did it proved invaluable. Now we arranged with him to test our fish. Jack had designed it and what's more he had volunteered to wear breathing equipment and manoeuvre it under water. Being only a moderate swimmer I didn't contest his right to play the part of a fish manipulator.

We decided to mould it in latex, the most up to date material available to us at that time. It meant sculpting an original in clay, taking a cast of it in plaster and recreating the original fish in rubber. It seemed a relatively simple job and we weren't anticipating trouble. But what we failed to appreciate was that we were dealing, not in pounds and ounces of modelling clay, but in tons. Even when the huge amount of clay we'd ordered ran out before we'd only reached the gills leaving us slightly perturbed. We ordered more, which ran out half way to the tail. Now we began to worry about the budget. But it wasn't just the cost that troubled us. We began to question the weight. Would we ever be able to lift the fish when it was cast and moulded? We knew that it would need neutral buoyancy in the water, but had already prepared for that – we were going to fill its interior with balloons.

We ordered more clay from a delighted supplier and finished the tail. We hadn't the experience to make the plaster case mould, neither did we have the space to swing it – the normal method for casting aqueous rubber – and so when we'd used up all our clay we passed the job of making a rubber fish to a specialist contractor. It took five people to lift the clay master off the bench and get it to their vehicle.

A week later our fish was delivered. It was as white as snow and despite its bulbous eyes and malicious lips, looked horribly dead. So the next thing was to paint it. It soon became clear however that we'd hit another problem – this rubber did not like paint; in fact it struggled so hard to rid itself of the offensive stuff that the paint was almost peeling off as we brushed it on. It was a problem we'd not encountered before. But Jack came up with an answer. He suggested that we should give it a primary coat of aluminium paint, the sort of paint used for industrial installations. He reasoned that if it would stick to boiler pipes and rusting iron it would stick to a rubber fish. He was right, it did. Furthermore it gave us a splendid base coat for coloured lacquers. Not only was our fish going to be brightly coloured, it was going to glow with brilliant iridescence.

The following evening we took it to the baths. Having no transport we had to carry it through the streets to Lime Grove and although it was getting dark our strange bug-eyed fish aroused considerable interest and many humorous comments from passers-by – the English are a witty lot.

We were met by the superintendent who had thoughtfully wedged all the doors open which enabled us to walk straight through to the main pool and lay our fish on the tiled surround. Anxious to get started we changed into our swimming trunks. He was intrigued by the fish and commented on its beautiful colours. We felt rather proud.

He had set out our underwater breathing gear consisting of a pool-side air bottle, long lengths of hose, demand valves and masks. Sensibly we had arranged for these to be sent over earlier in the day, but he was puzzled by the box of party balloons that had come with it. Now was the moment to test our theories. The balloons, once we'd blown them up, were inserted through the fish's mouth then we lowered it gently into the deep end. It sank like a block of concrete, plummeting through nine feet of water to the bottom; it was followed by a trail of escaping balloons.

Jack bravely followed it down but he hadn't yet donned the breathing gear and couldn't retrieve it before his lungs gave out. He came spluttering to the surface and told me, as if I hadn't realised it, that the fish was too heavy for him. The superintendent, seeing our predicament, went off to fetch a rope while Jack equipped himself with the breathing gear. But even with the rope and Jack, now in the mask, it took a good ten minutes to get the fish from the water onto dry land

– a task that would have been beyond us had we not cut a nine inch slot in the rubber belly to let the water out.

During this rescue operation I'd noticed a few flakes of silvery green paint floating on the surface of the water and had assumed these to have been scraped off during our strenuous attempts to get our fish out of the water. No such luck. The silver paint that would cling to pipes for a hundred and fifty years appeared to be allergic to chlorinated water. We inspected the fish as it lay on the tiles and saw that it was suppurating freely. But this was clearly a minor problem compared with the one of buoyancy. We blew up more balloons and stuffed them into the mouth.

Perhaps at this stage fate considered we'd suffered enough because with this further insertion of human breath the fish floated level and trim just below the surface. But the coloured scum that floated around it was looking ominous. I don't think it impressed our friend the baths superintendent because he went away to collect a bucket and mop. Satisfied that we'd beaten the main problem we got dressed and, after donating ten shillings towards the clean-up operation, carried our lustreless fish back through the streets. Our frame of mind can be judged by the fact that we walked past the White Horse without stopping. We did consider going in because we both needed a drink, but leaving a six foot long bug eyed peeling fish propped outside against the pub wall might have been unwise.

And, of course, we were to discover that fate hadn't really relented, it had simply paused before delivering another blow. Try as we might to keep the defunct fish away from our clothes we saw that we were now covered in iridescent paint. I might have asked Jack how long silver paint that would stay on pipes for years would last on a fifty shilling suit, but I could see he was too dispirited to answer.

We did eventually overcome the paint problem and Jack, equipped with underwater breathing gear made a brilliant underwater fish animator, but remembering the evening I spent at home trying to clean the paint from my jacket and trousers the dismal episode is one I prefer to forget.

H e a v e n ' s   A b o v e

The fish was not the only item on our list of commitments for *Tobias*; there was the small matter of the Flying Angel. For the principal roles Rudolph Cartier had cast opera singers, and the Angel was no exception. However, with hindsight Rudy might have looked through the pages of *Spotlight* in an attempt to find a circus performer with a good singing voice.

The role called for nothing special in the way of acting – a baritone who would play the part of a winged angel holding a sword. In opera they often carried weapons like swords or spears or scythes, but this sword had to be flaming. This requirement apart, it would seem reasonable to ask a singer to dress up as an angel sporting huge feathered wings and carrying something, but in this case there was an added dimension; this angel would be standing on top of a ten foot high column. To imply that a trained stuntman would have studied the contract in the presence of his lawyer might be putting it a bit strongly, but it gives some idea of what the part demanded. And at the end of his performance the singer was required to float gently down to earth, still singing lustily while raising his burning sword aloft.

The floating down to earth finale was to be achieved with the aid of the Kirby flying ballet system supervised and installed by a fully trained operator. Developed for theatrical work the Kirby system was designed to levitate such characters as Peter Pan who, supported by wires, could be manipulated by hidden operators to fly around a stage like a butterfly. In essence this apparatus comprises a number of fine steel wires attached to a leather body harness which is hidden under the costume. Lit skilfully the wires become almost invisible.

Although an easier matter to deal with on a large stage than in a television studio where close-ups can show light glinting from the wires, the problem, for once wasn't ours, it was a task for the lighting cameraman who would have to illuminate each shot in such a way that the wires, sprayed black, would not be noticed. The fine wires in the Kirby system are connected to thicker cables and from there to soft ropes held by the operator. An arrangement of reducing pulleys bolted to the studio gantry enable the operator to raise and lower a performer with ease and, at the same time, to move him from one side of the stage to the other.

The Kirby man was to haul our opera singer to the top of the column and (and this was the important factor) hold him safely on his tiny platform until the moment when he would be lowered, as gracefully as a butterfly, to the floor below. All he was required to do was to sing and, in the final moments, brandish the sword above his head. When we explained this to the singer he lost all fear and subsequently took to his part with such gusto that we had to restrain him from performing too vigorously. Jack and I were particularly worried about the 'flaming sword' because it presented such obvious problems. How does one define 'flaming'? Was this meant to imply that the three foot long weapon should be burning fiercely? The idea that this man clad in a Methuselian wig, a long flowing beard and wearing a voluminous white toga and large feathered wings would perform whilst holding a prop capable of incinerating him seemed unlikely. And so we decided to interpret flaming to mean glowing. But even this would be difficult to achieve. In the end we gave him a broad sword of Perspex behind which we fitted a domestic fluorescent tube. With this light tinted orange it looked good and when the artiste held it close to his body it bathed his costume in fiery light giving a suitably dramatic effect. But the problem was how to hide the 240 volt cable required to supply it. After one or two tests we found we could pass the wire under his costume and down his sleeve where it would be taped to his wrist. The rest of the cable would be hidden in his clothing and, emerging at his ankle would be formed in a loop to the back of the set. This, we reasoned, would ensure that it would not be seen by the camera and would not impede his plunge from the top of the column. With a limited budget we could make only one sword and were understandably anxious that nothing untoward should happen to it. Perspex, unlike forged steel, is delicate and one sharp tap would have converted our flaming sword into a smoking dagger. During rehearsals at Ealing we explained to the singer how important it was for him to follow our instructions to the letter, but presumably unaccustomed to being flown around on a wire he didn't at first grasp the fact that when the cue came for him to descend from the top of his column he must do nothing, absolutely positively nothing! Not even take a step forward. The reason for this is that in order to do his job smoothly the operator must have full control. We explained how essential this was – that the performer contributes nothing. He gave us a categorical hand-on-the-heart assurance that he would not even bat an eyelid. Happy at last that everything was understood we asked the operator to haul him to the top of the column. He was as good as his word, not even putting his feet on the platform until told he could do so.

Time was pressing and Rudy decided to go for a take without a rehearsal. The Kirby man took up his position and the angel held his raised sword correctly positioned; Rudy stood behind the camera while we looked to Paddy Russell to give us our cue.

'Camera running. Speed' intoned the cameraman. The clapper board was held in front of the lens and the words were read out. '*Tobias and the Angel*, Scene nine, take one'. Paddy dropped her hand and the sequence was under way.

The angel performed impeccably, brandishing his illuminated sword and remembering our instruction to keep it facing towards the camera. Jack and I relaxed, things were going well and soon the morning session would wrap and we could break for lunch. Silently we mimed the score.

Then came the moment for the actor to deliver his dramatic speech and descend from his column. Extracting every ounce of drama from his performance he flourished his sword in wild abandon and, completely forgetting our instructions, stepped off his perch. The Kirby man, expecting to take his weight, encountered nothing more than a handful of loose rope and, unable to brace himself in time, stumbled backwards. Jack and I watched in horror as events unfolded almost in slow motion. Blissfully unaware that he was now in free fall the angel played his part with enthusiasm flashing past the camera at a speed which left the startled cameraman filming empty space. My first thought was that when he hit the floor he would smash every bone in his body. My second thought was that he would break our sword. My third thought was that he was wrapped in a live cable. Fortunately the Kirby operator, trained to expect the unexpected, reacted swiftly, arresting the rope and halting the angel's descent before it took him through the studio floor. But the astonishing thing was that the delighted angel jiggling just inches from the ground seemed completely unaware of his lucky escape. He beamed at Rudy and asked 'Was it alright?'

A Regrettable Split

As is the pattern with most people's lives, my career with the BBC had its highs and its lows. The lowest point was when Richard Levin and I fell out. From the original blue-eyed boy I became a troublesome piece of horse manure.

The fault was mine, I over-played my hand and deserved everything I got – but the punishment was hard to take. Levin told me he would split the section if I found the set-up so difficult to accept – and he did. Jack would run the unit with all the existing designers, workshops and facilities – I would be in charge of the practical effects and would be responsible for explosions, rain effects, smoke and dry ice. I would also take over the armourers, a small unit of three chaps whose responsibility was to maintain, clean and issue all the weapons that appeared in BBC productions. These included hand guns, real and imitation, spears, swords, daggers, pikes and those studded knobbly ball things that hang on sticks. The awful thing however, was that I had to join these blokes in their basement workshop where I would become the great high over-lord of three wooden benches, some battered steel cupboards and all the spears, daggers and swords I could wish for. Richard Levin certainly knew how to punish wayward members of his staff.

A concrete room with a heavy steel door and two formidable locks housed the practical firearms which were regularly inspected by the local police. My 'office' was a space in one corner, a table and chair and, to mark my executive status, an in-tray and a metal coat hook screwed to one of the cupboards. I no longer rated even a bent wood hat rack.

Credit to the lads who ran the armoury because they kept it clean and tidy but it smelled overpoweringly of gun oil, a far cry from the lavender scented furniture polish of the offices above. The room was lit by ten overhead fluorescent tubes which were switched on throughout the day, the only natural light coming from a window high up in one wall. This window was level with the pavement outside that led to reception and all we saw were people's legs. Other luxuries included the distempered walls artistically decorated with magazine cut-outs of large breasted pin-ups. The chaps also had a battered radio which was permanently tuned to a pop music station. However in the afternoon the three hulking lads gathered round this radio to sip their tea and listen to *Mrs Dale's Diary*, a soap opera of village folk.

I wasn't entirely unfamiliar with life's tendency to deal out crushing blows; I had experienced them twice before. The first was when I was seven years old and was taken ill with double pneumonia and spent a whole year in bed (something worth thinking about when the cost of modern drugs is debated). I had caught a chill and being undernourished had succumbed to a disease which, at a certain stage, could prove fatal. My parents had put me in their double bed to separate me from my brother; my mother had a single bed alongside mine from which she could monitor my breathing and tend to my nocturnal needs. Where my poor father slept I don't know. I was in the care of the local doctor, a kindly man who seemed almost as concerned about my condition as my parents. The crisis point – the moment at which you either wake up and smile at everyone or you don't wake up at all – came eventually and, warned of this, my parents took turns in hovering over me as if to fend off the hooded reaper. I awoke and smiled at them

However, my memories of that year are not of misery at all, but of having a rather nice time. People brought me lovely books such as *Grimm's Fairy Tales*, beautifully illustrated, and toys such as the wonderful cardboard parade of shops comprising a greengrocer's, a butcher's and a confectioner's each with their wares fashioned from painted confectionery and a set of tin scales. I spent hours playing shopkeepers. There was a torch too, with coloured lenses that I would shine under the bedclothes to create eerie grottos. At one time I recall feeling too tired even to read or to play shopkeepers and the doctor came and kept looking at his watch and holding my wrist. Soon after the crisis had passed I was able to leave the double bed and walk around the house. But the misery I spoke of was about to follow. My parents had been advised that in order to make a full recovery I should spend the next six months breathing sea air and I was taken to the Isle of Wight where I was put into some sort of convalescent home-cum-boarding school run by nuns. These women seemed to get unnatural pleasure from beating young boys on their bare bottoms with a leather slipper – which they did almost daily. To ensure that we survived this punishment and were brought back to a degree of healthy fitness we were taken out by a retired army sergeant who, fortified with Brown Ale and protected by a coat buttoned to the neck, took us on long invigorating walks in a freezing wind. After this the beatings didn't seem the worst thing in our educational career.

The only comforts the school permitted were the morning delivery of incoming mail (outgoing mail was censored – 'We don't want your parents to worry, do we, boy? Rewrite this letter and leave out the bit about cockroaches in the porridge'.) and the school 'tuck shop', a small stone building with a minuscule stock of sweets which opened only on Saturday mornings and enabled us to spend our pocket money on such delights as Anchor Chocolate Toffees and Button's Coconut Squares.It's possible that I treat the custodians of that establishment less than fairly. I was a child away from home and family and it was a different time and a different age. Nevertheless it became my benchmark of misery against which all the other miseries in life would be compared.

The second time I suffered subterranean depths of depression was during the war when, in 1940, I was called up for national service. Strangely the circumstances were very like those I had experienced on the Isle of Wight. I'd left behind my father, mother and brother all who had said 'goodbye' with voices too choked to be heard, none of us knowing whether we would ever meet again. I had been assigned to the RAF and was to report for duty at Uxbridge. Arriving at the gates with about thirty other apprehensive young men I was escorted to a long room in one of the barrack blocks where I was allocated an iron bed and told to report in thirty minutes to another part of the building where I would be given my duties. When I got there I found a corporal sitting at a folding table. I sauntered up to him, gave him my name and details and told him I was to become a flight mechanic. He looked me up and down and asked if I had seen the toilets in the room next to the sleeping quarters. I replied off-handedly that I had noticed them. 'Right' he said, 'you perhaps *noticed* that they needed cleaning. You'll find a bucket and tin of Vim in there so you'll be able to clean 'em. When I get there in an hour's time I want to see them bloody spotless and bloody sparkling!' Dismissed, I crawled away. Could this be happening to me? Two days before I had left my job as an airfield lighting designer and the luxurious offices in the North Wing of Bush House (where three uniformed girls operated the lifts) and now I was expected to clean toilets. I thought of explaining to this lumpen idiot that I was scheduled for engineering, not bog sanitation and that there might just be some mistake, but I recognised the sadistic-nun syndrome and got out before he told me that I must also sweep the drill square.

Now, some sixteen years later, while a designer at the BBC, I was, metaphorically speaking, again made to clean the toilets. Richard Levin, I decided, was in the position of a drill sergeant and while, unlike a viperous nun, he didn't wield a slipper he was able to subject me to a form of humiliation that was far worse. I dragged myself to work each day not daring to tell my wife of my change in status and my shameful fall from grace.

During this period Jack and I continued to drink together, but we were on different planes and my misery was painfully obvious. I tried hard to convince him that everything was fine downstairs and that a new empire was being created, but he knew I was lying and desperately unhappy. To ease my grief he never talked about the marvellous programmes that were coming into his office, shows that I now had nothing to do with and saw only on the television receiver at home. Drinking together with few common interests became a depressing business and the intervals between lunches became longer and our conversation more and more stilted.

Perhaps the worst aspect of all was that I was now attached to the property department and my immediate boss was Bill King, the property-master – our former rival. The smirks on the faces of the prop-men were now undisguised as they remembered the times that Jack and I had lorded it over them and had appropriated their special effects equipment. Giving me time to settle in, Bill King summoned me to his office. By now I was prepared to hand in my resignation, but Bill was wonderfully compassionate. Realising the depth of my depression he produced a bottle of Scotch and two glasses and revealed his plans for the future. I left an hour later a much happier person thinking that perhaps I really could build a new empire from the nucleus of three oil-stained benches and my table behind the filing cabinets.

Eventually, Levin relented. I'm proud to say I didn't go down on my knees and beg for forgiveness, neither did I appeal to the Director General as I was entitled to do. I simply stuck it out. Levin had recognised that by despatching me to the basement he was losing the creativity that he so depended on. As a trained mechanical and electrical engineer I was the only technical person in a colony of artists. He'd also noticed that while Kine and Wilkie as a team had produced some of the better ideas, separated they were clearly not as good. I can't recall the moment when Jack and I came together again, but I do remember that it was during one of Levin's massive reorganisations. He did these shuffles quite frequently, believing that if people became too settled they would become stale. I think he was right, but his designers hated it. I saw one young designer in tears having been told he wasn't good enough to continue working in his present role and that he would have to return to drawing up other people's studio plans. Later on Levin reinstated him too, but the effect of demotion on this chap was traumatic. At the time I did my best to console him, because having been out of favour and later allowed to return I was a practical example of how things worked in design group. But he was of a nervous disposition and suffered a breakdown which kept him away from work for several months.

The reorganisation meant that on my return to the Visual Effects unit I wasn't simply coming back upstairs because now we were all to be relocated in Kensington House, the BBC office block on the other side of Shepherds Bush.

Television Design Department was now growing rapidly and the Design Block was bursting at the seams. Some reorganisation was called for and to make room for an enlarged graphics section we had to move out. Our new premises were in the basement of Kensington House but were, in many ways, superior to those at The Centre. They were large and comprised several separate rooms. This increase in accommodation enabled us to spread ourselves for the very first time. Moreover Kensington House had better car parking arrangements than we'd had at The Centre and it had its own club! The major drawback was that we had to travel back and forth across The Green to attend meetings with producers and designers. It also meant a delay if we were called to deal with a problem in the studio.

I am not sure how many people we had in our group at this time, but I do remember that it included Peter Day, Ricky Grosser and Ron Oates, all of whom turned up one weekend with Jack and myself to carry out the move. God, the junk we'd collected! Half the stuff went straight into the rubbish bins. By the following week we had sorted things out and given everyone decent accommodation, something we hadn't been able to do before. Furthermore we were able to set out two workshops and a materials store – the future once again looked promising and with a bit of luck I could put the past few months out of my mind.

Richard Levin and I resumed our relationship as if nothing had happened. I had been taught a lesson and served my sentence and, as if to offer a token handshake, Jack and I were invited to lunch at his home.

H R H ' s   M i r r o r s

Riverside Studios by the Thames at Hammersmith was conveniently situated to provide additional studio accommodation for the BBC's growing complex in Shepherds Bush. There was no set pattern for its operation it being used for comedies, dramas and documentaries as demand dictated. One day it was taken over entirely for a royal visit.

HRH The Duke of Edinburgh had recently been away on an extended sea voyage and, on his return, had been invited by the BBC to talk about his experiences in front of the cameras. He had taken a number of photographs on the journey and it was suggested that he might use some of these to illustrate his talk. But there was a snag. Riverside lacked resources. It was restricted in the number of cameras it could muster because the finite number of camera channels available in the studios limited their use. I think the maximum number of cameras on the day was four, three to cover The Duke and the interviewer and one to screen his photographs.

Anthony Craxton, the producer, was worried by these limitations and asked us if we could devise a method of presenting them on cue while the Duke was talking. It was unthinkable even in those days that they should be simply displayed on caption stands. Anyway the method of cross-cutting from one caption or photograph to another meant tying up two cameras and that was equally unacceptable.

Riverside had been chosen for security reasons, shielding the Duke from newspaper photographers and reporters. Being underused at that time it made an ideal location to record what was to be the first royal interview of its kind. It also meant that whatever solution to the photograph presentation problem we could devise we would have a whole studio to work in and would not be pushed into some out-of-the-way corner or behind the drapes. Not that this brought the solution any closer but it did give us a free hand.

When Anthony first asked us whether there were any means by which the Duke's photographs could be displayed using a single camera I assured him that it could be done. If the worst came to the worst we could always build a large Ferris wheel and drop each photograph into position. But this would have been an unsophisticated method – a Stone Age solution.

'It's all done with mirrors.' was a thought that kept running through my head and so confident was I that optics would solve the problem I was already working on a theory as we left his office. Jack was worried. 'Are you sure we can do it?' he asked. He acknowledged my Research Department experience and the fact that I'd had some training in optics, but this sounded a bit of a tricky one. How was it that the camera boys hadn't been able to solve the problem? Was I talking miracles? That afternoon I went to Woolworths and bought six handbag mirrors.

Back in the office I cleared a space on the bench and using blocks of wood and Plasticine I arranged the mirrors in a configuration where I became the camera and a coffee cup and a blue mug became the Duke's photographs. I was right, I saw that it was possible, but the mirrors reversed the image and I had to include another one to turn the pictures the right way round. The long and short of our thinking and setting up of countless arrangements of the handbag mirrors showed that my optimism was justified – we had the basis for a caption machine that would cross-cut between one photograph and another. We'd invented something that even by present standards was fairly sophisticated. I don't want to bore anyone with a technical description of the method, but suffice to say that my optical device finished up as a large plywood box on three self-aligning metal legs and contained no fewer than fourteen mirrors and sheets of surface-reflective glass. It had its own internal lighting and was viewed through a camera port in the front.

The Duke's photographs, mounted on numbered cards, were placed in holders on either side of the box and to make the changeover Jack and I, standing on opposite sides, turned a handle to bring the next one into view. The effect was that of a 'wipe' in which a line ran up or down one of the pictures revealing the next one. It was designed to hold about thirty or forty separate photographs. I am still proud of that design, but it was used only once more and that was for a general election broadcast when it was pressed into service to show the numbers of gains and losses.

The studio at Riverside was sealed off during the Duke's visit and security guards were employed to keep out enterprising news hawks and paparazzi posing as cleaners; those of us who were part of the production team were given special passes showing that we were to be admitted to the studio during the transmission – I still have mine.

Jack and I didn't see the programme because it was transmitted live. However we do know that it went without a hitch despite the fact that he and I were all too conscious of the awful responsibility we carried and our sweaty hands shook perceptibly as we removed the 'dead' captions and put them, in order on a side table.

Anticipating that one of us would be bound to forget which caption had to be withdrawn I had installed two mirrored viewing ports which enabled us to see what the camera saw and I had also fitted big red pilot lights on either side of the box to show which side was on the air. We knew that if the red light was glowing the photograph on that side must *not* be touched. We had seen the efforts of the scene staff who were forced to keep an eye on the cameras at the same time as their fingers hovered over their caption easels, a difficult task and I didn't want to risk removing a photograph and shoving it back in full view of the watching millions.

Although we had a list of the Duke's photographs and carefully ticked them off as we went along we were aware that a wrong move on our part could turn the Duke's performance into a parody of *Monty Python*. Suppose the Duke was talking about the captain of his ship and we were showing a picture of a baboon! I tried to put such thoughts from my mind.

Usually a bustle of activity the studio was strangely quiet with everyone speaking in whispers. Nobody was allowed to wander in and out and we had only a few key personnel to do the work normally done by a team. In the moments before we went on the air Jack and I tried to catch a glimpse of the Duke, but we and our lone cameraman had been placed at the far end of the studio and I don't think we saw the royal personage once. Installed in a small arrangement of flats he was out of our vision and, except for a distant muted sound of voices, also out of earshot. Once the transmission light went on we were too busy to look, concentrating entirely on our own responsibilities.

We received our cues via headphones which, fortunately, came to us firm and clear. Neither the Duke nor we got things mixed up and afterwards, while he was provisioned in a room specially given over to hospitality Jack and I, who weren't on the guest list, departed for the White Horse. It was closed.

Anthony Craxton showed his appreciation of our efforts however and, nice chap that he was, arranged for each of us to be given a special award of fifty quid.

S u p e r   M o d e l

Jack and I were both in the office when the PA came in. 'Hallo chaps.' he said, 'Is the model ready?' I couldn't recall that we were doing anything with a model but I saw Jack was looking flushed – a bad sign. Whenever someone asked us a question like that we usually had two replies. The first was 'Yes, it's over there.' the second was 'What model?' Jack wisely used neither but played for time. 'It's nearly finished but it needs another half hour for the paint to dry. We'll bring it over; how's everything going?' He was now looking *very* flushed, a terrible sign. When the PA had gone Jack scrambled to his feet. 'Christ!' he said with unintended aptness. 'Shaun's model of the site of the crucifixion'.

I remembered now. In a lunchtime conversation with Shaun Sutton we had agreed to make a model, but on returning to the office we'd forgotten to add it to the list. That's the trouble with lunchtime conversations, everything seems easy when you have a pint in your hands. And now they were expecting a model, a vital prop, to arrive in the studio. We tried to remember what Shaun had wanted. Jack's mind was more organised than mine and as he recalled the details it seemed more and more impossible. 'What's he using it for?' I wanted to know. 'God knows. I remember that is was a model of Calvary after the event' I recalled some of the details now. It should have depicted the scene with the wooden crosses on a mound and various animals and a couple of shepherds standing nearby. It was an impossible task but enlisting the help of the other members of the unit we sprang into action. Pushing aside the work they were doing they undertook various parts of the model. Peter Day would prepare the three foot square baseboard and mould the hill out of Plasticine and sawdust. Rhys Jones would make a donkey. Ron Oates would create the landscape with palms and rocks and Jack would paint a backing and make two shepherds. I would make the crosses and help with the two sheep. Without wasting time in discussion we got down to our various tasks. We looked like people in a speeded up film as we rushed to gather materials and although we didn't say a lot we did tend to cannon into each other.

An hour later saw us packing the finished items into boxes. We weren't proud of our work but it was too late to spruce things up. People who have tried to make model sheep look like model sheep and not like mouldy sausages on sticks – with less than an hour to do it will appreciate the difficulties. Perhaps a few minutes discussion would have been wise. Now, with everything packed in boxes, we rushed the model over to the studio. We set the base board on a table, fixed the backing and installed the animals and shepherds. It was awful. The shepherds looked more like replicas of the elephant man with an even more disfiguring disease, the sheep were lumpy and hideous and even the rocks looked misshapen (you've got to be either a genius or blind drunk to create a misshapen rock) but the goat was perfect. Unfortunately it was, comparatively speaking, about the size of a bus. We didn't know what to say. It was far too late in the day to remedy the situation besides which the PA was hovering nearby. He looked at each item as we unwrapped it with a facial expression I didn't understand. Could he not believe that a goat in those days might have been sired by a Hippopotamus?

When we'd assembled the model he ventured an opinion. 'That's marvellous boys – just how young children would have made it'.

Q u a t e r m a s s   a n d   t h e   P i t

In 1958, we were given our second *Quatermass*. Rudolph Cartier phoned us one morning asking if we were free to come to his office. He had Nigel Kneale with him and they wanted to discuss the visual effects for a new serial.

Normally phlegmatic, Rudy positively bubbled with excitement. I don't know what we were working on at the time but the mere mention of the name Quatermass was enough to have us hurrying through the corridors to Rudy's office.

Tom Kneale was already sunk in a chair. I say sunk because Tom ('Nigel' was his professional name but we always called him Tom) Kneale had a way of relaxing in a chair that seemed to put his head lower than his knees, but he untangled himself and got to his feet to greet us. We had met him several times since the previous *Quatermass* and it was good to know that we'd all be working together again.

He told us that this one was called *Quatermass and the Pit* and started to explain the plot but Rudy took over; I'd seldom seen him so animated. Jack and I were dying to ask questions but had the sense to sit on our hands and listen – Rudy did not like being interrupted. We were fascinated and occasionally glanced at each other as we saw the way certain effects could be achieved. When he'd finished he asked if we had any questions, but we replied with something diplomatic like 'not at this stage' and asked if we could meet again when we'd studied the scripts. Tom was obviously dying to know what we thought of the plot but I think he was able to judge from our expressions which could best be described as a mixture of starry-eyed and poleaxed. Remembering the press coverage that the previous *Quatermass* had received our mood of euphoria was easy to appreciate.

We walked back to the office muttering things like 'bloody marvellous' and 'bags of stuff in it for us' until we glanced at one of the corridor clocks – lunch time was over and the canteen was closed. The afternoon was spent in reading the scripts and waiting for the tea trolley. Occasionally we made comments as we marked the special effects in red, some of which were going to test our ingenuity to the full. There were mind-boggling marginal notes and directions such as 'the space ship starts to glow and melt' and 'pan from Sladden's terrified face to the gravel path beside him – it is moving, rippling as if hundreds of rats are running under it.' and 'In the underground workings there is this same hideous noise and everything – scaffolding, planks, ladders, tools fly around and are propelled through the air by some unseen force.'

Unlike the previous *Quatermass* this one had been given a reasonable budget. No longer would we forced to search for bits and pieces in the carpenter's shop, use spring-wound gramophone motors or beg for half-used tins of paint from the scene staff – we could actually spend money.

The alien monsters described by Tom as just over two feet high, insect-like with tripod legs and pointed proboscises, were crucial to the plot. For the first time the public was meant to see credible monsters from another world and it was important to make them as unlike the comic book Martians as possible; they would have to look menacing (although presumably dead for thousands of years) and not in the least like 'little green men'.

Jack came up with a design which, oddly enough, formed in his mind after seeing a painting by Tom Kneale's brother, the artist Bryan Kneale. We were at a party at Tom and Judith's flat in Holland Park where, over the mantelpiece, hung Bryan's abstract painting of a strange horny, lobster-like creature. It was enough to stimulate Jack's imagination and after discussing the design with Tom – who had wanted his Martians to look exactly like that anyway – he worked on a series of sketches that would become the aliens. Made in fibre glass they were almost as famous in their day as the Daleks were to become later on. They weren't required to walk thank heaven, because the tripod leg arrangement would have presented us with enormous difficulties.

When the monsters are eventually discovered they're seen hanging in 'gossamer-like fronds' in the cockpit of the space craft. Cartier watched as Jack and I hung them up on nylon fish lines and threaded yards of Boots' bandages around them. It was during this tricky operation that Jack accidentally broke one of the supporting threads, causing one of the monsters to drop about three inches before being brought up on its other two lines. Cartier saw this and leapt from his chair. 'That's it boys! I want you to do that when we record, exactly as you did it then.' He smiled hugely, having realised the effect this sudden jerk would have on the viewers. I watched that episode at home with my wife and when the creature dropped she jumped – and so did millions of viewers across the nation.

As a team, Rudy, Tom Kneale, Cliff Hatts (the designer), Jack and I got on very well, but during filming at Ealing Studios the pair of us upset everyone. Television technology was advancing and it was now commonplace for filmed excerpts to be edited into a programme during recording. This is known as 'telecine'. But telecine was expensive because the excerpts had to be pre-filmed. Nevertheless, Cartier had spent a long time working out the cost of the programme and had demanded (and had been granted) extra money to cover the sequences he would have to film. A schedule was worked out and arrangements were made to shoot the difficult items at Ealing Studios.

Jack and I enjoyed working at Ealing because the conditions were so very different from those at the Centre. In the film studio we had only one camera to work to, each sequence or change of angle being recorded separately. The atmosphere was different too. At Ealing the studios provided ample space, the floors were rough and made of wood and working practices were less restrictive – factors which enabled us to do things we would never have been allowed to do in the pristine studios at Television Centre. When the film camera was called upon to track it was placed on a dolly that travelled smoothly on sturdy aluminium rails.

One thing that fascinated us was the accessibility of the lighting gantries. We had discovered the iron ladders fastened to the walls during our original survey of Ealing. It wasn't the fact that they gave access to the hanging platforms so much as that we were allowed to use them. Still seemingly untouched, the lighting gantries were as dark and dusty as they had been on our first visit but up there was a mysterious world seemingly visited only occasionally by the studio electricians and ourselves. The best thing about them was that the lower ones offered us facilities for hanging or dropping things (without having to rig ladders and platforms as we were forced to do in the electronic studios) while the upper ones gave us the chance to have a cigarette out of sight, high above the studio floor. When I stopped smoking I also gave up the irresponsible pleasure of 'beating the system'.

On the first morning of the *Quatermass* shooting Jack and I packed the props and materials into the boots of our cars and arrived at the studios early. We made at once for the restaurant where we knew we could get a heavenly breakfast of bacon, sausages, eggs (fried, boiled or poached), hot toast with mountains of butter, freshly brewed coffee and clean ash trays. It opened early every morning to cater for the cameramen and technicians who took off from Ealing to locations all over the world. Satisfied with our double helping of almost everything we burped our way to the studio. We were looking forward to a good day but, as usual, we hadn't reckoned on Sod's Law. That morning we would upset everyone to such an extent that they would cheerfully have lynched us. Unable to do this they showed their displeasure by not speaking to us when we all lined up at the tea trolley and completely ostracising us in the Red Lion at lunch time.

It started with the sequence in which the Martians are seen in a hazy dreamlike video as armies engaged in lethal hand to hand fighting. This conflict spells the end of the entire Martian civilisation and nearly did the same for the crew on our filming. To produce this sequence we had cast a number of half-sized Martian heads in shell plaster which we filled with a mixture of spaghetti and tomato sauce. We thought the close-ups of shattering skulls and spattering brains would look 'interesting'. Unfortunately under the hot studio lights the ingredients (which had been in the skulls for well over a fortnight) decomposed even further and when the heads were broken open in our fight scenes produced the vilest of smells. Because the noisy studio ventilation plant had to be shut down during takes the unpleasant odour hung about in pungent layers. Studio doors were opened as soon as the camera stopped turning and the ventilation fans were switched to full blast. But the stinking mixture had been widely distributed during the battle scenes and the stench returned as soon as the doors were closed and the fans were again switched off.

Working in that atmosphere, our friends and colleagues were bound to be offended but after a while they forgave us, reasoning that anyone can make a simple mistake – like filling thin plaster skulls with rotting food. But what we did next turned their grudging forgiveness into near rebellion.

Clifford Hatts, the programme's designer, had created the huge spaceship which, in the final episode, had to glow and melt. This would have been virtually impossible to arrange on the full-sized fibre glass version and so we'd built a tiny model which we'd reproduced in paraffin wax. Earlier tests to melt this satisfactorily had revealed a number of problems. We'd started by experimenting with a small strip-light which gave a very satisfactory glow but the warmth of the strip-light was insufficient to melt the wax. Next we added a hot wire heating element which we hoped would do the job. However, although this combination worked well enough it still took far too long and looked unimpressive. We doubled the wattage of the element which certainly speeded things up but the experimental models kept bursting into flames.

Our second approach was to retain the strip-light and to pour Lyle's Golden Syrup over the model. We aimed to film it as the syrupy surface gradually oozed downwards. This, to our eyes, looked like a meltdown. It wasn't a classic special effect but we felt with skilful editing it would suffice. Set up on a rostrum as far away from the smelly area as possible we used several models and, flooding each one with lashings of golden syrup we shot them from different angles. The trouble came later when we'd completed that sequence and moved onto something else. Syrup is not only lethally sticky but it migrates and because we'd used it lavishly and not been too careful where we'd put the half emptied tins or the sticky models we'd finished with, the syrup eventually got everywhere. As we moved around we carried it from place to place on the soles of our shoes and on our hands. It spread to the iron ladders that led to the gantry, it was on every door handle and had even begun to travel outside - we could hear people clicking up and down the corridor. Our colleagues, already working in an atmosphere smelling like a refuse cart now found they were sticking to everything they touched or walked on. Our diminished popularity plunged to zero.

We cut short our end-of-day visit to the Red Lion (where even our placatory offer of drinks all round was spurned) hoping to clean up some of the mess. We bribed a studio cleaner to assist us, but with only one mop and bucket he made little impression on the rough wooden floors. Large traces of syrup remained and he grumpily abandoned the task and left the studio, pocketing our half crown and clicking his way up the corridor. We were left to clear up as best we could.

Fortunately not everything we filmed that week ended in disaster. Later on we had to produce the gravel path sequence where Sladden, played by Richard Shaw, collapses outside the church. Having tried to open the door into the spaceship's cockpit with a high powered industrial drill, the screaming vibration sends him mad. Frantically he flees from the underground workings and runs through the streets pursued by weird noises and 'manifestations'. Seeing a lighted church he heads for sanctuary. Unfortunately, exhausted by his flight he collapses before he can reach the door. Lying on the path we see him illuminated by a beam of light as the vicar opens the door and looks down at him. The pursuing blood curdling sounds grow louder – then, frighteningly, the path begins to ripple.

To achieve this effect we had nailed pieces of half round dowel to lengths of upholstery webbing which we laid out on the studio floor. These were covered by a tarpaulin onto which we tipped a few inches of gravel. On cue Jack and I slowly walked side by side across the studio floor, pulling the tapes behind us and creating the rippling movement that so intrigued the viewers.

Quatermass and the Pit quickly became another triumph for the BBC and in order that they shouldn't miss a single episode many people scheduled their affairs around the transmission times. Some pubs would be almost empty until the end of a programme when the customers would troop in chattering about that night's episode.

At the end of a television series most members of the production staff go their separate ways and Jack and I returned to the office and whatever was lined up for us. The contrast could not have been starker. We saw that we were scheduled to provide a puff of steam on an afternoon cooking programme.

I have always maintained that the most important person on any programme is the writer and Jack and I were very fortunate to have been able to work on those two remarkable series written by Nigel Kneale. The name Quatermass is still remembered by millions.

A   N a v a l   P e n n a n t

As the television service grew, the need for more office space prompted the administration to look at vacant houses around the Bush. Lime grove had been expanded by the conversion of a few properties next to the studios, but it became necessary to acquire some in the Goldhawk and Uxbridge roads. To modern office staff, the concept of walking from one house to another, some more than half a mile apart might seem an imposition, but in those carless days we all walked to these temporary offices without even thinking about it.

We had just come through a world war in which houses, streets and towns had been blown to pieces and the slight inconvenience of carrying an umbrella and wearing warm clothing was, by comparison, no hardship at all. Fortunately the BBC had a priority on new phone lines (a waiting time of months or years existed then) and direct communication between the various outposts was quickly established. Nevertheless messengers had to carry their satchels of internal mail to these houses, operating a timetable that whatever the conditions, was strictly adhered to. It might be sheeting with rain or swirling with snow but people would still ask each other 'What time's the next post?'

Jack and I had been asked to meet a producer whose office was on the first floor of a house in Goldhawk Road and as we hadn't been there before we left in good time. We found it easily enough and going in through the front door and up a flight of stairs met the man himself, a jolly tubby chap who wore bright red braces and introduced himself as John Hunter-Blair. Introductions over, he produced a bottle of wine and three glasses and without even asking us if we liked the stuff thrust two glasses of white across the desk. We knew we were going to get on with this chap.

He told us he was producing a new programme for children and that it was going to be big. He emphasised the bigness in the manner of a Hollywood producer, waving his arms and talking excitedly hoping that we would rise to his own level of enthusiasm. He needn't have worked so hard, he was preaching to the converted; with a mere whiff of something new Jack and I were away on flights of imagination to rival his own. The glasses were refilled and we all talked big shows and scribbled on sheets of paper. Later we were to know John by the nickname 'Hunter Bunter' coined by someone who presumably saw his likeness to Billy Bunter.

He wanted his new show to be quite unlike other children's programmes which were small and confined to the corners of studios. Away with table tops and armchair storytelling, Hunter Bunter was going to fill an entire studio with excitement – even sometimes spilling out beyond the studio doors. He painted a grand scenario with marching guardsmen and massed bands and animals, lots of animals because children loved them. He wouldn't have one presenter, he was going to have a team of two or even three!

History shows that despite Hunter Bunter's grand design many people remember the early shows not for marching bands, but for the egg boxes, yoghurt pots and sticky-backed plastic used by the incomparable Val Singleton on the sort of table top that H.B. wasn't going to have.

Having outlined the size and shape of the programme he asked us if we had any ideas, stressing that ideas were needed to make every edition different from the one before. He despised set patterns and wanted novelty such as canal boats and balloon trips, African safaris and lion taming.

Jack and I, in our enthusiasm, had rather forgotten that we'd gone there, not for the wine tasting, but for the purpose of offering suggestions, a purpose that was somewhat redundant because Hunter Bunter's proposals had exhausted just about every combination of ideas we could have thought of. We told him we'd like time to think about it, assuring him that we would make any special props or devices that he might need.

In the end our early contribution was to provide a space in our workshop for Christopher Trace the first male presenter. Chris wanted a bench on which he could build models and small gadgets. I think H.B. came to realise that the close-ups of a presenter's hands and models provided a necessary counterbalance to the large events which filled the rest of the studio. The animals did appear (the baby elephant that wet the floor and then slipped and slid around in the mess, pulling his unfortunate keeper behind him has become a classic) and it was decided that a winsome dog should join the team. Later the show included outside broadcasts with John Noakes climbing London monuments and defying death on land and water. I don't recall that Jack and I came up with a single memorable item for the programme, because it quickly developed its own style and momentum.

Before leaving his office one of us asked Hunter Bunter if he had a name for the programme. He spun his chair and pointed to a naval pennant fastened to the wall behind him, 'I'm going to call it *Blue Peter*.' he replied – and *Blue Peter* it is to this day. Originating in 1958 it is still considered one of the most successful children's programmes on television.

Blue Peter has changed over the years in order to reflect the tastes of a modern audience and has gone through a range of presenters and a succession of dogs. It has constantly pioneered new methods of presentation and there can be little doubt that Hunter Bunter's influence on children's television in elevating it from the cosy corner in the studio to the brashness of a three-ring circus moved it forward by several years.

Jack and I are grateful that we were there that afternoon to share H.B.'s enthusiasm and his wine. I'm sure that our subsequent support in providing dry ice effects, smoke sequences and prop-making repaid his hospitality.

We   F i n d   t h e   H o p   P o l e

I don't know how Barry, Jim and I got the idea, but when it came it seemed very appealing. It was to take every alternative route home that we could contrive – without deviating more than three miles either side of a mean line. The distance between Television Centre and the village where Jim and I lived was 22 miles and while we didn't suppose that such an achievement would impress the compilers of *The Guinness Book of Records* it would enable us to take a more positive interest in the rather humdrum journeys home.

The combination of roads offered a surprising number of permutations but it meant that sometimes we would be travelling along a connecting road from east to west and by using another route driving along the same road from west to east. This became very confusing when in the mornings I drove to work alone. At that hour my mind was usually preoccupied with the day's problems and did not concern itself with navigation. Doing the same thing, day after day, my autopilot tended to take over and I would have only the slightest notion of where I was. So when travelling along one of the connecting road, and suddenly coming back to life, I would wonder where the hell I was going.

Our record-breaking took on another and even more interesting dimension when one of us suggested that if we could vary our journeys why not our pubs? Why not have at least one drink in every pub on every route? (not all at once you understand). This plan had instant appeal and I seem to remember that Barry was elected to keep a tally. Traffic congestion often dictated the route we would take and so too did the weather. On fine evenings we would sometimes go through Richmond Park to Kingston or to Raynes Park via Wimbledon Common – or Parkside. On wet nights we might travel to Sutton via Putney, all of them with uniquely different environments and all of them with a choice of hostelries.

And so it happened one dark night that we chose to visit The Hop Pole in Wandsworth. It was a pub we had passed many hundreds of times on buses and in the car and, we all thought, looked run down and unappealing – not at all the sort of place we would normally go in. Nevertheless we had to visit it simply because it was on one of our routes. We parked down a side street and walked back. Close up it appeared to be even more run down than we'd supposed. The paint was peeling and grubby and the only exterior light came from a street lamp across the road.

When we went in we were conscious of the smell; it was an odour composed of beer, hops and cigarette smoke. Nowadays pubs have very few smells likely to be a mixture of aerosol polish and lavatory cleaner. But the aroma of The Hop Pole was the one we associated with a 'good' pub; it was ingrained in the woodwork, impregnated in the dingy paint, and lovingly preserved in the worn upholstery. The bar was almost as poorly lit as the outside and was apparently empty, but before we could rap on the counter the sound of movement came from behind a faded curtain which hung from the ceiling and divided the room. Then we saw an old man who had been reading a newspaper slowly getting to his feet; he smoothed the pages and asked us what we wanted. We assumed this meant what did we want to drink but because he was on the customer side of the bar and looked bad tempered it could have meant 'What do you buggers think you're doing here?' If this old fellow was the landlord then we had clearly got off to a bad start. We ordered three pints which he served in silence and then, looking at us as if daring us to order anything else, he shuffled back to his seat behind the curtain.

This silent hostility was disconcerting and we leant on the bar and conversed in the hushed voices normally reserved for funerals. Deciding that we had honoured our commitment we took large gulps anxious to empty our glasses and depart, but then an old lady emerged from a back room and came behind the bar. She was everything that the old man was not. She was cheerful and hospitable and soon had us in animated conversation. She even switched on another light.

We left feeling that maybe it wasn't a bad pub after all; it certainly had character, the beer was well-kept and the glasses sparkling clean so, perhaps, who knows, we'd pay it another visit sometime.

And we did. Abandoning our quest to try every pub along the route, we returned again and again to The Hop Pole, soon making it our regular stopping off point. The old couple became firm friends and were disappointed if we didn't turn up each evening. Their names were Arthur and Maisie and although they soon knew our names they referred to us collectively as 'Freeman, Hardy and Willis' (after a well-known chain of shoe shops) which was somehow rather nice. There's a great deal to be said for the familiar and comfortable, and only on the evenings that we were forced to take a different route did we drink elsewhere.

Maisie and Arthur had a son and two daughters, one of whom was married to a lighterman who worked a barge on the Thames (or was he a bargee who worked a lighter?) The other was married to a delightful Frenchman. As the years passed we got to know them as a family and on the occasions when the old folks had time off the others would take over. Their son worked abroad but even he appeared behind the bar whenever he returned to England. The magic thing about the Hop Pole and something that would have taken us there even if Arthur had been a serial killer and the bar had been frequented by pirates was a truly remarkable beer called Winter Brew.

Lovingly created by Courage's it was absolutely amazing. Finer than Champagne, Nuits St George or even celebration Burton, Winter Brew surpassed them all. Drawn from tiny oaken casks cradled on the counter it cost half a crown for a half pint (which in the days when you could get a respectable pint of best bitter for just over a shilling says everything.) Winter Brew was legendary and I won't attempt to describe its flavour – indeed I couldn't. Suffice to say that the first sip produced the effect of angels singing, the second transformed the pub into a flowery dell and the third gave the sort of feeling that must, I believe, be associated with winning the National Lottery. Winter Brew was produced in the days when brewers were more concerned with pleasing their customers than benefiting their shareholders but even here they were up against it. Winter Brew was too expensive for the average drinker and because it was supplied in those small casks a percentage of it went sour and had to be thrown away.

In later years the Hop Pole was run by the old folk's son-in-law, the Frenchman whose name was Charles but by then Winter Brew had ceased to conform with the accountant's money-making policies and, like other exquisite beers (such as Barclay Perkins's ten year ale – bottled and protected in straw sleeves and the wonderful Aylesbury Brewery Company's light ale), it was consigned to oblivion. Nevertheless, The Hop Pole remained our favourite pub and a journey home without calling in would have seemed an evening short on contentment.

T h e   E m p t y   R e s t a u r a n t

Although the Visual Effects Section was now an established part of the Design Department and could not easily have undergone a major reorganisation, the same immunity could not be guaranteed for its location. Outgrowing our first office we were moved to two larger offices further along the corridor. These offices had the advantage of being alongside the light-well and the open roof. But before this move took place we had a period in a caravan.

Faced with a shortage of accommodation, the Beeb hired some industrial office units which were set up in the car park. These portable offices were heated, well-lit by windows on either side and were equipped with drawing boards and plan chests. However, they lacked workshop space. We got around this by working outside in the car park whenever anything big was called for and using the tops of the plan chests for painting and prop-making. I forget how long this lasted before the caravan accommodation was needed for someone more important and we were moved again. This time it was to be the restaurant block.

The restaurant block, newly built, was empty and although equipped with lighting, toilets, lifts and central heating had not yet been furnished with the stainless steel counters and kitchens for the three floors (snack bar, waitress service and self-service cafeteria) that were planned for the final stage of its development. Until the building became operational the ground floor was being used as a rehearsal room, the first floor was used to store incoming kitchen equipment and the top floor was completely empty – that was the floor we had been allocated. Told that we were being moved there Jack and I went to inspect it. Oddly enough, we had never set foot in this building before and knew it only from the outside. We went up the stairs, looking into the other sections as we passed them until we reached the top floor. Going through some double doors we found a vast open space with only the supporting columns to break up its emptiness. We were impressed by its size – here was all the space we could possibly need, now or forever; it was nearly as big as the scenic workshops, but it had nothing in the way of usable facilities. Neither of us knew what to make of it. Large windows ran the entire length of the side and end walls, but because there were no power points anywhere near them we chose the back wall, reasoning that it was better to sacrifice a small amount of natural light and the aerial view over a nearby public park (where young girls in short skirts played tennis every lunch time) for a sufficiency of power sockets.

We couldn't possibly make use of all that space and so we opted for a modest area just inside the entrance doors.

The next thing was to enclose it, to put up a barrier between ourselves and the barren concrete wastes of the surrounding area. Although we had been assured that it was only a temporary arrangement we didn't fancy living and working in an environment that resembled a deserted warehouse. Sizing up the area which we figured would be suitable for our needs we plodded around marking it out with a piece of chalk and a tape measure. Eventually, satisfied that we'd got the best of the available resources, we went to the property department and borrowed ten low-level counter units. We assembled these end to end around the perimeter of our marked out space. The next step was to mark the positions for our desks and work benches.

We were happily engaged in furnishing our new quarters with chairs, small oak tables and another bent wood coat rack (we never knew when we might want some dowelling) when one of us needed to go to the toilet. It was then that we discovered to our horror that the nearest loo was on the floor below. There was a toilet on our floor but it was clearly marked Ladies. While it was unlikely that the few females using the rehearsal floor, where they had a toilet of their own, would need to come up to the top floor we weren't going to risk a chance encounter – besides which it had no urinals.

Without water we were going to be severely handicapped. We couldn't wash our paint brushes or mix chemicals and although it was hardly possible that the concrete, protected as it was by about nine hundred over-head sprinklers, would catch fire, if it did we would have no means of putting it out. This was serious.

We discussed ways and means of bringing water to the top floor. Here was a problem to test our ingenuity. Initially we considered installing yards of garden hose but dismissed the idea because the double doors were fire doors and couldn't be closed over a hose pipe. We realised that we would have to provide some sort of arrangement which would not only give us fresh water, but would incorporate some sort of a drainage system (and that didn't mean chucking it out of a window after dark.)

Working on various ideas we settled on a portable unit with a small hand basin of the type used in caravans and two medium sized containers or drums underneath. One of these would contain the fresh water and the other would be used for the waste. We knew where we could find such things and we knew where to get a battery operated pump which, at the press of a button, would transfer a thin jet of clean water to the wash basin. We drew up the plans and a list of the various items we would need to construct it and, eager to be fully equipped in our new domain, started work straight away. When we'd built it, and given it a coat of bright blue paint, our sink unit looked quite smart but there was a snag. To refill it with water and empty the waste tank meant wheeling it to the lift, going down one floor and trundling it into the gents. Ever the optimists, we thought this would be merely a tiresome operation, but we discovered on trying it that it wasn't just an irritating chore but was fraught with danger. In wheeling our sink unit to and fro we would slop dirty water all over the floors going down and, on the return journey, lose half our clean water in a similar manner. It spilled in the lift and it slopped on the floors – particularly while trying to hold the fire doors open and manoeuvre our contraption through at the same time. Furthermore, we found it almost impossible to tip the waste water down the urinal without soaking our shoes – had we learned nothing? Although we remembered those early days when we'd had to empty the dry ice bath at Lime Grove all we could recall was that we had to start very, very slowly. But at The Grove we were simply handling full buckets – here we had a container holding fifteen gallons of dirty water and the chances of tipping it very, very slowly were slender. The drum tended to shift its centre of gravity as it was being lowered and invariably caught us unawares, with disastrous results.

Ian Beynon-Lewis had assured us that these premises were an interim measure, an arrangement expected to last only a week or two and with his jovial sense of humour told us that the planners had no intention of incorporating our workshop in the self-service restaurant or to provide us with a permanent space in the kitchens. Producing the gin and tonics from his cupboard he asked us to make the best of things until they found us somewhere else to take our hat stand. Naturally we wondered how temporary was temporary because the main building was some years short of completion. The restaurant block wouldn't, we reasoned, be required until the building was complete and fully staffed.

Within days of moving in we were joined by two other displaced persons, Cliff Michelmore and Aubrey Singer. Cliff at that time was producing children's programmes and Aubrey was a high powered executive who seemed to spend most of his time on the telephone to

New York. They were given two chairs each, a table and a telephone apiece (I think Aubrey was given two) and you've guessed it, each was given a bent wood hat stand. It was obvious that somewhere there was a warehouse full of these things – ordered perhaps by a clerk who had put a decimal point in the wrong place and nobody had discovered the error until the first hundred thousand were delivered.

Having no contacts in the scenic servicing departments and unable to enclose their territory as we had done, they looked like evicted flat dwellers who had fallen behind with the rent. They too had been told that this was merely a temporary arrangement and that as soon as the Clerk of Works needed to install the catering equipment they would be rehoused somewhere more suitable.

Aubrey was, in later years, destined to become Managing Director Television and, had we known that, might have offered him some of our counter units, but even without such grovelling overtures he remained a good friend throughout our BBC careers.

I don't recall how long we all spent in the restaurant block, it was probably only a month or two, but our stay wasn't measured in time, it was counted in trips to and from the loo wheeling the bloody sink unit up and down and drying our suede shoes on a radiator. It always needed refilling at a moment when, with dirty hands and paint brushes dripping all over the place, one of us would press the pump button and hear only the hiss of air. Fortunately they relocated us before we got so fed up with our brain child that we wheeled it across to a window and flung it into the ring road. But on sunny days we did miss the young girls with the short skirts.

We   Make   Smoke

We sat in the office trying to blow smoke rings. It's supposed to be easy – you light a cigarette, draw in a mouthful of smoke, open your lips, tap your cheek and smoke rings emerge, getting bigger as they flow into extinction. They didn't for us. I don't mean they didn't get bigger, they just didn't materialise at all. A great deal of choking and spitting, but definitely nothing you could call a decent smoke ring. We hoped this wasn't a bad omen; if we couldn't make smoke rings what hope had we of filling an entire studio with dense white fog. Well, we were about to find out.

We were having a break before going upstairs to the concrete roof where we planned to test our prototype smoke gun. It stood on the bench, handsome in a blaze of polished brass and wire-brushed copper. Neatly coiled beside it was a thirty foot length of mains cord and a plug. To a casual observer our gun might have looked like a pump-up garden spray – which is what it was, but in its conversion to a practical smoke gun we had fitted a large cylindrical heater at the spraying end. However it hadn't been fully tested, and this morning we were going to give it its trial run. Opinion has it that 'the better the day, the better the deed' and this day was perfect. The sky was blue, the sun was shining and the air was warm and calm.

We had made our smoke gun because, apparently, no such thing as a theatrical smoke maker was obtainable. The few devices that did exist were used chiefly in the film industry and were made by individual effects men for their own use. Any attempt by us to discover the secrets of their design came to nought, the nearest thing being the pencil-like vapour trails used to test wind tunnel model aircraft. It seems strange now, when almost every type of theatrical smoke is catered for, that no manufacturer in the early fifties seemed to produce equipment that could be hired or bought off the shelf. It took the television industry to show the need. Smoke generators can now be bought or hired in sizes ranging from small hand-held devices to monster machines that are wheeled out on location to spread fog over vast landscapes.

In those early years if we were asked to provide smoke, we relied upon pyrotechnics (of which there were many varieties). These were bearable in the open air but really horrible in the studio. Drain testers were the worst with their pungent smell of sulphur and bitumen which impregnated our clothes and hair to such an extent that if we got into a lift other passengers got out.

Pyrotechnics cannot be extinguished, not even by submerging them in water so the need for a controllable smoke maker was clearly evident. Smoke generators, or smoke guns as the hand held variety are usually called, work on a common principle. A proprietary smoke liquid (or oil) is heated to a temperature at which it turns into smoke. The oil in a domestic chip pan, before it bursts into flames, produces the same effect. In a smoke gun the super-heated oil vapour is trapped in the heater unit and so, virtually bottled up without oxygen it cannot ignite. The heated oil is turned into vapour by forcing it to travel along a small bore tube which is coiled around a heating unit from which it emerges as dense white smoke. If this sounds perfectly straightforward, it isn't. A design for a smoke gun must be far more sophisticated than that. Get it wrong and one of two things will happen. Too low a temperature and the pressurised oil will not turn into smoke at all but stays as oil which is squirted out at searing temperatures, well above that of boiling water.

It is said that actors have been known to leap several feet into the air screaming as a malfunctioning smoke gun, handled by an incautious operator, squirts boiling oil over their socks and shoes. Marginally worse is the other condition where the smoke gets too hot and ignites spontaneously on leaving the nozzle. This turns the gun into a flame thrower of awesome potential. Strangely this flaming malfunction usually makes people laugh, unless of course they happen to be standing in the line of fire, in which case they don't say much.

It didn't take us long to realise that we were working in an area of technology outside our experience, and despite my own years as an engineering designer I had no answer to the vagaries of a malfunctioning smoke gun. Evidence of our many tests – patches of melted tarmac or blackened brickwork – may still be found at Television Centre.

There is another factor to be considered when designing a theatrical smoke gun – everyone involved will have to breathe. It might be feasible to record the opening scene of, say, *Macbeth* with the witches wearing respirators and throat mics but this would be bound to upset the make-up staff.

By chance Bill King, our property master, had previously worked in a film studio where he had acquired a rudimentary smoke gun that he kept locked away in Props. Having tried it once, he lacked the courage to ever try it again. Without hesitation he handed it over to us. We were delighted but never got it to work. But Bill knew where to obtain the special smoke fluid that we would need if our prototype was to pass the BBC's medical inspectorate. The stuff we wanted, he told us, was the oil used to lubricate ship's engines. Below decks, seamen are forced to work in places where the lubricants are continually vaporising on hot metal and the need to keep the men alive had already occurred to marine engineers. Bill said that if seamen could work in the fumes, so could actors. I appreciated his logic but Bill spent his days in an office whereas Jack and I spent ours in the studio. If the smoke was going to affect anybody, we would be the first to succumb.

To heat the metal coil in our smoke gun we used an electric element from a heavy duty soldering iron. Unfortunately this meant that our smoke gun could be used only while attached to a mains cable, but with so many power points around the studio walls this would not be a handicap. (Designs using bottled or camping gas are now available and can be used anywhere, outdoors or in). The reason we had chosen to make our smoke gun from a garden spray was that it had a container that would hold the oil and was pressurised by a tiny hand pump on the top. We decided to include a thermostat in the heating unit because we saw it as an insurance against overheating or a talisman to ward off conflagration. This thermostat (and many of the other bits we used in our effects) was bought in London's Oxford Street which at that time boasted a large shop selling 'war surplus.' It was an Aladdin's Cave of green painted tank radios, aircraft compasses, bomb sights and packs of field dressings. This shop was a magnet for male office workers who loved browsing through redundant equipment in their lunchtimes. I was tempted to refer to it as a 'junk shop', but having seen the Union Jack mugs and plastic policemen's helmets now sold as souvenirs in Oxford Street I realise that by comparison our war surplus store was on a par with Aspreys.

This was not the only shop of its kind because, tucked away in Lisle Street, a small shady thoroughfare behind Leicester Square, were the radio shops. These shops supplied the hobbyists – the people who built their own radios and television sets – with their trays of resistors, condensers and components of every kind. They became a valuable source of supply for Jack and me and we soon depended on them for many of our projects. However, we seldom went there alone because some of the flats above the shops were rented by prostitutes and in the afternoon the girls would emerge to trap the unwary. Their introductory spiel ranged from the unambiguous 'Want to come up and have a quick one, lads?' to the puzzling 'Can you help me? It's stuck' (I imagine the ploy was to lure a helpful male indoors to free a reluctant zip fastener). One of these predators once approached me with the offer to 'strip and take things off. I never worked out what she might have taken off once she had stripped, but she was old and repellent so my curiosity was never satisfied. Suffice to say that in that shadowy street of staircases and doorways Jack and I avoided capture by staying closely together.

But I was talking about smoke guns. In the workshop that morning we had admitted defeat; we gave up blowing smoky spit, stubbed out our cigarettes, gathered up the box of tools, oil, funnel, cleaning rag and the shiny smoke gun and went up the iron staircase to the large flat roof above. We had recently moved to our second office, a much bigger room further along the corridor which, situated alongside one of the two roof-wells, enabled us to take an extension cable out of a window and up to the roof above without it impeding anyone's progress.

We half-filled the brass tank with marine oil, pumped it up and switched on the heater, then we lit two more cigarettes and stood back while our gun slowly achieved its working temperature. What would happen when the lever was pressed? Would we have a flame thrower or shiny equipment that produced boiling oil?

Seeing the blue haze that hung over the nozzle Jack picked up the gun, pointed it well away from the pair of us and pressed the operating lever. It was incredible! No scorching flame, no boiling oil – just a great cloud of wonderful white smoke. We could scarcely believe our eyes. I called to Jack to keep it going: this was a momentous occasion and I wanted to enjoy it to the full. As the smoke grew in volume it slowly drifted away and collected in the corner of the offices on the top-floor. It was fantastic. The gun had performed almost beyond our wildest expectations. Jack swept it from side to side and up and down; it didn't falter. The sounds of windows being slammed shut told us that not everyone shared our enthusiasm for smoke. Fair enough, you can't please everybody but some day those designers were going to be grateful for our smoke gun. But what we had forgotten was that as well as the designers' offices there was a conference room on the top floor and on that morning it was being used for a high level meeting of managers. Behind those windows the controller and heads of all sections (including our own, Richard Levin) had assembled to discuss a most important matter and they were listening to the third speaker of the day. It was warm in that room and the windows had been fully opened – allowing our smoke to enter unmolested.

Now I can't vouch for what happened in that room, I was on the roof with Jack, but this is how someone recounted it to me. At first no one seemed to know what was happening. The sky had darkened and a grey mist was coming indoors. The speaker, who considered he had a firm grasp of his subject, paused, wavered and stopped; everyone looked at everyone else. Two young men anxious to show their superiors that they were capable of instant and decisive action leapt to their feet. One went to the windows and the other to one of the two doors. It was an understandable manoeuvre, given the circumstances, but unfortunately they chose quite the wrong sequence. The eight windows should have been closed first. As soon as the door was opened, the smoke, now smelling pungently of burnt oil surged across the room turning what had been a slight mist into a thick fog. This was too much for the departmental heads who, intent on removing themselves and their expensive suits from the acrid smoke, moved rapidly to the other door. An even more unfortunate sequence because at that moment the lady bringing the tea trolley was about to enter. She never made it; the tide of managers swept her and her trolley backwards down the corridor. She told us later that most of the sandwiches survived and that the tea urn was alright, but the milk jug had tipped its contents onto the carpet and the Black Forest gateau was smeared along the wall.

Once again we were summoned to the office of Ian Beynon Lewis and once again we were threatened with dismissal. But this time we had a trump card. We pointed out that we had developed a successful smoke maker, something demanded by directors, designers and even the fire chief and while we were sorry for what had happened he should weigh the pros and cons. Ian sensed the logic of this, but he had to give us a wigging and he did so. It was short, to the point but wholly lacking in conviction. He finished with a wink and took a bottle of gin, three glasses and some tonic water from his cupboard and we settled down to discuss the potential of our invention. We told him about Lisle Street and the habits of certain females, stringing it out to allow him to pour more gin. In fact I recall that the latter part of our telling off was a discussion about gin and the superiority of a certain brand when served with a slice of lime and a slice of cucumber

On the whole we reckoned that it had not been a bad day as days go, but our smoke gun was not always to perform so well, in fact it proved to be a right bastard and was eventually consigned to our junk box. But more about our smoke gun later.

Mr Tate, the Chief Fire Officer, was responsible for Lime Grove, Television Centre and Riverside studios. He wore smart suits befitting his rank and was diligent at finding transgressions and discovering any flouting of the rules. He was disabled and moved with some difficulty using a walking stick for essential support. He found this stick very effective in pointing out things which were wrong. Amazingly, for a man so handicapped he would appear out of thin air whenever Jack and I were engaged in a bit of rule flouting. Nevertheless, although our interests were as far apart as those of poachers and gamekeepers, we were friends and Jack and I, while trying to outwit him at every turn, respected and liked him.

Knowing that the odds were on our side (how could anyone expect to outsmart someone whose job it was to think up illusions and ways of fooling people?) he probably spent more time and effort in trying to nail us than he spent on any of the other transgressors. We cheated and admitted it, but to balance the odds he had an army of firemen to pounce on us whenever we unloaded our bits and pieces in the studio. They would surround us looking into the cardboard boxes, examining suspicious cans and sniffing anything that appeared to contain inflammable solvent. On the whole, I think that at the end of our careers the honours were more or less even.

The sort of tricks we got up to might be exemplified in our tactics where, to ensure that certain inflammable materials such as cloth or canvas (which we had either forgotten to fireproof or had had no time to process) was treated at the last moment with an application of fireproofing liquid around the edges. A fireman visiting a studio had authority to test any material and, if necessary, to have it removed. But the only way of testing cloth was to apply a match to one edge. I'm sure Tate knew what we were doing, but short of destroying suspect material by trying to ignite it in the middle there was little the firemen could do.

Jack and I were not deviants; we were, in fact, as safety conscious as the firemen and never once did we flagrantly ignore the code of practice. However, occasionally it seemed to us that the regulations were probably drawn up centuries ago for old fashioned theatres by people who never lived to see a modern TV studio and under some circumstances were nonsensical. Nevertheless, knowing that we would be held responsible for anything of ours that caught fire we were extremely careful not to take risks.

Oddly enough the one thing we were permitted to do was to smoke in the studio, a perk we shared with actors who had to light up as part of the action. For everyone else smoking was strictly forbidden. Our reasons for lighting a cigarette were usually to produce small amounts of smoke on models, or around things like soldering irons to add a touch of realism - effects which could be achieved at that time in no other practical way. Sometimes this rare privilege backfired on us as in the case of *The Grove Family* and the smoking electric iron. This prop had to be left on the ironing board, scorching a garment. To achieve this we blew cigarette smoke through a thin rubber tube which, painted black, purported to be the power cord. If the action had to be repeated or the smoke sustained for long periods we would, even when sharing the cigarette, finish the sequence with tongues like kippers and eyes artistically red-rimmed. After such a session we would never, ever want to smoke again. I sometimes wondered if Mr Tate was up in the control room urging the director to replay the scene 'just once more'. Any director (they were also forbidden to smoke) might just see the justice in such a request.

The time when we really frightened Mr Tate however, was when we were demonstrating our new brass smoke gun. Its performance was still unpredictable and despite our many attempts to tame it we never overcame its tendency to either overheat or underheat.

On that day, at Riverside Studios, we were booked to create an atmospheric mist across the surface of an artificial lake and Tate had demanded that before we could even take our gun into the building it must be demonstrated to him personally. Accordingly we'd arranged for a demonstration on the concrete walkway that ran alongside the river at the rear of the studios. We were worried because if during this test it were to suddenly flare, Tate would condemn it and then Jack and I would be truly in the midden, floundering in a situation of our own making. Very few directors will listen to excuses and this one was not one of the few. We could see ourselves working like maniacs with bee smokers if the gun was condemned. Lying alongside the wall at the rear of the studios were some scaffold tubes and one of us hit upon the idea of discharging the smoke down a seven foot length of it. It was a brilliant idea. Smoke, deprived of oxygen and cooled by seven feet of steel jacket could not possibly ignite. We tried it and were proven right.

Quickly, because the time for Mr Tate's visit was drawing near we wiped everything down with rag, refilled the oil container and stood by to show him that his visit had been quite unnecessary. Tate arrived punctually and we showed him the rig, explaining away the scaffold tube as the means by which we would direct the mist across the water. He examined it and seemed reassured, but even so he was not prepared to stand near it while it was switched on. Stories of flamethrower smoke guns had evidently filtered through to him and not being as agile as other people he had no intention of being incinerated. Sensibly he took up a position at the far end of the scaffold tube and even then prudently stood to one side. We primed the gun, checked it for working temperature and pulled the trigger, crossing our fingers behind our backs. It worked perfectly. At last we could relax. We smiled at each other – the tube had worked and the smoke looked almost as good as it had done on the day we'd first tried it on the roof. Spreading along the concrete path and drifting out over the River Thames was the finest white mist anyone could wish for. But Tate required the ultimate test; would our smoke *support* fire? Taking a cigarette lighter from his pocket (he didn't smoke) he bent down to apply a flame to the end of the tube, but before he could operate the flint wheel there came a strange sort of hollow rumble up the tube. This was followed by a sheet of flame that would have scared the wits out of a trained stunt man clad in an asbestos suit.

There are those who believed that Mr Tate, incapacitated as he was, could never move quickly. We proved this to be a fallacy. He grew from a bent five foot four inches to an astounding vertical six foot eight, moving at the same time to a position yards behind the two of us. Jack and I were horrified; our lovely gun and its scaffold tube had let us down. I tried to remember where we'd stored the bee smokers.

But the authoritarian Mr Tate was also compassionate and noticing our stricken expressions gave us permission to use the gun for that one performance providing that it was employed only for the mist over the lake sequence. To ensure that we complied, he brought in two extra firemen equipped with fire extinguishers and sand buckets. He told us that they must stand beside the smoke gun throughout rehearsals and transmission. He smiled broadly (unusual for him) as he left because he knew that the additional costs would be charged to the production and we would have to answer for it. The sequence went perfectly and the effect of low lying mist over the water gave the director ample opportunity for artistic tracking and craning shots. Jack and I were pleased, particularly when he thanked us afterwards, but our satisfaction was slightly overshadowed by the knowledge that his budget would now have to include additional overtime payments for the extra firemen, a fact that we didn't reveal to him.

Some you win, some you lose, but we knew the extra costs wouldn't surface for a couple of weeks and if the programme had been a success the producer would surely forgive us for the overspend. But it was the death certificate for our smoke gun and it was never used again

The Finest Club in the World

We had been told that Television Centre was to get its own branch of the BBC Club, and having been many times to the very grand one provided for the staff of Broadcasting House we were keen to discover what was planned for The Centre. We had been sent a duplicated sheet which gave the date of opening and the location, a room on the fourth floor. These instructions hinted that we might be able to wine and dine there so long as we were bona fide club members and had good table manners, didn't wear muddy boots or bite our nails and so on. On the day it was due to open we forsook the White Horse and made for the fourth floor.

The corridors in the central part of the building are circular so if anyone couldn't remember which room they wanted they had only to keep going until they found it – or tried another floor. We walked around the fourth floor several times, once in the reverse direction asking people and sniffing the air for any aroma of exotic cooking. There was no sign of the club – only the light entertainment offices that we knew so well. But eventually we found it because on our third circuit the door had been propped open. We saw a twelve foot long refectory table set with fine plates, cutlery, silver-plated condiment sets and menus; it looked very expensive. Polishing our toe caps on the backs of our trousers we went in.

Two drama producers were already sitting at the table, a fact that puzzled us. Did they have special influence or did one have to be a Freemason? Perhaps they'd slipped in while we were searching the other side. Nodding acknowledgement, we sat at the table. Within minutes we were joined by Charles Lawrence and Gordon Roland, two fellow designers, and then another director, until nearly all the chairs were taken. The atmosphere was that of a doctor's waiting room with everyone speaking in lowered voices and reading and rereading the menu. To our relief this was written in English (at that time it was customary to use French in smart places) and the food was modestly priced. However the wine list confused us. What, we wondered, was a carafe? We wondered if we dare order a whole bottle but decided, after much whispered consultation, to purchase a couple of light ales. The meals on offer were quite ordinary, lying somewhere between Brown Windsor and Potage de choix provencal.

The two waitresses stood silently at the end of the room; they seemed nervous and may have been recruited locally. If so, it must have seemed an enviable job when they'd applied, believing perhaps that they would be waiting on the stars and celebrities. Feeling guilty at having to disappoint them we peppered our conversation with the names of actors, assuming that when they got home they would be able to tell their family that there had been a diner there who'd said he'd worked with another person who'd actually met Arthur Askey. It was nice to live posh for once because, on the salary we were getting, aspirations soared no higher than a chicken sandwich and a pint of bitter.

Altogether it was an enjoyable experience and we hadn't endangered our holiday savings. We tipped the waitresses when we left and said it was lovely and we'd come again.

This was the introduction of the BBC Club at Television Centre and Jack and I went there several more times. However, this tiny room with its single long table was in the nature of an experiment and with a capacity of only ten or twelve diners was quite inadequate. Its popularity grew until we couldn't be assured of getting a seat even if we arrived punctually and so we returned to the White Horse where we could get beer by the pint and a large chunk of ham and eggpie without having to buff up our shoes or leave a tip.

As membership of the club grew, the dining room was replaced by large new, purpose built premises on the fourth floor situated conveniently (for them) opposite the light entertainment production offices. Soon, in response to members' demands, a licence was applied for (and granted) and the new club eventually featured a very well- stocked bar. One might have supposed that management would have objected to such an outrageous scheme but it was probably better to allow people to drink on the premises than to have them wandering off to the various watering holes around the Bush. An unfortunate casualty was a nearby newly built up-market pub with a classy restaurant that had, presumably, been designed specifically to attract BBC production staff.

The White Horse also suffered a loss of custom, but TV staff never made up the bulk of its customers and during the lunchtime it seemed as busy as ever.

The Club went through several conversions; the last in my time – and unquestionably the best – provided a roof garden with a splendid view over London and comprised two legendary bars. The smaller one was favoured by light entertainment and the larger one by drama and the other departments. This demarcation was only notional and everyone was free to use whichever bar they fancied. The Club soon became a renowned meeting place for actors, producers and writers from all over the country as well as their counterparts from abroad. It was a power house of creativity and did more to establish the BBC's reputation than all the press officers, media men and publicists laid end to end. The Club was smoky, noisy and awash with booze and was a truly marvellous place to congregate and discuss work. Despite the fact that it was roomy and had plenty of bar space people tended to make for the same spot day after day. Dennis Main Wilson was always to be found slightly to the right of centre at the small bar where he held court and drank his beloved Bells. And there was Eric Sykes who always stood in the middle of the floor and puffed one of his large cigars – and Dave Allen with his Champagne and... well a list of people who gathered in those two bars would have rivalled the index of *Spotlight*.

As well as the actors there were composers, writers, reporters, musicians, agents, designers and extras who wanted to be noticed and bought everyone drinks – they all gathered there. Jack and I usually made for a settee by the window in the well of the large bar where we could sit down, eat and drink our pints and scribble designs on paper napkins.

As the reputation of Television Centre's club became established visitors from European networks made their way to W12 to discuss and exchange ideas. Later, when I'd retired from the BBC and was directing comedy for German Television I discovered that many of the people on the unit had been to the club at the Centre. Even my close friend, Rolf Spinrads, the Head of Light Entertainment at Westdeutscher Rundfunk revealed that he'd developed a taste for whisky by drinking Bells with Dennis Main Wilson!

Because it was a club, admission was restricted to members but each member was allowed to bring two guests, a perk that gained us many influential friends. To be invited to the club where one was sure to rub shoulders with the famous personalities of television was for many people an unrivalled experience. Even company directors were quite happy to dine on sausage rolls served on paper plates for the privilege of being there. Jack and I milked this arrangement to the full and several times were able to get things done quickly or cheaply simply by introducing the contractor to someone well known in showbiz.

Now it has gone. When social historians write about the decline of the BBC and the end of intelligent television they need look no further for a significant date than the day when some purblind committee decided to remodel the bars on the fourth floor. This was done apparently to appeal to a more youthful employee and to cater for the tastes of an enlightened, health conscious generation. I'm told (although, thank God, I've never seen it) a large area has been given over to a gymnasium where staff can 'pump iron' in their lunch hour. Out have gone the cigarette-burned carpet, the worn settees and comfortable chairs to be replaced by a truncated counter and steel frame furniture. It gives me mild satisfaction that the health conscious, lettuce eating, iron pumping employee still has a taste for alcohol – although in moderation no doubt – and the floor is now covered in, heaven help us, vinyl tiles. The spartan tables and chairs, placed around the floor at regular intervals would be more appropriate in a package tour airport. The celebrities and the stars have gone; so too has the creativity. Eric Sykes would no longer be able to stand in the middle of the floor puffing his cigars but would be asked to sit down at a table where such vile habits are grudgingly permitted. I don't think Eric would like that – and as for working out in the gymnasium – I know exactly what Dave Allen would say.

An Inflatable Monster

In his autobiography, *A Point of View,* Barry Took refers to Michael Mills, a TV producer of the post war school and a pioneer of considerable talent. Barry says 'in his erratic and traumatic career, Michael Mills was either loved or loathed in spite of his many foibles I was extremely fond of him and miss him greatly'.

I echo those sentiments (although I'm not too sure about the foibles – I don't think I know what a foible is.) Michael Mills was an ex-naval officer and was happiest when working near water. Despite this handicap, we found him innovative and pleasant. But he was not given to praising or even thanking those who had done a good job. He considered that the cachet of being allowed to work on a prestigious show should be reward enough, and he was probably right. However, Jack and I had become accustomed to being lavishly praised for our contributions and in our way had grown as autocratic as Mills. But he held rank because Jack and I were unable to claim officer status in our war service and Michael Mills knew it. The fact that aeroplanes didn't have funnels apparently placed the RAF on a par with the Pioneer Corps and as for the western desert – just sand. If you hadn't been to sea you were nothing. However it was Mills' affiliation with water and boats that gave Jack one of his favourite moments.

Michael was producing and directing a programme about the Loch Ness Monster and wanted us to provide a life-sized 'Nessie' that could be transported by rail and filmed on a Scottish loch. This was tricky. Firstly came the problem of manufacture; to create a forty foot aquatic monster in a small office was clearly impossible and so we got in touch with a contractor who agreed to fabricate an inflatable monster from sheet rubber. The second problem concerned the method of propulsion. A third problem might have been the one that arose when Michael Mills decided to run the entire show himself. It had been arranged to film the monster on a loch that was well off the tourist map and offered facilities for launching and stabilising it in shallow water. The location also offered a high vantage point from which to get some good establishing shots.

On the train to Scotland, travelling with Jack (who had undertaken to look after the special effects – and the monster), the cameraman and PA, Michael Mills redeemed himself by producing a half bottle of whisky and passing it around. This was confusing, because although he changed in later years, up to that time Michael had never bought either of us a drink. We were landlubbers.

Our inflatable monster was certainly easy to transport but it required a hell of a lot of air to fill it – a fact to which we had obviously paid too little attention. We had never tried to inflate it at Television Centre but had seen it in all its glory standing proudly on the contractor's factory floor. It seems silly now, but we had decided on a foot pump to do this (Jack was assured that he had hours in the morning). Clearly, it required a motor driven compressor but the budget, already overdrawn, was causing concern. So on the day of filming Jack found himself on the grassy banks of a Scottish loch with forty feet of limp rubber and a foot pump. While the cameraman and sound crew bustled around getting their equipment in place, Jack connected the pump and started to inflate. After about half an hour the rubber monster still lay flat upon the ground and all that Jack's pumping had achieved was to smooth out the wrinkles. Taking ever lengthening periods of rest he eventually appealed for help.

Michael Mills, using all his wartime training, summoned the ratings and explained Jack's dilemma. He got about five volunteers who were deputed to work in relays. They all seemed cheerfully robust to start with, but after a session on the foot pump, they sat about on the grass, grim-faced and mutinous. After about two hours the rubber had unfolded and had begun to look like a dead Loch Ness Monster – and it still needed more air. Without sufficient pressure the neck buckled and the head trailed on the ground. Jack seems to recall that it took another hour of pumping before it could be launched.

Our planning – that had failed to see the absurdity of inflating a huge rubber monster with a foot pump – had, nevertheless, taken care of the buoyancy and stability. Underneath were eyelets from which Jack was to hang six or seven sandbags. But here was another problem. We has assumed the shores of a loch to be composed of sand and pebbles and the empty sacks now lay on the bank waiting to be filled. Alas, loch shores are made of mud and roots and Jack had to despatch someone to have the bags filled at a builders' merchant in Oban.

To tow it through the water the unit manager had hired a twenty foot clinker built boat with a rugged in-board engine. Normally engaged on harbour work, this vessel was owned and operated by a rather craggy lady with a fine line in highland invective and a face so weather beaten that at first Jack didn't know whether she was a man or a woman. Her vessel was to tow the monster behind it on a long length of sash-cord (weighted to keep it out of sight below the water) while Michael Mills and the cameraman, also in the boat with Jack and the craggy lady, got their footage of the monster travelling through the water.

When all was ready Michael Mills (who was sporting his naval cap and binoculars) stood up and issued his orders. Jack was to pay out the line as they cast off and the cameraman, crouching low by the transom was to get his pictures almost at water level; Captain Craggy was to steer the boat and regulate the throttle. Once out in the water the monster travelled well. It didn't 'porpoise' or 'snake', but rode upright with its head proud and its neck firmly erect. Jack was pleased to see that it was leaving the traditional wake pattern across the surface. Michael Mills called for more speed whereupon Captain Craggy, no doubt used to towing ocean liners, gave the throttle a generous couple of notches and the tow line snapped.

Jack felt that Michael, a seasoned mariner, should have foreseen the impending disaster but, possibly because he was peering through his binoculars he didn't comprehend. The line came zinging towards him at high speed. In the last few micro-seconds he attempted to duck, but was far too late. The wet sash cord hit him fair and square in the chest, knocking his cap from his head, soaking his shirt front and causing him to lose his footing. Jack swears that Captain Craggy, who appeared to have less humour than a block of granite, hung over the wheel convulsed in helpless mirth.

M i c h a e l   B e n t i n e

It's a Square World was primarily a sketch show. It featured Frank Thornton, Clive Dunn, Leon Thau, Dick Emery, John Bluthal, Anthea Wyndham and Janette Rowselle – to name but a few and, of course, starred Michael Bentine.

Michael Bentine was one of the original cast of *The Goon Show,* the zany ground-breaking radio show. Teamed with Peter Sellers, Spike Milligan and Harry Secombe he kept audiences glued to their loud speakers and, it is believed, even the young Prince Charles went around imitating their voices and repeating their catchphrases.

But like Milligan who, with Neil Shand, went on to write a surreal comedy series known by the letter *Q* and a number, Michael Bentine wanted to go it alone. He starred in his own puppet show *The Bumblies* in 1954 and *Yes, it's the Cathode-Ray Tube Show* (snappy title!) written by Bentine and David Nettheim in 1956. But it wasn't until *It's a Square World* was accepted for TV that he really had a chance to show the breadth of his comic invention.

Although *Square World* was renowned for its funny sketches, the items that most people remember are the flea circus and little Irishmen that featured in the model sequences. As far as the effects were concerned, it was indisputably Jack's show because he was so good at making intricate and complicated things (and the models on *SquareWorld* were certainly that). The fleas didn't exist of course; they were established by their props which were made to move as if being manipulated by some tiny beings. For example the flea on the high wire carried a miniature parasol which twirled as it traversed the wire, while the flea that leapt off the little diving board was shown to exist by the fact that the board bent under its weight and sprang back again when the flea leapt into a barrel of water. To substantiate that, when the invisible flea did actually perform this daring stunt a tiny plume of water shot into the air and water flowed down the barrel's sides.

A sound track of high pitched 'little' voices accompanied every action and made the invisible fleas seem entirely convincing. But as performers the fleas in the circus were limited to conventional circus acts and so Michael, needing to extend the possibilities, came up with the idea of the little Irishmen. These were supposedly inhabitants of a mythical tiny Irish village and took part in all sorts of adventures and dramatic plots including drunken funerals and sozzled weddings ('Take yur coat off and say that again, you ill bred biled potato!') They had the same little voices as the circus performers, but now they were given an Irish accent.

An early item of the genre had Michael Bentine explaining the art of making and putting ships in bottles. He first showed a bottle with a human hand in it allegedly amputated from the sailor who hadn't quite got the hang of things. He then showed two more bottles, one containing a miniature destroyer and the other a submarine. He turned his back on these exhibits and continued to talk to camera. We heard the two crews in their high squeaky voices preparing to open fire. Looking past Michael, we saw a ripple on the green baize table as a miniature torpedo apparently traversed the sea between them. It finished with a loud bang and Michael turned to see the destroyer with its bows in the air sinking below the plaster waves in the bottle. A retaliatory bang and the submarine suffered the same fate.

For most of the series Jack had the assistance of one of our visual effects designers – the legendary Tony Oxley. The two of them complemented each other perfectly and in creating those extraordinary models and having the skill to operate them they were able to produce anything Michael could dream up. Never did he have to think 'I wonder if Jack and Tony can make that?' Large or small, he knew the pair of them would produce it but when he conceived the idea of having the great white whale searching for its baby and running it to earth in The Natural History Museum it must have seemed wildly impracticable, particularly the concept of a great whale making its way along London's Exhibition Row and climbing the steps of the museum.

This sequence was followed by one that showed the whale gliding past the glass cases to where its offspring was incarcerated. This was the other end of the scale from the flea circus and did a great deal to advance the scope of television entertainment in general – and the reputation of our section in particular. Rehearsals for the first sequences, which were to be filmed on the Welsh Harp, a reservoir in London, were almost as bizarre as the ones finally recorded. On this occasion, Jack was supported by Jim Ward another of our early assistants. It was Jim's task to work a stirrup pump to produce the traditional water spout (no easy task while bobbing around a few inches above water sitting on a plank and unable to see what was happening from the inside of a fibre glass whale).

It was Jim's responsibility to see where they were going and to do this he had to lean forward and peer through a small slit in the whale's mouth. This meant him leaving his pumping duties to check on their progress which in turn resulted in the water spout fluctuating between an ooze and a dribble.

In the event steering the whale proved almost impossible because Jack had installed an out-board motor to propel them through the water. Regrettably (as he was to discover) an out-board motor does not respond in the same way when installed in a fibre glass whale as it does when screwed to the transom of a fibre glass dinghy. No matter which way he swung the steering bar the huge whale failed to answer to the helm, preferring to lurch through the water like a drunken sailor. Furthermore the interior began to fill with noxious fumes and the drunken sailor could be heard coughing all the way up the reservoir.

The sequences that followed were less difficult because they took place on dry land. Filmed early one Sunday morning in South Kensington the fibre glass carcase was 'walked' by a gang of chaps hidden inside the body. They were just as visually deprived as Jack and Jim had been, the leader having only the most slender view of the road ahead. After one or two practice movements they managed to totter in unison and the whale travelled smoothly with someone in the street shouting directions.

To create a whale in fibre glass was expensive and used up a good part of the overall budget, but producers in those days weren't governed by irksome financial restraints; they were given a sum of money and how they spent it was their own business. Of course they exceeded the budget over and over again, but I'm sure the programme organisers made allowances for overspending and had contingency funds tucked up their sleeves.

It was natural that Prince Charles as a fifteen year old devotee of *The Goon Show* should want to see behind the scenes of *It's a Square World* and a special demonstration was laid on for him in our workshop. He seemed delighted with the setup and watched with obvious fascination as Jack and Tony operated the various moving parts from beneath the table. Jack felt that, given the opportunity, the Prince would have loved to take part in the recording.

I took over the show when Jack went on holiday and it fell to me to sail a Chinese junk up the Thames, where it was supposed to open fire on the Houses of Parliament. Although the river police had given the project their approval, they were still worried by the fact that from mid-river we were firing straight at the windows of the House of Commons. A police launch sent out to keep an eye on the proceedings found the junk crewed by Orientals, 'Do any of you chaps speak English?' one of them asked and was reassured by a coarse reply which certainly wasn't in Cantonese. We had to show them that the gun was made from a cardboard tube charged with a simple pyrotechnic flash and the only people in any danger were those standing near it.

Two weeks before in a real 'stranger than fiction' occurrence Jack was driving to work wondering how he was going to create a Chinese junk when, looking across the river, he saw – a Chinese junk. He almost crashed his car. The owner of the junk was traced and he readily agreed to pilot his vessel for Michael Bentine and so, garbed in traditional Chinese costume and waving a fearsome broad-bladed sword he not only played his role to perfection but at the same time managed to navigate the boat (which had an inboard engine) and take care of the steering controls. I don't remember what part I played but I do recall that Michaeljohn Harris, one of our effects team and the most impressive Chinese war lord on the boat, fired the cannon. Michaeljohn, in later years, became Head of Visual Effects when Jack and I had retired.

The sight of a fully rigged Chinese junk on the Thames would have been reason enough to cause pedestrians on Westminster Bridge to pause and stare, but when the crew started shouting and waving fearsome cutlasses they behaved like true Britons and walked past pretending they hadn't seen what was going on down below.

Michael Bentine may have been the first to use the running gag and the saga of The Doomsbury Lifeboat was a classic example of the genre. Each week the business of trying to launch the lifeboat was repeated. Clive Dunn was cast as the bumbling idiot entrusted with the job of knocking the shackles free with a hammer. But each week, despite his valiant efforts, the lifeboat remained on the slipway, the one exception being the occasion when it was launched smoothly and without incident

– and without its crew. On another occasion Clive's hammer wielding resulted in the propeller falling from its shaft, and there was the moment when, anxious to make amends, he acted prematurely and the lifeboat was launched before the bloke down the other end had opened the shed doors. On the final occasion I think the shed itself slid smoothly down the ramp while the lifeboat remained shackled at the top.

There were so many original sketches in *It's a Square World* it would be hard to pick one that was outstandingly eccentric, but some of the laurels must go to The Game of Drats, a contest played out entirely off screen. Held in a country pub the contestants went out through the door and were never seen from that moment on. The viewer heard crowd noises accompanied by occasional grunts and moans while the customers in the bar were looking through the half open door and commenting on an exciting game the viewer could only guess at. With the customers speaking in a broad Mumbleshire accent the commentary went something like this.

'He's fumbled his dottle. No, dang me, he's double cobbled!'

'Taint possible, not without his other boots on.'

'The ones soaked in Goat's milk you mean? He's faster with yon on – he's faster than Michaelmas!'

We hear a loud cheer.

'He's done it. He's dratted!'

Big groan from outside.

'No he baint – fuddle me, he's been and gone and nurdled!'

Making notes for this book I would have liked to have discussed that sketch (and many others) with Michael, who some years ago moved to a house in the next village to mine. Unfortunately I never caught up with him until he was suffering from terminal cancer. I saw him and his wife Clementina just before his death when we met by chance in the reception area of the Royal Marsden hospital. Although confined to a wheelchair he was still performing and, predictably, the people who had gathered around him were convulsed with laughter. It was coming up to Christmas and he and I chatted happily about the old days and the many memories he and Jack and I had shared. Before leaving, he invited me to his home to continue the conversation and to play with the model train layout he was constructing. This was something both of us would have enjoyed and I thought I'd ring Clementina and pop round after Christmas. It was not to be because poor Michael was taken back to the Marsden where he died shortly afterwards. It says much about the man that he was visited by His Royal Highness Prince Charles just before the end. Aware of the impending visit Michael, now suffering terribly, sat up in bed and swapped jokes with the Prince as if he were suffering no more than a common cold.

Michael Bentine was a wonderful man and Jack and I and the many others who had enjoyed his friendship over the years were deeply saddened by his all too early departure from a life in which he still had so much to give.

A Trip Round Birmingham

Jack and I had become so used to working together that when we had to take on programmes individually it became clear that two heads are better than one. By the same token, two pairs of hands are better than a single pair and drinking alone in a pub is no fun at all. Nevertheless, when I volunteered to do the effects for a burning house sequence in Birmingham it was a commitment I was happy to take because it meant that I could stay with some friends in the Cotswolds.

Whenever possible, Jack and I allowed each other to choose any location that particularly appealed to us, either because we liked the area or because we had a particular interest in the show. In this case it was the lure of the Cotswolds and the chance to spend the night in my friend's vicarage. The weather on the way down was perfect and I chose the pretty route taking in a few of the villages and beauty spots that abound in that part of the world, but later in the day when I entered the outskirts of Birmingham I felt vaguely uneasy. I can read a map, but I seem to have a deficiency in the orientation department – in short, I couldn't find my way in Birmingham, a place for which you need a very good foreknowledge of location. Apart from my few visits to BBC Pebble Mill I knew nothing of the city at all. Now it was beginning to get dark and I regretted having taken such a leisurely drive down.

I had been given a script and a photocopied map of the area, but in the gathering gloom it was difficult to read the passing street names. I must have stopped a dozen times and, as usual, there was never anyone around to ask. Eventually I found the road, a quiet backwater of expensive houses and large gardens, but few of the houses had any numbers that could be read from the car. But then, quite by chance, I found the one I was looking for. Its name was prominently displayed on a sign beside a gate post. Relieved that I'd reached my destination I parked in the driveway and got out to look around.

The house, which had been hired for the filming was, of course, empty but I had expected to see some signs of our film unit – a location catering van or a mobile generator, or even some lamp stands and cables. There was nothing. I got back in the car and settled down to wait, but after half an hour I became restless. Looking at the schedule I saw there was an earlier location and assumed the unit had been delayed. It was pointless wasting time just sitting in the car so I thought I'd see if there was an open door or window or any other means of getting in, but a circuit of the building showed the doors and windows to be firmly shut. The front door had a Yale lock and this seemed like a good opportunity to try my hand at house-breaking. I'd been told that a Yale lock can be opened by slipping a thin piece of plastic between the tongue and the door frame and as I had some stiff plastic amongst my props I thought I'd try it. Fetching it from the car I cut a piece from the sheet and inserted it close to the lock. It wouldn't budge. I pushed firmly and it buckled into a Z-shape. I tried another piece which snapped. I wondered if the bloke who'd told me about this method had ever used it. It was while I was trying to retrieve the broken bit of plastic with a pair of pliers and a torch that the light from another torch shone on the door. At last. I turned round and saw that two of the cast, already in their police uniforms, had arrived. They came up to the door and asked me what I was doing. I think I replied 'Waiting for you buggers of course'. I believe I added that I was testing my house-breaking skills and that this something or other plastic Yale lock theory didn't work. One of the two took my arm and said in the typical plod voice, 'I think you'd better come down to the station.' I told him to stick to the script, which strangely didn't produce a witty riposte. I saw a puzzled glance pass between them and I had that icy feeling that comes when at a wedding you ask a fellow guest 'Who's that drunken old hag over there?' and he replies that the lady is his wife. I shone my torch on them. 'You're not real bloody policemen surely?' There followed a long and confused set of questions and answers in which they told me they'd been alerted by a householder across the road. Despite the hollow feeling in my stomach I knew I could prove my innocence and produced my script and the map which showed quite clearly the road and the house. They were still puzzled because they hadn't been given any information that filming was due to take place. In such an event the local police must be notified and as far as they were concerned no such notification had been received. A call to the station over their car radio produced a blank, but when the desk sergeant phoned around he discovered the location had been changed to another house in another district. Unfortunately I had been on holiday during the preceding week and the unit hadn't been able to contact me.

I thanked the two policemen but it was now quite dark and I would have to set off again looking for street names with my torch and getting totally lost in Birmingham's fiendish one-way system. Birmingham's road network seems to be designed to send you anywhere providing it's via London. But when I explained my difficulty one of the policemen said, 'You follow us and we'll take you there'. I don't often feel the urge to kiss a male policeman, but I did on that occasion. Praying that I wouldn't run into the back of their car but equally afraid that I might lose them, I stuck to their rear lights as if we'd been chained together. Eventually we reached the new location, which I would never have found without their help. The unit was preparing for a take. Explanations as to my late arrival could come later but I wanted to make sure that the two policemen were rewarded with hot coffee and blackberry pie (say what you like about the BBC – their catering was always top class). Thanking the two policemen for their help I wondered what would have happened had that observant and thoroughly commendable neighbour decided it was none of his business and had not dialled 999.

That location taught me to make sure I knew where I was going before driving all over the county gawping at beauty spots. And I was about to learn another valuable lesson.

The sequence called for the house to be full of smoke and I had gone through all the necessary safety procedures before lighting two or three smoke pots. The rooms, staircase and front hall were soon obliterated by the dense fog which made it difficult to see. Stupidly I had cut off my own retreat but it didn't matter because I was at the rear of the house and there was a convenient window I could open to get some fresh air. I flung it wide and filled my lungs with smoke. Perhaps it was the wild ride through the streets of Birmingham or the double helping of blackberry pie that had dulled my senses but I had forgotten to check the wind direction. Opening the window caused the smoke to pour out and although I stuck my head out as far as I could I was still in a smoke-filled environment. Taking one last gulp in the hope of ingesting at least some oxygen, I clutched my handkerchief to my mouth and groped my way to the back door where I leant against the wall and tried to clear my lungs of bitumen.

Newspaper headlines kept coming to mind – 'They had tried to escape but had been overcome by smoke. The funeral is on Friday.'

I swear for the next five minutes I exhaled black breath. When I had recovered sufficiently I tottered over to the catering wagon where I had some hot coffee and another slice of blackberry pie.

D o c t o r ,   D o c t o r !

DoctorWho was created as a quirky science-fiction story for children but soon became a favourite with viewers of all ages. The episodes, written by several top-line TV dramatists ranged from stories which took place on Earth to adventures on strange and forbidding planets. What made the programme so unusual was that the journeys through space and time were undertaken in the TARDIS, a London police box – and you can't get more bizarre than that, particularly when you are asked to accept that the police box is much bigger on the inside than on the outside.

Throughout its long run it became necessary to change the actor who played the Doctor and this was done by a form of metamorphosis. Nevertheless, although no more implausible than anything else in the series, I'm convinced that ardent viewers found it difficult to adjust when a new Doctor was brought in to replace the current one, even when the ploy of superimposing the new Doctor's image over the old one was meant to explain the substitution. It must have upset youngsters when it was explained that the Time Lords had decided the Doctor's life had run its course and, like it or not, the youngsters would have to get used to a new one.

It was just as hard for those of us who were closely associated with the series because it meant that we too would have to lose a friend and accept a stranger. The new Doctor would know nothing of our ways of doing things, a situation which for a short time could easily result in a degree of chilliness between the incoming Doctor and the studio staff. Like all friendships, time was needed for them to ripen, but eventually the new boy became a good friend until he too was moved on and the whole sad ritual of farewells and end-of-series parties established another milestone in everyone's career.

Doctor Who hit the screens in 1963. From its unpromising beginning it eventually gained the status of a cult programme supported by fan clubs, magazines and merchandise. It even spawned two feature films with Peter Cushing as the Doctor.

Jack and I were responsible for the special effects from the first episode, but the early stories called for very few effects, relying chiefly on the work of the costume designers. If we did supply anything it was usually a hand-over prop that we would pass to the production unit – which accounted for the fact that we never got to know William Hartnell, the first Doctor.

He was followed by Patrick Troughton, a Doctor of a very special kind. Pat was a lovely bloke with a wicked sense of humour and an easy charm, attributes that helped many of us cope with tedious rehearsals and mind numbing periods of inactivity. Jack and I were not the types to sit around for hours reading newspapers or solving crossword puzzles, we were intensely active and wanted to be doing something – anything other than sitting on a table in a studio. And, of course, we had a mountain of work to get through in the workshop and anything which interfered with that meant that we had to toil late into the evenings. Hanging about was part of the job and one or other of us had to face up to it. Nevertheless, it could be frustrating when at the end of a long period spent sitting in a corner of the studio we were required to operate a simple prop or squirt fog or smoke around. It would have been fine if the timing had allowed us to go back to our workshop and get on with our other work but a director having paid for someone to be in the studio for a day didn't want that someone wandering off. Fair dos, but when one has sat in the studio listening to the millionth agonised scream of 'Doctor! Doctor!!' it's easy to become disenchanted – even bloody rebellious.

Under such conditions a querulous actor can make life doubly miserable for everyone: petulance, in all its forms, can permeate through the production bringing bad temper from the most placid of people. Excused as 'temperament', displays of pique can fray the nerves of the director and cause the floor manager to exhibit qualities of restraint well beyond the terms of the job description. With Jack and me it induced a variety of emotions ranging from a desire to shout out 'Why doesn't someone tell the silly bastard to shut up?' to furtive whispering about how a generous pinch of laxative in coffee is said to go undetected and even improve the flavour. We were never driven to try it, but it gave us pleasant thoughts during our periods of inactivity. Strangely enough, this temperamental behaviour seldom came from the principal actors; nor did it come from the 'noddies' – the extras with only small parts to play, but, surprisingly, it sometimes came from actors who had substantial roles. It's possible that being cast for only one series, fussy actors would be intent on getting their character exactly right and the constant stopping and starting during rehearsals would unsettle them.

When Pat Troughton was cast as the Doctor it proved a tonic for everyone. He was patient, undemanding and able to keep us smiling with his satirical observations on the plot, the implied illegitimacy of the director and droll observations on his fellow actors. Pat would tell us during long periods of silence from the gallery that the director had either fallen asleep or had buggered off to the pub. We enjoyed the shows with Pat.

Another Doctor to become a great favourite was Jon Pertwee. He too had a witty sense of humour and while it differed from Pat Troughton's it enabled us to get through long days in the studio with a minimum of tedium. Jon was not beyond having a barney with the director, but only after a series of technical hold-ups had forced him to repeat his lines over and over again. He suffered back trouble which meant that long periods of standing could be painful.

Location filming for *DoctorWho*, like most outdoor work, was invariably fun, but it could be tough. The inactivity in the studio would be replaced by frenetic effort as we prepared our props and devices and carried tools and materials from our cars (which could be a long way from where we were filming). It is expensive to take a crew on location and the need to have everything ready on time for the director was essential. But there were occasions when the area chosen for our work was already occupied by electricians or scene staff preparing their stuff for other sequences. One cannot lay out long firing lines and set explosive charges when the scene boys are laying down runways for Daleks or the ground is being churned up by vehicles transporting cameras and lighting equipment.

As with all location work we were very dependent on the weather, but in this Jack and I were unusually lucky. Nevertheless we felt sympathy for any unfortunate producer who, on being told that the unit he had so carefully set up was marooned in pouring rain, would have to reschedule all his arrangements. As well as checking the availability of actors any hold-up could mean that the production unit would have to extend contracts and sometimes the writer would be called upon to rejig the scripts.

Although the gods were kind to Jack and me we heard plenty of horror stories from other people – such as the cameraman peering at the sky through a neutral density filter and calling out for the fiftieth time, 'There's a clear patch coming up' only to find that when the clouds had drifted away from the sun, the patch had changed shape and gave less than three seconds to record the shot. Our hearts bled too for the luckless costume designer as she hung up more and more dripping clothing in her inadequate caravan around an impossibly ineffectual heater hoping that by some miracle they would dry out in time for the next sequence.

Although I worked with several Doctors and their assistants I never worked with Tom Baker feeling at that late stage in my career I'd had as much of *Doctor Who* as I could take. Jack and I were running a very large department by then and consequently had the luxury of being able to select the programmes in which we would become personally involved. However, being curious to know how this new Doctor would fit in I decided to go into the studio on his first day. Moving inconspicuously about the floor I listened to his conversation with the director – and I was not impressed. I thought him arrogant and pompous, a bloody actor who on his first day was already showing signs of temperament. I wondered if laxative really did make coffee taste better. Now, many years later, having read his autobiography I realise that poor Tom was probably petrified. His book *Who on Earth is Tom Baker?* reveals an early life that could best be described as unsettled – he even became a monk for Christ's sake! If I harboured any evil thoughts towards him in those days I have since changed my mind. This change of heart came about when I discovered that we had very much in common (although I didn't become a monk I did spend a chunk of my life incarcerated in that catholic institution on the Isle of Wight) and I visited many of the London pubs that Tom went to in the years following the war. It was at the time when I was working for the Air Ministry and I thought that if I went to the watering holes around theatre land and the West End I might find someone who would offer me a job as an assistant stage manager. I never did of course but I met many jobless actors, writers and directors also looking for work, and of course the drinking was excellent.

Having watched Tom Baker's *Doctor Who* and his performances in other roles I realise that he is a fine actor and I wish now that I'd stayed with the series – he could have been as much fun as Pat Troughton and Jon Pertwee. One part of his autobiography caused my normally dormant hackles to rise however because he refers to K9, the robot dog, as 'the insufferable K9' and later as a 'boring, expressionless little robot'. He even admits that K9 was 'the tin dog that I disliked so much.'

It is held that actors dislike sharing the stage with children or animals (or props that look like animals) and so a robot dog was bound to offend Tom. K9 was temperamental because, packed with batteries, electric motors, gear boxes and radio control it could hardly be anything else. In a TV studio where there are numerous electronic signals transmitted or carried by wire to items of equipment such as headphone talk back systems, studio monitors, boom microphones the poor dog was occasionally confused by alien signals it didn't understand. Furthermore because they interfered with camera signals K9's own command messages had to be reduced in power. This caused it to run wild on its first appearance, careering into walls and generally behaving like a rogue elephant with a bee up its bum.

K9 was designed by Tony Harding and Chris Lawson, with radio control expert Nigel Brackley designing the command signals. Charlie Lumm was responsible for K9's maintenance and operation in the studio and he and Tony would dread the anguished phone calls from the studio telling them that the bloody dog was not responding to commands. Then one or both of them would have to rush to the rescue, carting heavy batteries and boxes of tools from the workshop at North Acton to the studios at White City. As Tom Baker points out, K9 would grind to a halt if it ran into a matchstick, but one doesn't plan for matchsticks on the studio floor.

Having no electronic aids we sometimes faced great difficulties in providing what we were asked for, a prime example being the shots of the TARDIS spinning in space. To get this effect we hung a small model on a thread and wound it up. On being released the threat would slowly unwind and the model would spin satisfactorily. Unfortunately, an object spinning freely like this generates a build-up of opposing forces causing it to wobble uncontrollably. Dozens of modifications in rehearsals were necessary before we could be sure that the tiny model would perform smoothly without either lurching from corner-to-corner or jerking up and down like a demented spider.

Having beaten that problem we faced another – the difficulty of hiding the thread. Despite all efforts to paint it matt black it would invariably catch the light and reveal its presence. When it was flaring like a neon sign it would show up as an obvious black line against the bright star-scape behind it. The answer lay in the lighting and the cameramen would spend hours trying to mask out the maverick thread. We, in the meantime, would paint out all the stars directly behind it.

Spill light was always a problem. In lighting the model it was difficult to keep light off the background and it was only when we adopted the technique of pricking holes in black paper and illuminating a sheet of tracing paper behind that we finally achieved a convincing star-scape.

A sequence which demanded that the TARDIS should not only revolve in space, but should travel towards or away from the camera brought fresh problems. The technique of dollying the camera towards or away from the model didn't work because it showed quite clearly that the star-scape and the model were a fixed distance apart. In real life, any movement of that kind would have no impact on the stars, which being so far away would remain unvarying in size and area.

Moving the model to and fro would have been impractical because it would not only have been jerky, but the entire lighting arrangement would have to move with it. The only answer I ever came up with was to fix the background to the camera in order that the two would move in unison. This called for an arrangement of long wooden battens, stick tape and G-clamps which was a triumph of gimcrack engineering. Compared with some of our assemblies, those of the celebrated Heath Robinson looked positively hi-tech!

The TARDIS console was another prop that gave us trouble because, unlike a Dalek, which comprised a bottom and a top with just a few simple bulbs and batteries that could be bashed about and mishandled without suffering a fit of the vapours, the console was heavy and if misaligned was likely to jam the central column. The TARDIS control desk was a simple arrangement of plywood panels fitted with dummy levers, switches and a few practical lights and its sole moving part was the Perspex drum containing tubular mains lamps and an array of plastic dressing which went up and down, accompanied by spine-chilling sound effects. However, in order to make it possible to transport (too wide for a scene truck) and to erect it in the studio it was constructed in three parts: the desk, which was split across the middle and the drum and its lifting gear which could be handled as a separate unit. The lifting gear, a well-designed unit of cycle chains, electric motor and switches, would have run forever if it had been allowed to remain in a permanent position, but at the beginning of each show it had to be taken to the studio and assembled. At the end it was carted away when the scenery was struck. Those who have worked in television will appreciate the full implication of such comings and goings; anything less robust than a Centurion tank is bound to suffer damage of some kind in transit. The raising and lowering gear which was built to lesser specifications than a tank became distorted when placed within the two halves of the console and would seize up at the most inconvenient moment – usually late in the day or, worse still, during recording. This presented a problem. If the fault lay with the motor then the electricians were supposed to deal with it. If the fault existed in the gears and chains the work was 'engineering' and the sparks wouldn't touch it. The only people authorised to deal with the whole problem in those days were the special effects personnel and so we were called to the studio whenever there was a malfunction. On a bench in the workshop, maintenance would have been relatively simple but in the studio where we had to scramble around underneath the console with a torch and a handful of tools it was far from easy.

This demarcation of responsibility epitomised the BBC's trade union relations at that time. Never mind the fact that the BBC paid their wages and provided excellent working conditions the 'bolshies' saw the Beeb only as a milch cow which would give in to their every demand.

Consequently they dedicated themselves to extracting as much as they could by twisting their employer's arm to breaking point – and beyond. Some of the trouble could be attributed to weak management but the necessity for keeping shows on the air meant that no one was willing to confront the militants and so they got away with murder. The rule book, which was flourished at every implied infringement, took precedence over everything else. These restrictive practices were hated by the moderates, the people who actually preferred working to sitting idle, but they had little effect on the outcome. Any attempt to flout the party line was discouraged by the militants and so the moderates remained silent.

Despite these battles – or perhaps because of them – *Doctor Who* grew progressively sharper and more sophisticated. The writers and production unit rose to the challenge and designers and backstage staff would handle their requests with imagination and enthusiasm. Perhaps *Doctor Who* epitomised the ideal format – a programme which was not only a great favourite with the public but inspired everyone who worked on it.

C u r s e   o f   t h e   D a l e k s

Mention *DoctorWho* and most people think of the Daleks. To millions of small children around the world the Dalek was a frightening monster to be watched from behind a sofa or the security of a repositioned armchair; to their parents it was an intriguing part of *DoctorWho* which promised *thrilling* moments of excitement and anticipation

To many of us in the Design Department the Dalek became an icon and one with which we were secretly proud to have an association. Even the lads in props could claim that they had sole charge of them between shows. My own association has been a special one because many years ago I designed some exhibits for the *DoctorWho* exhibition at Longleat (the home of Lord Bath) and am now part of an organisation responsible for the several *DoctorWho* exhibitions around the country.

In the beginning the Daleks were stored at Ealing Studios where there was room to house large, infrequently used props, but the available space was soon used up and it was decided by management to have a clear out. The Daleks hadn't been required for some time so they were among the many items to go. To be fair, the manager responsible for scenery and property storage had some awe-inspiring decisions to make and in the case of the Daleks two were disfigured (having been dramatically exterminated) and one had been accidentally damaged. Should a new Dalek script be written they could be recreated simply by reordering them from the company that held the moulds. This would have been a cheaper option than repairing and storing them for long periods.

And so it happened that when my colleague Ricky Grosser and I were on our way to Ealing Studios one morning we encountered a Dalek. It should have been a sight to strike terror into the hearts of all Londoners – a yellow dustcart moving slowly through the streets of Ealing with a Dalek on board. This Dalek however was a dead Dalek. It was, to paraphrase John Cleese's protestations in the famous parrot sketch, no more; it was defunct; it was a departed Dalek. Lying on its back with its sink plunger pointing pathetically towards the sky, it threatened no one, not even a passing bird. Half-buried in a pile of broken scenery the monster that had terrorised the world and frightened millions of young viewers was on its way to the council rubbish dump where it was about to suffer cremation at the hands of council employees. What an ignominious end for one of the conquerors of the universe!

We saw the dustcart and were prompted to offer a valedictory two-fingered salute to the 'dear departed'. Ealing council were about to achieve something that *Doctor Who,* and all the forces of good ranged against the invincible Daleks, had failed to do – exterminate the monster in a Corporation incinerator. The irony didn't escape us. But then Ricky had an idea. 'Hey, why don't we get it back? Your boys would love it'. Of course! I did a sharp and illegal U-turn and five minutes later (and ten bob poorer) I had a Dalek strapped to my roof rack.

It meant little to me at the time or even during the years my kids exterminated the milkman and scared the hell out of passing motorists, but this particular Dalek was one of the first three ever made and, with the other two having been written off, could be regarded as number one – the true progenitor of all those that followed. I'm sure if I had offered it to Sotherby's it might have proved a nice little earner and repaid me for the years of aggravation I suffered at its prongs. It still exists. Abandoned by my grown up sons and mouldering in my barn it now features as an original artefact in a BBC *Doctor Who* exhibition.

Doctor Who fans might ask how I can be sure that this really is the first of the Daleks? Well, because I was invited to the conception and was present at the birth. It was late one evening when Jack Kine and I were asked to join Ray Cusick in his office where he wanted to discuss a design problem. Ray, as *Doctor Who* aficionados know, was the designer of the first programme in which the Daleks appeared and he is, of course, their creator. Ray showed us his sketches for this new and interesting monster and sought our advice on its construction. The problem lay in the time scale. The Dalek would be an expensive and complicated prop to make and Ray needed to know if three of them could be produced in the time available and at a price within his budget. Jack and I believed they should be made in fibre glass by one of our specialist contractors, but because it was late on a Friday evening we couldn't contact them on the phone. It was clear that we would have to make some educated guesses.

Having had experience in fibre glass production I was worried by the size of the mould it would require and took another look at Ray's sketch, a tall pepper pot as smoothly contoured as a baby's posterior. I asked him if he would be prepared to compromise. If our firm couldn't meet either the deadline or the price, we'd be forced to construct them in plywood – which meant using flat sections for the main part of the body. Ray agreed and drew a few lines, faceting the lower torso.

The following Monday contracts were issued and, in the stipulated two weeks, three Daleks were delivered to Television Centre. They had been successfully moulded in fibre glass but the makers had worked to Ray's alternative design and had retained the flat sides. The fault was mine. I should have explained to them that the flat sides were simply an alternative. But Ray had a further problem that evening. How could he make the Daleks move around? Radio control and electric motors were plainly out of the question, so we agreed that we'd use manpower. But this still left the problem of propulsion; how would the operators move and control them. We sketched a tricycle undercarriage with two small wheels driven by pedals and a single steerable one in the front. It looked possible, but common sense prevailed and we settled for castors and human pushing power. In those pre-supermarket days none of us had experienced the vagaries of shopping trolleys or we might have thought differently. Stick someone inside, we reasoned, provide them with BBC carpet slippers and we were home and dry. Ray agreed, but realising that the operators couldn't stand all day trapped inside a fibre glass shell, he included a seat in the design.

The upper part of a Dalek is removable to allow an operator to climb in, resulting in some of my most enduring memories. The sight of an inexperienced pusher, one leg over the side, trying to get into something which ran away from him every time he tried to climb on board would have had even the most compassionate onlooker in hysterics.

Getting out could be equally traumatic because it needed two people to lift and remove the top. Until studio staff were organised to do this it was not unknown for luckless operators to be left behind in the studio while everyone went for a coffee break. Attributing the silence to a long and important take they would sit patiently, not daring even to whisper a question. It was hardly surprising that on being released they dashed, not for the tea bar, but for the loo.

It wasn't long before the script writers decided to deploy Daleks in locations away from the studio. This undoubtedly benefited the series but it gave the scene boys and the designers more than a few headaches. On the level floor of a TV studio they would glide smoothly and effortlessly, but in a stone quarry they become a tad less reliable – in fact they looked ridiculous. On even relatively smooth ground they nodded their heads like ducks in a shooting gallery. They would jerk convulsively as their operators struggled to prevent the castors digging into soft soil or coming to an abrupt halt as they encountered even a medium sized pebble. The solution, it seemed, was to lay down sheets of block board, but the edges where the boards abutted could often prove as hazardous to these masters-of-the-universe as a set of step ladders.

Sharp eyed viewers were often puzzled by the unexplained cuts in some sequences, but these were employed to hide the embarrassing sight of an invading army of Daleks appearing like arthritic old men convulsed with hiccups.

It is reasonable to ask what would have happened had Ray's design been more slickly mechanical or 'bug-eyed' and less weirdly humanoid? Designed without a personality, the world famous Dalek might have been written out after the first series. As it was, Ray's unique design became an outstanding success.

In the commercial world Ray might have benefited hugely from his design but as a BBC employee he was not permitted to capitalise on his work. He was, I believe, eventually awarded a small sum of money in recognition of the fact that he had been denied the real plums, but that's the way it works. Had Ray been allowed to profit from his creation, other designers would have had cause to complain. Programmes were invariably allocated to those thought most likely to work well in a particular field; hence a set designer in, say, light entertainment would have had little chance to originate a world famous science fiction monster. It could be argued that a writer contracted by the BBC should be subject to similar restrictions and that the Beeb should be the sole benefactor, but that isn't the way of things. Not endowed with the wisdom of Solomon I can offer no opinion on this anomaly but when one considers the possible monetary gains that the creator of such an icon might have expected to make in the commercial world one can't help feeling that a more equable system could be devised.

I c e   W a r r i o r s

For us, every episode of *DoctorWho* had its problems but few were more traumatic than the introduction of the Ice Warriors. Starring Bernard Bresslaw, this story called for four or five tall, green aliens to be discovered embedded in the ice wall of a glacier. Found by a party of explorers they are standing upright and 'frozen in time'. The director, Derek Martinus, was adamant that they had to be in an upright position as this would emphasise their menace and size. Supine, he reasoned, they would look just like any old dead bodies. I could see his point but how was I to make an ice wall ten feet high? In the end we compromised by having the base of the ice buried slightly below a snow bank of polystyrene granules – leaving me with just eight feet of ice wall to make. As we discussed it we could both see the picture, and an exciting one it was. We imagined the scene – with the explorers, helmeted and goggled, making their way along the glacial chasm and, centre frame, pausing for a rest. One of them wipes snow from the face of the ice and sees something unusual. He clears more snow – 'Ugggghhhh'

Imagination is a marvellous thing and I'm addicted to it, but real life and practicality can ruin the most vivid of illusions. While the director went away with his expectations intact I was left with the business of turning his expectations into practicality. Ice looks like ice because of the way it refracts light. A glass bottle looks like a glass bottle and clear plastic, the material I intended to use, looks just like clear plastic. If however, you fill a clear glass bottle with water it refracts light in the same manner as ice and by the same token, putting water behind bent plastic has the same effect.

Enough of the science. Visual effects designers are paid not so much for their skill in making things, but for their ability to come up with good ideas, and in the case of *The Ice Warriors* I had come up trumps in the ideas department. But in the event, it was my ability to make things that was to be tested. At first I had toyed with the idea of using real ice blocks but quickly rejected it. Even sculptured and pared down they would have been far too heavy, and of course, there would have been the melt water to contend with. In the end I opted for Cobex (a malleable clear plastic) intending to fabricate a number of shallow tanks which could be filled with water and assembled on a steel frame. I figured that the joins between them could be disguised with white paint and aerosol snow.

Each Cobex tank was to be four feet high by two feet wide with a flat back and a distorted front sheet the two being held together with sealant and rivets. My assistant at that time was Ron Oates and, full of happy optimism, he and I made our first tank. The front sheet was distorted by heating it with a blowtorch and (where we didn't burn it) looked quite convincing. It was then riveted to its back sheet and given a hole near the top to provide a filling point. It looked good, but while it was empty it could be seen for what it was, a tank with a distorted front. We carried it over to the sink and with a length of hose connected to the tap, set about filling it. As the water rose the transformation was apparent. The plastic tank that had looked like a plastic tank began to look just like a block of ice. Ron and I were delighted and, assured that we'd solved the problem, became quite light hearted. All we had to do now was to make five more.

We became slightly uneasy when we realised that our prototype tank was taking a long time to fill. We'd made it as shallow as possible, a mere four or five inches at its widest part, and hadn't expected it to hold more than a gallon or two of water. But this was far more than a gallon or two. Cautiously we tried to lift it and were surprised by the weight. Nevertheless we reasoned that once the tanks were fitted into the upright metal frame they wouldn't be moved; we had discussed it with the director and he'd arranged for the actors to get into position from behind.

The tank was just over three-quarters full when it burst. Ron and I were both looking at it when it happened and saw the entire bottom seam open up like a sardine can. We collided with each other as we leapt to turn off the water.

Time for a bit more science! It wasn't the volume of water, but the *head* of water that had caused the tank to rupture. Those who know about these things will understand what happened, indeed may have foreseen it. I will explain it thus: A hypothetical saucer, a mile in diameter, would hold millions of gallons of water without any ill effect on the saucer, whereas a hypothetical cup a mere twenty feet tall would burst long before it could be filled. It's all to do with the pressure. As the head of water rises, so does the pressure at the bottom. There was no doubt about it, we were in deep trouble. Time was running out and we didn't have an ice wall – we didn't even have a tiny ice wall for midgets!

We did however have a lot of water. It was flowing all over the floor. We grabbed mops and buckets and rushed to clear it up. Our colleagues, alerted to what had happened, came to our aid, some helping with the mopping up, some giving advice. Both were welcome. The consensus of opinion was that we should use a different type of sealant – one that was also a strong adhesive. It was also agreed that we should double the number of rivets. Armed with so much sensible advice we returned to our labours. We drilled out the existing rivets, cleaned the Cobex and applied the new adhesive sealant. Then leaving it to dry and being in need of a drink, we went to the club.

At the end of lunch things looked better and much of our former optimism had returned. Ron and I had sat in the usual corner by the window and assured each other that we really had beaten it. The new adhesive would work and the additional rivets would hold the two sheets even more firmly together. We returned to the workshop in a much happier frame of mind. We tested the adhesive and found that it had stuck the two halves firmly together. We then drilled the extra holes and pop-riveted the sides and bottom; surely this would work? We covered the floor with rags and newspaper as a safety precaution, but were convinced that we wouldn't need them. We reconnected the hose but this time the fact that it looked like ice didn't arouse the same emotions, we were far too concerned with the water level. It rose and rose until the sound of water on the floor shattered our concentration. But it was merely the fact that the tank was full and was overflowing. Ron turned off the tap and carefully withdrew the hose. Nothing happened. We examined the tank and could see that none of the seams had failed – there were no cracks and no seepage.

We decided to leave it in position, moving it might impart strain; we then set about making the other five. From time to time we returned to our prototype, examining it for faults, but it continued to give solid reassurance. Eventually it was time to go home and it was with a light heart we put away our tools and departed. Ron had syphoned out the water using a tube and a bucket and we had cleaned and tidied around the sink area. We had considered leaving the tank filled overnight, but we didn't want to take any chances – gallons of water on the workshop floor might have affected the friendly relationship we had with our lady cleaners.

Rehearsals were the following day and we took our tanks to the studio. At no stage did we allow them out of our hands. There was the usual chaos that precedes a recording, with the harassed designer, Jeremy Davie, trying to supervise everything at once. We didn't want to add to his problems but when we found that the frame that was to support our tanks had not been erected we naturally asked him where it was. His response was unhelpful. 'I don't know, they were supposed to have done it by nine o'clock. I'll see if I can find somebody.' And with that he went off to deal with more important problems – we went off to look for the frame. We found it in pieces on a scene truck.

Suffice to say between us we got it done – just before the lunch break. This meant that to get the tanks in place and ready for the afternoon rehearsal we would have to miss our lunch but that was par for the course. The important thing was to get the tanks in place. In those days rehearsals started immediately after lunch and all studio work was supposed to be finished. Any hammering and banging which was necessary during the rest of the day was halted during the actors' rehearsal. By working through our lunch hour we had managed to clamp the tanks to the frame and dress them with artificial snow to cover the joins and the burnt bits and now all we had to do was to fill them with water. This would have been a simple operation if we had been near a sink, but we were in the middle of the studio – about as far away from a sink as it was possible to get – funny how the little things like essentials sometimes get overlooked. We took it in turns to carry buckets from the studio tap, but, using a plastic funnel and a length of hose, it was pitifully slow; I decided to call in some reinforcements. A phone call to the workshop produced another pair of hands – those of Rhys Jones. Rhys brought with him two more funnels and enough hose to get from the studio tap to our array. He also brought a load of rags to mop up spillages. Filling the tanks by hose would not only speed things up but would save a great deal of mess. However the operation had to be authorised by the Quenton Annis, the floor manager, because a hose laid across the studio floor would cross the fire lane and would also obstruct the camera routes. He agreed to our plan providing we removed the hose whenever one of the pedestal cameras had to traverse that part of the studio. But although we agreed, this would have been difficult. We would have to disconnect and drain the entire length of hose every time a camera wanted to operate in that area. We had a word with the cameramen who obligingly compromised by allowing us to lift the hose so that they could pass underneath it.

Studio taps are not like domestic taps; they are huge, great brass monsters with the sort of pressure that could demolish a brick wall; our garden hose was never going to fit that. I phoned the head of studio maintenance who, like the cameraman, was very helpful. He told us that he not only had an adaptor and a fitting for garden hose, but he would send up a chap to fix it for us. I promised to buy him a drink when next we met, but at the back of my mind there was the burgeoning suspicion that things were now going too well.

The filling process speeded up from then on. With luck we might get a chance to pop along to the crash bar for coffee and a sandwich. I climbed the step ladder to fill the top three tanks. With no warning at all the left hand lower tank began to gush water – waves of it flowed across the studio floor. I froze. For ****'s sake – not again!

Fortunately Ron had surrounded the area with hessian and newspaper, anticipating some spillages during the filling operation, but never for one moment had we anticipated another burst tank. Ron and Rhys leapt into action, mopping and wringing, wringing and mopping while the maintenance man and I ferried buckets to the studio drain. Quenton came across to tell me that the ice wall was to be the next sequence. It was no good debating the point, the Ice Warriors were already moving into position. We ceased operations while the director rehearsed the scene at the ice face with Bernard Bresslaw leaning back on a pile of dry rags. Glumly I realised that I had been right – things had been going too well!

By transmission time we had managed to repair the faulty seam and had more or less built an ice wall. It wasn't the ice wall I had visualised and there was a great deal more white paint and polystyrene snow than I had reckoned on but it showed Bernard Bresslaw's head clearly embedded in ice and the director was happy. 'It had just the right amount of mystery.' Derek assured me later. I was grateful to him for that.

C y b e r m e n   a n d
C y b e r m a t s

Although Daleks and the TARDIS fascinated young viewers, few props has so many people writing in to buy them than the Cybermats. Visualised as small animals, these were created by Ron Oates. They were a cross between silver fish and guinea pigs. Metallic, they had big eyes and flexible fish-like tails. They glided around the floor without the aid of legs. They seemed to move around without supervision, disappearing and reappearing later is if on some vital secret mission. The fact they had a low key role made them mysterious, but they also looked cuddly and if BBC Enterprises had been able to make and market them they would've made a fortune – and promoted a new genre of mechanical toys.

Ron and I had a brush with Cybermen the year before. We were asked to create an animated wall map to show global weather for Kit Pedler's serial *The Moonbase*. It was designed with two rear wave-pattern projectors, one scanning vertically and the other horizontally producing a sequence of patterns that was, in those days, quite revolutionary. Nowadays any form of animation can be created at the touch of a button, but those days we had no such facility. To show an advancing ice field we lowered a sheet of Perspex with a lightly graded pattern sprayed onto its surface. [PUBLISHER'S NOTE: We suspect this may have been for *The IceWarriors*]

This particular episode was memorable because the control room of the observatory was being made by an outside contractor who, the day before they were due to be delivered to the studio, was taken ill. On the day of transmission, the four desks that comprised the central area of the scene lay in his workshop only partly finished. There were no lights or instruments on them and the plywood shells had not even been painted. Despite his illness the contractor had battled through the night to complete the work, but finally collapsed.

Hiring a van we went to his workshops, collected the unfinished props and returned to Lime Grove where we took them straight into the studio. It was now the dinner break and we had less than an hour to turn them into a credible looking control centre. Fortunately there were still people working in the effects workshop and we summoned them urgently to the studio bringing with them everything that could be regarded as instruments, banks of switches and rows of pilot lights.

There was no time to paint the desks so we sent out for rolls of white Fablon which we cut and stuck to the raw plywood. Fablon doesn't adhere well to absorbent surfaces but we prayed that it would stay in position until the end of the show – which fortunately it did.

We cut holes to accommodate the working lights and instruments, but to make up the deficit we cut pieces from magazine adverts and stuck them around the panels to resemble sophisticated monitoring equipment. Manned by actors, the desks looked quite good, but the fact that the actors had had no chance to rehearse with them gave everyone some anxious moments.

P y t h o n

To be associated with *Monty Python's Flying Circus* was an experience with a difference. Unlike other programmes in which we became part of the team, in *Python* there seemed to be no cohesion, nothing to latch on to. The stars were plainly happier writing, planning and organising the entire show themselves and we, the servicing departments were simply part of the apparatus needed to put the show on television. And I for one was content to be part of the show even though my contribution was merely to read through the script and provide the special props it called for.

The producer and director Ian McNaughton arranged for some of the major location work to be filmed in the Scottish highlands where many a sketch was performed in the heather. Whether this was because the script demanded a Scottish background, or whether the remoteness and the freedom to perform without intrusive members of the public flourishing autograph books I'm not sure, but I do know that it suited me very nicely, thank you. I had long been a lover of the wild and rugged country that is so special to Scotland and this for me was as good as a location could get.

Strangely enough I can't remember any of those sketches, but I do recall that away from London and the pressures of the studios everyone seemed more relaxed and more convivial. Although still not part of the 'inner circle' I became closer to the unit than I ever was in London. Having observed the way in which the stars of *Monty Python* have developed their individual careers since those early days one must commend Ian McNaughton on the tactful way he allowed them to express their individual personalities while at the same time trying to suppress any *prima donna-ish* behaviour and overt attempts to gain superiority. They were, as everyone recognises, extremely talented people and with so many brilliant performers in one team, all of them determined to demonstrate their own skills as writers or comedians – or even directors – it wasn't easy for him to keep control. I feel that the part Ian played in shaping *Monty Python* was never fully appreciated but I do know that he had a hell of a job.

A cherished memory of mine was when I went with Eric Idle to Scotland. We had arranged to meet at Euston Station where we boarded the train for Glasgow. The forerunners of today's intercity trains these were known as express trains and although they clocked up quite a speed they weren't nearly as fast as their modern high-speed counterparts. Eric and I knew that we were in for a long period of inactivity and in order to pass the time started off by attempting to complete his crossword puzzle. But we soon became bored; there is only so much interest one can maintain in solving esoteric clues involving nine letter words beginning with Q and ending with T, so we folded the paper and considered more rewarding pleasures. We could either play 'I spy with my little eye' or have a drink; Eric went to the refreshment bar and bought four cans. Unsurprisingly, the long journey to Glasgow didn't seem so tedious after that. Finishing the cans faster than we'd done the crossword puzzle I went to the bar and bought four more. We talked of this and that and it was all rather pleasant.

The scenery outside had changed from the smoky bricks and mortar of London to the softer grass and farmland of the Home Counties and then to the very different landscapes of the North Country. We felt so good we kept buying cans.

I suppose we had lunch on the train – we must have done and when we returned to our compartment I think we bought some more cans of beer.

It was getting dark when we arrived in Glasgow where our hired car and driver were waiting to whisk us off to our hotel. I say 'whisk us off' as if it were just around the corner but it was a very long journey to the Cairngorms. Reaching Loch Lomond we decided that a 'comfort break' was necessary and we asked our driver to stop at a convenient spot. He spotted one immediately – it was a large hotel on the side of the loch. By this time we were feeling we might have a wee top-up so we made our way to the bar. It seemed rather full of men in smart suits engaged in jovial conversation. The fact that the assembled group was almost entirely male led us to think that it was some sort of a convention but whatever the occasion they were obviously having a very good time. One of the men looked round at us and turning back had an urgent conversation with his companions. The sudden silence from that group communicated itself to the others and they all looked at us. Then one of the men came over and enquired of Eric 'Excuse me sir, are you Eric Idle?' From that moment our fate was sealed. We were, for heaven's sake, in the middle of The Scottish Whisky Distiller's Association's annual junket! Soon people were crowding around and plying us with glasses of fabulous liquor. 'You must try this', they kept saying. 'It's distilled from the dew that collects on the Northern slopes of the Island of Ictalochorrie' – or attributes of that kind. Eric and I could not have been more appreciative. It could have been refined from liquid gold, but our palates, blunted by so many cans of beer, were incapable of differentiating between fine Scottish Whisky and cat's pee. The effect was powerful though and we would have been happy to spend the evening with these splendid chaps but, outside, the evening was turning into night and Eric kept reminding me that he was due to meet Ian and the others to hammer out a script needed for the next day's filming. Eventually we got away, thanking them for their hospitality and regretting that we'd had to leave so many unsampled tumblers.

We resumed our journey, dozing in the car while our cheerful driver ploughed on through the night. Needing another comfort break we asked him again to pull up at any convenient spot. We were thinking of some bushes by the roadside but he'd found a pub. In all the blackness, by the side of the road, was just the place he thought we were looking for. In a sea of nothingness he'd spotted the welcoming fairy lights strung along a facia board and a pub sign illuminated by two flood lights. By that time I suspect that Eric and I were scarcely in a condition to tell a pub from an ocean liner but we went inside. It was amazing. It was as if we were still in the bar of the Loch Lomond hotel. It was crowded and jolly and a young man was playing a large and expensive electric organ. Eric was recognised instantly and the young man immediately stopped playing and going behind the bar he asked us what we'd like. 'Drinks on the house', he offered. He said it so charmingly that we couldn't refuse. Besides which we were about to make use of his toilet. 'Just very small ones please' we pleaded. It turned out that he was the son of the licensee and whilst his father and mother were away on holiday he and his wife were managing the pub. When he'd made sure we had tumblers filled to the brim he returned to the organ and the merry sing-song continued. Only when our driver came in to find out what was happening did we realise that we should have left hours ago. For the second time that night we thanked a gathering of strangers for their hospitality, wished them well and went back into the night.

We eventually reached the highlands hotel where the team was staying, arriving there at some unearthly hour. I don't remember too much about it but we made our way, somewhat unsteadily, to the bar where we were due to meet the others. Because of our delayed arrival we expected to find everyone had gone to bed, but no! They were all still in the bar. Despite the late hour they had stayed on waiting for Eric. Grim-faced and looking as disapproving as a collection of Cardinals about to sentence a pregnant nun they watched our entry in disapproving silence. Graham Chapman who had been waiting for Eric since dinner had, like the others, enjoyed a jolly evening but at that hour the beneficial effects had worn off; now, tight-lipped he showed his disapproval.

For once I was glad not to be part of the team and picking up my bag, I cravenly slunk off to bed. The Cardinals were clearly preparing to burn someone at the stake and I didn't want to be a witness.

M o r e   W h o

It was called a 'sonic screwdriver' and went through more modifications than the tilting train. The problem was that it was small, and small props get lost. With the Daleks it was easy to know how many we had and where they were, but when it came to the sonic screwdriver no one could ever remember where it was or who had it. Was it in props, or had it been put on a shelf in the Puppet Theatre? We knew that it didn't appear in the last three stories – or did someone call for it two weeks ago in that scene where Jo was trapped in the cage? And so it went on. Seeing it in the script I would underline it in red to alert the effects designer to the fact that someone might have to provide a duplicate. But what did it look like?

One way of finding out would have been to simply rerun an episode in which it appeared and note its size and shape; somebody actually suggested that once. Unfortunately in an organisation geared to transmitting hours and hours of programme material the system has to be fairly well regulated and to get a glimpse of an errant screwdriver it would have been necessary to check the episode in which it was known to have appeared, book out the reel and then either arrange a viewing time on telecine equipment or acquire a non-transmission copy of the film to run on the editing desk. Having done all this, one would find that the screwdriver never appeared in close-up except for a subliminal shot in which it was taken from the Doctor's pocket hidden in the palm of his hand. A fruitless exercise like this would use up valuable time and money and was rarely employed. Instead, the luckless designer would make an intelligent guess as to its shape and size hoping that no eagle-eyed kid would spot the substitution. Of course, I might have taken a Polaroid of it but would we have remembered where the photograph was?

Members of the *Doctor Who* fan clubs must have known that the Daleks themselves changed over the years, the later versions being of significantly different proportions from the originals. The early ones were narrow at the base while the later ones were fatter and more stable. When the writers became more inventive and called for them to appear in various locations, the designers and ourselves had the task of creating studio conditions wherever the Daleks popped up. I recall only one episode in which the location conditions were so perfect that the Daleks travelled flawlessly, but that was not 'outdoors'. It was the London Underground.

I thought this story was one of the most convincing, and the most spine-chilling, and I still regard it as a classic. My opinion was somewhat affected by a sequence in an earlier and unrelated drama in which I had had to blow up an escalator and in order to get reference photos I spent a couple of hours wandering round an Underground station that had closed for the night. An empty Underground Station is a strange place, full of echoes and implied menace and is, to my mind, far spookier than many a haunted castle. [PUBLISHER'S NOTE: While this could relate to *Day of the Daleks*, we suspect Bernard is thinking not of Daleks, but the Yeti in *The Web of Fear*.]

All too familiar with the difficulties of Dalek locomotion in rough terrain I should have dodged *Colony in Space* which was scheduled to be filmed in the china clay pits in Cornwall, but the lure of an exotic location proved too tempting. Furthermore there was the challenge of creating the unusual vehicles called for in the script. For these we hired two Austrian Hafflingers, amazing little off-road vehicles in which the suspension, cab, body and tiny engine were all assembled on a single steel tube.

The work and the slog long since forgotten, I nevertheless remember the location with affection. The terrain was permanently wet and muddy because china clay is mined, not by digging, but by using high pressure water jets to blast it from the ground. The quarry is worked in a series of descending levels in order that the mixture of water and the clay can flow down a central culvert to a lake where the two eventually separate – the clay settling below and the water clearing and being reused. From the lake it is dug out and taken by sea to various parts of the world. One might have thought that a quarry subjected to high pressure hoses that swept the prescribed area automatically, filling the air with mist and spray would have been the last place to film an episode of *Doctor Who* but there were other areas which remained comparatively dry providing excellent science-fiction terrain for our story.

The days were sunny, and when not required on the set, colleagues Ian Scoones, Colin Mapson and I were able to explore the surrounding countryside. The incredible lake where the china clay settled out was particularly fascinating, because it was bright blue. Filming was relatively trouble free but for a number of memorable incidents. One that stands out was when Ian Scoones volunteered to propel a wheeled object (I think it was called the I.M.C, Robot) which had to slowly travel across the ground and perform a series of lumbering manoeuvres. This robotic device was supposed to be highly automated but, to operate and propel it, it had nothing inside to work it other than Ian's legs and hands. The shot was mute and Ian was given his cues by the director standing next to the camera. I stood on the other side and watched. The sequence started with the director calling out in calm and measured tones, but, as the action progressed his voice changed to a worried shout. The robot, instead of performing smoothly, was clearly in trouble. It lurched, it staggered and, at one moment, came to an unscheduled halt; then it shook itself and carried on in a series of hops. Having seen Ian rehearse at The Centre earlier in the week I knew there must be something wrong and I had this sudden dreadful fear that the sun playing on the exterior had turned this prop into a solar oven – an oven in which Ian was clearly suffering from heat stroke. My fears were realised when the sequence finished and we got him out. He looked awful, his face was pale and he was breathing heavily. When he could speak he explained that one of the six-inch castor wheels fitted to the base had been damaged in transit and that instead of being able to wheel the robot around he had had to carry the whole thing on his back. Remembering that it took three of us to get it out of the prop van I knew what a Herculean task this must have been. You hear of actors who 'give their all' summed up by the phrase 'the show must go on' but I doubt whether their sacrifices can surpass those of an effects man who runs into buckled castor trouble during a take.

Another incident that gave me anxiety concerned one of the Daleks which had to appear on the top of a cliff – a cliff with a very nasty drop in front of it. This particular Dalek was being operated by the doyen of Dalek operators, John Scott-Martin. He was delighted to undertake the sequence, despite the obvious risks, but we had worked together for several years and he trusted me to take care of such eventualities as his lifeless body ending up in a pile of shattered fibre glass at the bottom of a cliff.

Visibility from inside a Dalek is limited and cresting the rise at the top of the cliff there would have been little chance of John being able to stop on a mark. Drawing a line on the cliff top would have meant him looking down at his feet and the movement might have been hesitant as he searched for the mark. However, even if he had had a perfect view and a precise method of stopping I would still not have allowed the action to take place without adequate safety measures. The safeguard on this occasion was a stout line fastened to the back of the Dalek and anchored to an iron spike driven into the ground behind him. But first

I had to determine the length of the line. This was critical because the Dalek had to be seen coming right up to the edge – there would have been no drama in a view of the top half of a Dalek peering nervously, yards from the rim. I anchored the rope and pushed the Dalek to within perhaps a couple of feet of the edge. Then, satisfied with the restraint, we were ready to shoot. John climbed in and we closed the top. Ian stayed above to organise the take-off and to relay the cues while I went into the quarry to watch events from the camera position. Action was called and after a suitable delay the Dalek came into view; it moved menacingly and swiftly to the cliff edge and my marker point – and beyond. My heart went into a spasm as John came to the very brink before stopping – I had, of course neglected to allow for the momentum of a heavy moving object. I felt slightly sick. The rope would have restrained the Dalek, but would it have prevented it from tipping forward and dropping John into the quarry below?

The fact that it came right to the edge enhanced my reputation as an expert on fine judgement – thoroughly undeserved – and I offered up a silent prayer of thanks to whoever it is that looks after fools like me. Whether this or a subsequent take was used I don't know, but I did shorten the line for take two.

Some time ago there was a TV comedy in which Lionel Jefferies, sitting in a car, was to be propelled into a lake. It was alleged that as the car began to drift into deep water it started to sink and, because he couldn't get out he came close to drowning. I know nothing of the circumstances but it exemplified my own personal nightmare – the fear that a stunt would go wrong and endanger someone's life. Fortunately none of our effects ever did, but this is a risky business and one is often working close to the margin. There were, from time to time, a few singed eyebrows and perhaps a piece of cardboard maroon hitting an exposed leg, but nobody was ever called upon to take risks that we would not have been prepared to undertake ourselves. An unwritten rule, it was nevertheless accepted by everyone in the section Whether this attitude came from our regard for human life or whether it was because we were determined to protect our reputations I can't be sure, but in hindsight I feel our reputations may have been the over-riding factor. It's well known that if you do a good show it is soon forgotten whereas if you cause an accident or are responsible for a dangerous incident, the account of it, often much magnified and repeated, will haunt you for ever. [PUBLISHER'S NOTE: This action relates to the similarly titled *Frontier in Space*]

A   B r i d g e   T o o   D e e p

It was raining torrents as we drove home from work, and at times the windscreen wipers couldn't cope. Fortunately I'd sold my pre-war BSA and in 1959 bought a Standard Eight. The old BSA would never have survived such a downpour. In its day it was a lovely car but it had wooden floor boards and if one became careless and drove through a puddle over a quarter of an inch deep, water would spout up through the generous holes made to accommodate the gear lever, handbrake and foot pedals. Rubber seals were presumably meant to prevent this but they'd perished and the water always shot up my trouser leg. I was, therefore, instinctively wary of puddles even in the new car, but I was not prepared for the one I encountered under the railway bridge.

My two chums and I had had enough of driving through the blinding rain and were aiming to reach The Hop Pole and rest up there until the downpour abated. But a few yards before The Hop Pole a railway bridge crossed the road and its builders, wisely assuming that trains could not be expected to negotiate a hump back bridge, had lowered the road and kept the railway line level. I suspect that this decision was taken some years later when it was found that double-decker buses kept smashing into the ironwork. Whatever the reason, the road below the bridge dipped several feet. But this gave the road engineers a drainage problem – the dip, surfaced with tarmac would have filled with water when it rained.

Fortunately the river Wandle flowed nearby. For most of its length it travelled in tunnels or culverts, but here it was open between high grassy banks and so capacious drains, installed under the bridge, were able to discharge into this.

But tonight, in the atrocious downpour, the Wandle was flooding and couldn't cope. I don't know how many inches of rain had fallen that evening, but it probably amounted to trillions of gallons and the road under the bridge, no longer able to clear, had flooded. I might have decided to risk it, but in the middle of the 'puddle' was half a post office van with water almost up to its windows. We parked on the roadway, locked the car and walked the few yards to The Hop Pole along the pavement, which mercifully follows a straight line well above the dip in the road.

We hurried in from the rain looking forward to a quiet drink and a chance to relax, but we were unprepared for what we saw. Dripping crates of bottled beers had been dumped all over the place and were now forming puddles on the carpet. They covered the floor and some of the tables and a few were even stacked on the bar. Of the landlord there was no sign, but the door to the narrow flight of stairs that led down to the cellar was wide open. We heard footsteps, faltering and laboured and then, out of breath, coming up the stairs was Fred the publican's son-in-law. He staggered into the bar carrying yet another dripping crate. He was soaked to the waist and despite his occupation as a lighterman on the Thames, looked red-faced and totally buggered. He explained that the Wandle was backing up into the cellar and all the crates, bottles and barrels were floating in deep muddy water. This was serious stuff and we immediately pitched in to help, ferrying the remaining crates of beer to the bar by passing them from hand to hand up the wooden stairs. Very soon we were almost as wet as Fred.

It transpired that in the cellar there was a drain which, like the one in the road under the bridge, emptied into the Wandle. To prevent river water flowing back up during times like these, it was fitted with a rubber float which rose up and sealed the drain. It was necessary to keep this drain clear – clear of dirt, draymen's delivery notes and wayward bottle stoppers. That night it was probably jammed open by all three. The trouble was that the river hardly ever gave cause for concern and so the drain hadn't been properly maintained.

Having rescued everything except the barrels, we all four gathered in the bar. We were surrounded by crates of Guinness, Brown Ale and Oatmeal Stout but even with so much beer on hand it was difficult to feel convivial.

These days the entire cellar stock would be condemned by Health and Safety officials and because everything would be insured, the bar staff would be unlikely to attempt any sort of salvage operation; they would simply close the pub, the insurance problem would be dealt with by the brewers and we'd all pay a little more for our beer. In which case this account would read something like this: It was raining heavily so we decided to stop off at The Hop Pole. It was closed.

F i r e p o w e r

Every generation invents toys and games to entertain its children. The Victorians indulged their offspring with hoops and whip tops, or dolls and cardboard theatres. Today we have computer games, television cartoons and mobile phones. In the twenties and thirties, when Jack and I were youngsters, we had the yo-yo, model trains and fretwork. And we also had fireworks! Well yes, fireworks had been around for centuries, but we had the means of making them. The ingredients: saltpetre, powdered charcoal and sulphur and even mealed gunpowder could all be bought at the local oil shop, and in the library there was that famous manual – the illustrated instruction book written by Alan Brock, *Pyrotechnics: The History and Art of Firework Making.*

Brock's book gave formulae for coloured fire and flash powder – and it gave the ingredients for rockets and their methods of construction. It even gave instructions for making elaborate set pieces. It seems a pity that modern children can't have access to that book and that wonderful hobby – how sad to think that they can't experience the esoteric pleasure of setting fire to their father's shed or melting the tyres on their auntie's bicycle.

When I was twelve years of age, unfettered by modern health and safety legislation, I looked forward to bonfire night and the opportunity to show everyone my arsenal of exciting devices. For weeks beforehand I had manufactured exotic pyrotechnics including my Roman candle specials. These were made in cardboard tubes acquired from the local draper's shop and measured about two feet in length. Sawn in half, these tubes were ideal for my purposes, but because my meagre resources wouldn't permit me to waste money trying them out I unknowingly adopted the showbiz creed that they'd be 'alright on the night' and my masterpieces were packed away untested. In the event they invariably produced more flame and smoke than colourful display, but intent on making them burn for as long as possible I made the intervals between the coloured ejections boringly long. To produce the coloured lights I would often cannibalise shop fireworks, extracting their vital components and assembling them in my long-lasting tubes. The cheers, oohs and aahs, which followed each manifestation probably ranged from the sympathetic to the ironic, but I was too besotted with my own creations to notice.

To improve the visual effect I fixed the tubes high up in the branches of a large horse chestnut tree that grew beside the garden wall and because I was older than my brother I gave him the job of applying the match. This meant climbing the tree in the dark (which he could do with ease) but unfortunately he never seemed to grasp the fact that it is easier to climb a tree with your eyes open than it is to descend with them tightly shut. I admit that when your night vision has been completely destroyed by a magnesium candle erupting four inches from your face it doesn't matter a damn whether you climb down with your eyes open or closed, but I'd assumed he would have had the sense to know that blue touch paper, even when it was grey and made from newspaper, should always be ignited at the end furthest from the firework. Now that time has healed the scars I think he would agree that making dodgy fireworks was far more rewarding than pressing buttons on a computer keyboard.

Regrettably, Brock's book can no longer be found on library shelves but perhaps that's no bad thing. I imagine the assistants in Boots the chemists would be confounded by a request for strontium nitrate or copper sulphate. The demise of the old fashioned oil shop and its ready supply of raw materials has undoubtedly safeguarded the nation's garden sheds and bicycle tyres but, for God's sake, where's the fun?

En passant you might be wondering why we could buy gunpowder in a London oil shop. One answer lies in the construction of the domestic wash boiler, or 'copper' as it was usually called. These were built in the servants' quarters of the larger London houses and were constructed of brick. For boiling the water they had a large copper bowl which was heated by a small coal fire underneath. Unfortunately the flue pipe was at the back and could not be swept with brushes and rods without first removing the copper bowl, a tedious and filthy business that was put off for as long as possible. However, the men in our street had cracked the problem. The trick was to buy two pennyworth of gunpowder, wrap it in newspaper, light it, close the iron door and stand with a broom, holding it shut. The soot either fell back down the flue pipe or was shot into the sky.

My father usually undertook this chore, and one Sunday lunchtime, returning bright-eyed from The George, he decided it was time to clean the copper. My mother, doubtful of his ability to do the job safely, didn't dare say anything because she had been nagging him for weeks to do it. Whether he had bought the gunpowder earlier or borrowed some from a neighbour, I wouldn't know, but he was confident that he was going to make a thorough job of it. Wrapping the powder tightly in newspaper he lit the bundle and stood with his broom against the fire door. He then got up from the floor where he had been thrown by the blast and wondered where his broom had gone. Looking up he saw that it was suspended in the shattered glass of the scullery door. My mother, tight-lipped, didn't say a word but set about removing a layer of soot from a bowl of custard that had been set down in the scullery to cool. My brother and I were the only ones at the dining table that day.

And now, Jack and I had a Home Office licence authorising us to make fireworks and use explosives, albeit with many stipulations. But we were actually licensed to make fireworks – we could hardly believe our good fortune. No longer did we have to hide our activities from grown-ups or apologise to our maiden aunts – or even explain to Headmasters why the toilets were belching orange smoke.

But our work in television was demand led; we had to develop techniques which would meet the requirements of producers and writers; if a script called for a volcano it was our job to create it, and the more skilful and experienced we became, the more the production teams would expect us to do. We didn't mind of course, because life for everyone in the early days of television was a challenge.

To simulate a fire scene in the studio necessitated using smoke, and here we came into conflict with the engineers. They were concerned by the effect smoke had on the electronic cameras which, because they had to be cooled by an internal blower, sucked in air from the studio. This air was directed at the contacts, transformers and the very expensive image-forming tubes. Should the air be contaminated with smoke, the cameras had to be dismantled, cleaned and tested which, understandably, the engineers didn't care for at all. During an acrimonious debate resulting from my trying to smoke up a set and the cameramen trying to stop me, I suggested that the cameras should be fitted with smoke filters. I pointed out that viewers paid their licence fees, not to protect the engineer's bloody equipment, but to watch a programme. If this called for smoke then smoke they were entitled to have. This didn't go down at all well and the engineers threatened that if I persisted they would remove their cameras from the studio. Faced with a walk-out I retreated to the prop room where, in a fury, I stuck a wedge of cotton wool on a batten of wood, wrote the word SMOKE on a caption card which I pinned underneath and returned to the studio where I stood it against a settee. The engineers didn't even smile.

On location, fire scenes were much less restricted. Unless they took place in rented or domestic buildings there was almost no limit to what we could do. Conditions on location were better even than those in a movie studio where the reliable film cameras were airtight, and if the cameraman was able to breathe for the duration of the take it was considered safe to carry on. Most of the film cameramen wore immaculate suits to mark their lofty status, and these absorbed the smell of paraffin and burning wood like olfactory blotting paper. Even on location, they seldom deigned to wear sensible clothing lest, God forbid, they might have looked like special effects riff-raff. But there was a price to pay. At the end of the day we would toss our smelly work clothes into the boot of a car whereas the smart suited and odoriferous cameramen would often have to travel home with the car windows open.

One of our greatest problems was the constancy of smoke. When a change of angle was called for we had to ensure that the smoke looked the same as in the preceding shot. Too much or too little and the change of viewpoint would be distracting. The one thing we could rely on for consistency was the fire produced by flame forks. These were an arrangement of copper tubes terminating in a variety of nozzles and were fed from gas cylinders. They could be adjusted to any degree of fierceness simply by turning a knob, and unlike practical fires could be shut down instantly. This made them safe to use in the studio. Flame forks were handheld and could be employed for fire sequences under any conditions or wherever they were staged. They were used in buildings, vehicles and boats. They could be fixed below windows (so that from outside it would appear that the building was ablaze) and for local effects behind furniture, and, providing the operator stayed with them, they could be kept burning for as long as a sequence lasted. Outdoors, supplemented with smoke canisters, they could produce the illusion that vast areas were on fire.

One ploy (rather overused I'm ashamed to say) was to crouch below a camera and waggle a flame fork in front of the lens to create the impression that there was a widespread conflagration. Supported by smoke and a few small patches of burning material further back in the scene this provided a clear area in which actors could perform safely and yet appear to be in mortal danger. Flame forks were the mainstay of all our fire sequences and I believe are still in use today.

The constancy of smoke was not the only problem with fire sequences; we had to be aware of continuity in other directions. During a large fire scene many items became charred, blistered or smoke-blackened making it difficult to recreate pristine conditions for retakes. Where curtains or drapes had to burn it became something of a nightmare. To ensure that they weren't seen to change in length from shot to shot meant that we often had to hang new curtains and pre-burn them to the same degree. A fire sequence that might last for no more than two or three minutes in screen time could often take a day or more to re-rig and shoot.

Flickering flame effects are employed in the studio where 'flames' from a log fire are required to illuminate the walls and ceiling or, perhaps, flicker across the faces of actors sitting around the hearth. For this effect we made a crude device which we called a flame drum. However, when I refer to it as crude it was considerably more sophisticated than the device used by the studio electricians who until then had created a flickering effect by waving strips of rag fastened to a length of batten in front of an orange light.

Our flame drum consisted of a large cylinder of black paper with cut-out slots, fastened to two wooden sticks in the form of a cross to hold it open. With a strong light shining through them, the angled slots, passing each other gave the effect of flames moving upwards at different speeds. It's an old idea and is used even now to simulate flames at the back of some electric fires, but our achievement was to make it run all on its own without human supervision or the use of an electric motor. We simply hung the drum on a very long length of thread which we tied to the studio gantry. The thread was wound up by rotating the cylinder in a reverse direction and letting it unwind on its own. Winding it up was an extremely tedious job and took forever, but fortuitously, when it unwound its natural rotation produced just the right speed of flicker to look like flames and we employed it in many different ways. Used with a combination of smoke machine and flame forks it was possible to create the effects of burning rooms and with actors rushing around it would look very convincing.

We were now using Taylor-Hobson smoke machines, designed and built by an engineering company and which, unlike our original brass contraption, were able to run safely with a minimum of supervision. These machines contained cylinders of carbon dioxide gas to pressurise the oil and some of the CO_2 gas was diverted to the nozzle where it quenched any flames which could have turned the machine into a flame thrower.

Another of our later discoveries was to use charcoal tablets (the type used in ecclesiastical incense burners) which we would place on sheets of asbestos or in tin lids. These tablets were used to provide areas of local smoke and combined with pieces of fire-lighter could be used safely in the studios. Once lit the charcoal tablets would slowly become red hot and would remain like that for up to thirty minutes. They burned without producing smoke, but when primed with a few drops of machine oil they would smoke gamely for anything up to ten minutes. When the smoke tailed off and the oil was used up it required only a few more drops to start the whole thing going again. Charcoal tablets could be positioned anywhere and were placed under domestic 'coal' fires (gas burners and plaster coal) in open hearths and kitchen ranges They were also used to imply that equipment was overheating and in studio 'roof-top' chimneys.

Another discovery was that a red hot charcoal tablet seen under normal lighting does not *look* red hot, only in the dark are they seen to be glowing. To assume therefore that they had gone out because they looked grey and ashy – and to pick them up with bare fingers – was an intensely emotional experience.

A technique which we pioneered on *The Forsyte Saga* was the outdoor set. I know that it had been used from the earliest days of movie making but it was a novelty for television and seemed jolly clever to us. The sequence was one in which Eric Porter (Soames Forsyte) had to rescue valuable paintings hanging on the walls of his burning library. Knowing that if we staged this in the television studio it would be limited to the amount of smoke and flame we could use (too much of either would set off the sprinklers) I arranged for the library set to be built on the lot at Ealing Studios. Here I could safely burn as much of the scenery and as many of the props as required. Fortunately the fire happens at night which made it practical to film in the open air after dark. The set had no ceiling and was open to the sky, furthermore, it was constructed of only three walls. This meant that the front was wide open and should the fire get out of hand, Eric was free to stroll off the set. His role called for him to tear the paintings from the walls and, after rushing across the room, throw them from a window (theoretically upstairs) to the servants in the grounds below. There was no window there of course, being in the non-existent wall, but all Eric was required to do was to hurry past the camera shouting something like 'Look out below, you dozey lot. If you drop 'em or damage them I'll have you flogged!' To ensure a full measure of drama I held a flame fork below the camera which I carefully placed in Eric's path. His comments were pithy. 'You Bastard!' he said. 'If you make me jump over that bloody thing again I'll smash the next something painting over your something or other head – and when you're lying on the floor I shall kick you in the somethings'. I gathered from this that he was perhaps less interested in dramatic realism than saving himself from cremation. I took the hint – perhaps he had not forgiven me for trying to kipper him in a smoke scene during the *Age of Kings* at Stratford on Avon. Funny, but he was always a friendly bloke in the pub.

One of the most bizarre events I can recall occurred during the filming of a burning building. We were on location in an empty house in a road near Ealing Studios. Because it was a day time sequence we were using photocine flares laid in trays of sand to produce an intense glow inside the top rooms. These flares produce a bright white light and a large amount of smoke, but to boost the smoke, which had to pour from the windows, I supplemented the cineflares with smoke canisters. The cineflares had a duration of only two and half minutes so nobody could afford to hang about. While my assistant lit those in the lower rooms I raced from the rooms above where, lighting each flare as I came down we would both exit the building more or less at the same time. It remained only for me to yell to the director to start filming before hiding outside at the back of the house. As I came down the stairs two at a time I saw my assistant go out slightly ahead of me and, as arranged, leave the door open for my exit. I could not believe my eyes therefore when I saw a man and a woman emerge from a back room holding a piece of paper. One of the essential safeguards when filling a house with smoke, is to ensure that the property has been vacated, which I had done. I had gone from room to room opening and closing every door making sure the crew had left. When the place was entirely clear I went upstairs calling down to my assistant to light his flares; at the top of the house I did the same. So where these people had come from I hadn't the faintest idea. The possibility that they were ghosts briefly crossed my mind, but surely, ghosts don't cough or wipe their eyes. Hustling them into the garden I asked them what they were doing, and by way of explanation I was shown the sheet of paper. It was an estate agent's leaflet and an appointment to view. They spoke very little English so it was no good questioning them about dates or times or explaining that we were filming a burning building, but I did wonder what they thought. Was it 'strange people these English, they use big joss sticks that smell of tar'?

R a i s i n g   T o w e r   B r i d g e

It was a dull Sunday morning in Central London and we stood on Tower Bridge looking down at the river. The area was strangely quiet – no traffic and no pedestrians – there was nothing on the entire bridge except the two of us leaning on the handrail and wondering what it would be like. Somewhere a bell rang and instinctively we clutched the hand rail. Too late now to pull out. Slowly, noiselessly, we drifted apart. This wasn't at all what I'd expected, I'd assumed we'd go up. But we were apparently sliding sideways.

Earlier that day Ian and I had arrived in a van which was now parked on the road at the city end of the bridge. Our team had unloaded a seventy foot long banner which was tightly folded and trussed with string. There were also two specially designed metal foot plates and enough stout rope to reach from one end of the bridge to the other; these things were now all in place. The rope was fastened to the two bascules and the foot plates had been bolted to the balustrade. The team were lined up behind the barrier and were standing around, laughing and joking and awaiting events. With them were several policemen and I wondered now if I should have booked an ambulance crew and a team of trained skin divers. Perhaps the policemen had a boat somewhere or were trained to carry out resuscitation. It didn't look like it; they didn't seem to be at all concerned. I doubted if they even had a first aid kit between them and I could see no sign of a boat – or even a raft.

We were filming an opening sequence for *Not Only… But Also* starring Peter Cook and Dudley Moore. In an inebriated moment one of them must have said: 'I know – let's stand on Tower Bridge while it's going up!' And the other may have replied 'What a splendid idea and let's have a banner which unfurls revealing the name of the show.' And as their visual effects designer, here I was on this Sunday morning, testing my theory to see if these things could be achieved. And not only had I to figure out how it could be done but I also had to try it out for myself in order to make sure it would be safe for Pete and Dud.

Ian and I really were ascending now. As the two arms of the bridge were slowly raised our angle to the roadway changed and we had to alter our positions on the stepped foot plates. These footholds were made of heavy sheet metal and had been fastened to the cast iron balustrade bordering the pavement. They should have been strong enough to support our weight and I'd stood on them in the workshop, but out here they seemed pathetically flimsy.

Looking at the Thames far below I could see that between the stone foundations the river was surging and frothing like a white water maelstrom; it looked decidedly ugly. On the other side of me and now almost as far away as the river, was the section of road that doesn't move. Composed of steel and tarmac with, I suspect, a foot or more of reinforced concrete in between, it looked even more uninviting than the water. Were I to fall from my position at the tip of the bascule there would be nothing to halt my descent before a final squidgy bounce finished a promising career.

But something was wrong. The safety belt that anchored me to the iron balustrade was pulling my body into the shape of a butcher's hook. I clung to the handrail, not daring to let go but desperately wishing I could unclip the belt and move it to a higher position (not a good idea really and one that would certainly have invalidated my insurance policy). With my hands now at shoulder height and my waist pulled at right angles I rethought my design. We needed longer safety belts – about ten feet longer if my tortured spine was anything to go by. From that height Ian and I should have been enjoying a magnificent view across London, but agonisingly restrained by the belts we were wholly disinterested. It was then that I remembered our schedule; we were marooned up here while the Tower Bridge engineers carried out their weekly inspection of the motors and hinges of the lifting mechanism. I recalculated my chances of survival. I could die slowly and horribly from a fractured spine or I could unclip my belt and leap into the Thames. Or of course I could just go mad. In the end I did none of these things. I let go of the handrail and hung limply in my harness.

Catching sight of the flapping sailcloth below I could see that the banner had unfurled automatically as planned. Neatly folded it had been hung below the bridge, trussed in loops of thin string. It was supported by the thick rope which had a loop in the middle also tied up with string. I'd worked out that with the ends fastened securely to the balustrades on either side the strings would snap as the two bascules rose into the air and the banner would unfurl and hang artistically between the two raised arms. They did and it had. I was pleased with the success of this part of the operation but why hadn't I thought more about the bloody belts? I was very thankful that I'd set up this test before subjecting Peter and Dudley to a similar fate – they really would have loved me.

After what seemed hours Ian and I felt a slight movement and were going down. As our tortured waists were released from purgatory and our feet shuffled back to their original positions we came together in the centre of the bridge. I saw that Ian's complexion had undergone a marked change, a condition brought about not by altitude sickness, but by suffering a restricted – blood flow in the spinal area. I should have apologised to him, but there wasn't time – we had something important to deal with, albeit something I had anticipated (Well, I had to get something right). Small vessels move freely under the bridge at all times and our unfurled banner was now hanging down in the shipping lane, ready to snatch the radar and navigation lights from any passing masthead. Such was the stoutness of our rope it would have dismasted all but the largest vessel – in which case it would probably have wrenched away one or more sections of the cast iron balustrade. I visualised insurance claims with so many noughts that the BBC would have to abandon its entire summer schedule. Ian and I shouted urgently for the team to bring some lines but they were already responding. Galloping along the road with coils and hooks they quickly and efficiently hoisted the banner onto the bridge rolling it up and tying it into a bundle. I signalled the all clear and the police released the traffic to travel once again across the bridge.

It had been an amazing experience and one I suspect that has been shared by very few other people. We thought of forming the 'Bascule Up Club' and having a special tie made with a discreet emblem of Tower Bridge woven in silk but on reflection a human backbone shaped like the letter S would have been more appropriate.

To film the sequence on the bridge it was decided that the camera must be situated in the middle of the river – which meant hiring a vessel. The producer opted for something quite big in order that the deck would be stable and that the camera would not bob up and down. As so often happens the plus is cancelled out by the minus. Because of the fast flow of water under the bridge the vessel could not hold station and it drifted away downstream. At the same time the cameraman zoomed in, the one cancelling the other. Furthermore black smoke from its single funnel blew towards the bridge and occasionally blotted out the picture. Unfortunately, the official time table governing the raising and lowering of the bridge was inflexible and there was no hope of a second take.

N o t O n l y . . . B u t A l s o

Starring Peter Cook and Dudley Moore, *Not Only… But Also* was an unusual type of light entertainment programme and the Tower Bridge opening title device was but one of their imaginative ideas. *Not Only* became an immediate favourite with the public and was quickly elevated to the level of 'cult' status. Moore and Cook had been part of the very successful stage show *Beyond the Fringe* so they weren't new to show business but now, unsupported by the two other members, Alan Bennett and Jonathan Miller, they formed a perfect double act. They're probably best remembered for their characters Pete and Dud, the two shabbily dressed customers of a seedy pub who narrated their outrageous fantasies over pints of beer. 'Sophia Loren came to me last night. I found her trying to climb in a window calling Petter, Petter I lurve you.' Much of the beer was spilled as Dudley tried to mask his giggles at Peter's adlibs and unscheduled deviations from the script. Fortunately for me however, Peter and Dudley indulged their real life fantasies by dreaming up more and more outrageous ideas for the programme.

One of these involved launching themselves from the deck of the aircraft carrier *Ark Royal* while playing a piano and singing their closing song *Now is the Time to Say Goodbye*. Having entrusted me with the Tower

Bridge sequence they presumably thought that I could cope with such trivialities as using the hydraulic catapult on the *Ark Royal* to fling a piano hundreds of yards out to sea. And so it was arranged that Ian and I should accompany Dudley and Peter and the production team when they were flown out to the *Ark Royal* which was cruising at sea. We were taken by helicopter from the naval air base at Yeovilton, a flight for which we had to don full survival gear and memorise instructions on what to do if the helicopter was forced to ditch. I hoped this wouldn't happen because the instructions seemed very complicated and for someone not conversant with naval terms I would have found it easier to drown.

We landed smoothly on the flight deck and saw for the first time the enormous size of the *Ark*. It was more like a town than a vessel and I, who until then had regarded the Navy as a load of poncy sailors who drank pink gin (a libation at which even Beynon-Lewis drew the line) was forced to reconsider my opinion.

We were shown to our quarters – two cabins six floors down – and invited to take drinks in the officers' mess when we had divested ourselves of the survival gear. This, we realised, was a civilised life and in honour of the Navy I chose to drink pink gin. I didn't become a convert but as an alcoholic stimulant it certainly acted fast.

The planned sequence on the *Ark Royal* called for Peter and Dudley at their piano to be brought up from the hangar below on the huge aircraft lift. They would then go into their closing routine singing and playing *Now is the Time to Say Goodbye* in a tight shot after which the director would change to a long shot showing their dummy counterparts at a piano being fired into the ocean. Now, of course, I wasn't allowed anywhere near the controls of the hydraulic catapult; my task was simply to supply the dummies and the piano – and watch from the side lines. All the tricky technical stuff was in the hands of the Navy which was quite a challenge for the officer in charge. Because the catapult was designed to deal with fighter aircraft weighing tons (against which our piano and the dummies were the equivalent of a paper bag) it meant that the whole set up had to be recalibrated. The operation went without a hitch, which was just as well, because there was no contingency for a second take. A motor launch was used to recover the remains of the piano and the dummies because the piano, floating level with the surface, would have endangered yachts and small boats and the dummies would certainly have been mistaken for dead bodies.

As much as I enjoyed organising this gag it was the *Ark Royal* that was the real star of the show. Everything Ian and I saw was impressive. The huge aircraft hangar below decks, the sight of a Buccaneer or a Phantom with jets going at full blast being catapulted from the deck and the sheer smooth speed with which the *Ark* itself travelled through the water. The Navy gave us a tour and showed us the bakery, the enormous food preparation areas, the laundries, the cinemas, the sports centres. I likened it to a town, but it would be a good town that could rival the facilities on the *Ark Royal*. And of course, it was a fighting ship with all the equipment and armament that was required to make it so.

Ian and I were privileged to have spent even such a short time on that amazing vessel and would have welcomed the chance to extend our stay. But having completed our part of the job we were returned to dry land. Once again we and the team were to board a Sea King for the journey back to shore and after thanking those who had helped us and been so hospitable we accepted a final pink gin and headed for Yeovilton.

Dudley Moore had a passion for Marmite sandwiches and following our flight and transference to the coach that was to take us to the building were we would divest ourselves of our survival gear, he produced a loaf of bread, a packet of butter and a jar of Marmite. His idea was to make sandwiches for us all to occupy the time on the rather boring coach ride. But, unexpectedly, the coach drew up at our destination. For a reason none of us could comprehend, the coach that had taken all of twenty minutes on the way out now, after only three or four minutes had come back to the same place. Poor Dudley was left holding a mountain of sliced bread, buttery knives, paper napkins and an open jar of Marmite which he had to gather up, repack in his case and scramble off the coach.

I have only happy memories of *Not Only… But Also* but there was one occasion when I saw what the pressures of writing and performing can do to a person. We were filming on a sports ground in Hangar Lane, London and having nothing to do at that point I went to the bar in the club house. It was an uninspiring wooden structure, ill-lit and barren but marginally better than the field and the weather outside, which was miserably cold and grey. Peter was already in there, smoking and holding a half-filled glass. He accepted my offer of a top up but without enthusiasm and I joined him on the wooden bench seat. He seemed depressed. Within minutes the PA came in and told Peter that the director needed at least two pages of new dialogue. Peter looked at him blankly and picked up some sheets of paper while with the other hand he groped for a fresh cigarette (there was one already burning in the ashtray). As he struggled with the task of thinking up funny lines in such a depressing atmosphere he looked completely disorientated and seemed almost on the verge of tears. When the PA left I went too. I wanted to say something to Peter, but I sensed that words of sympathy, even flippant ones, would not have helped. Turning to shut the door I saw him sitting there alone, staring at the blank sheets of paper.

D a v e   A l l e n

Some comedians and personalities present themselves on TV as charming and lovable; so amiable do they appear that the viewer believes they must be the friendliest people in the world. In my experience the reverse is often true; the more overtly friendly they appear the greater the likelihood that they are mean, petulant, querulous and spiteful. On a scale of one to ten of human virtues, I rank the worst of these as being double zero – lower even than dog's droppings. Those of you hoping that I am about to name names will be disappointed because despite the urge to tell all I feel that it would be unfair for me to defame anyone, living or dead, on the grounds that in my opinion they – are totally repulsive.

I was nearly always supported in my assessment of these people by the makeup girls, costume designers and assistant floor managers, all of whom had to endure impossible demands and spiteful sarcasm without being able to complain. In later years I became the assistant director for a German pop-music show and found that some of the visiting UK pop groups were just as objectionable.

Which brings me to the people I have written about here. Whilst not prepared to name the troublesome ones I have no hesitation in naming the nice ones: all the people, comedians, actors and personalities mentioned in this book are, or were, genuinely nice people. They were quick to show their appreciation when things went well and kept quiet when things were going badly. Conversely I don't want you to think that because I haven't mentioned a famous performer that he or she must be on my hit list; the fact is that I can only talk about those people with whom Jack and I worked or came into contact with.

As our section grew in number, he and I were able to select our own programmes and arrange the schedules. If we didn't relish the prospect of spending hours in the studio with actors who were boorish or directors who were intolerant we would allocate the programme to one of our assistants. We did this without compunction, reasoning that they had to gain experience as we had done and anyway, at their job interviews hadn't they assured us that they were willing to take on anything?

And that is why I chose to work with Dave Allen. On or off stage he was a genuinely funny comedian and a nice chap. He didn't invite his television audience to love him, all he wanted was for people to share the joke and laugh with him. Consequently he surrounded himself with a supporting cast of likeminded people, Jackie Clarke, Robert East, Peter Hawkins, Michael Sharvell Martin and others of a similar temperament. His director, Peter Whitmore, having been responsible for many editions of *Crackerjack* was the perfect man to direct that sort of sketch show and he in turn wanted a crew in tune with the quirky and irreverent Dave Allen type of comedy.

Because the sketches and quick-fire gags invariably included scenes that couldn't be recorded in the studio, much of the show was filmed on location. However there were a number of sequences that had to recorded in the studio and for that reason we were allocated time either at Ealing Studios or at Television Centre prior to transmission. Many of the sketches in the *Dave Allen Show* ended with a bang, calling for explosions of every kind. I was particularly fond of the running gag of 'el Presidente' in which Dave played the part of a peasant intent upon getting rid of the tyrannical president. These sketches ended with el Presidente escaping all harm while Dave suffered the consequences of his own bungled assassination attempts. Quite often these explosive pay-offs were tricky and had to be rehearsed and tested before being taken on location – an operation which would normally have meant booking time on an army range. However, because I lived in a rural area, I was able to carry out some of the tests in the fields surrounding my house without arousing complaints from neighbours.

One ingenious writer devised a sketch in which Dave was to swing the bomb, Bolas fashion, on a long line. It fails to hit el Presidente but the cord, still travelling in a circular motion and coming to the end of its length rewinds, wrapping itself around the luckless peasant's body. The bomb, with a smoking fuse, finishes up hanging from his waist and, because he is now trussed like a chicken, he can only react with resignation. 'Kerboooomm!' and the unlucky Dave disappears in a cloud of smoke. When I tried this out in a field, whirling the line around my head, it worked perfectly just as the writer said it would. Whether he had drawn his inspiration from those steer-roping cowboys one so often saw in the movies or whether the idea had come to him in the middle of the night I wouldn't know, but it worked. To test it I used a block of wood on fifteen feet of cord and whirling it around my head I paid out the line as far as it would go. Then, dropping my arms by my sides, I awaited events. The line under the momentum of the wooden block rewound itself neatly around my body. However, because each revolution shortened the line, the block speeded up. It must have been doing fifty miles an hour when it crashed into the back of my head.

For those who wonder how you can blow up somebody without causing them harm, the technique used is known as a jump cut. The sequence in which a bomb explodes and the character disappears works like this. The camera records the first half of the sequence and is then switched off allowing the performer to walk away. He is replaced by a pyrotechnic and the camera, without being moved, is restarted. After a second or two the 'bomb' is exploded and the two parts of the film, with all the superfluous frames removed are spliced together, showing what appears to be continuous action.

I did this for a sequence in which Dave, as an army officer, is marching a small group of soldiers along a country lane; he is looking for a suitable place in which to instruct them in the technique of grenade throwing. Coming across an old stone wall he decides this would be an ideal spot because they can take cover behind it. The grenades are dummies, so knowing they will neither endanger a nearby cottage nor damage anything in the garden, Dave goes through the sequence of actions ending up by directing them to lob their Mills bombs at 'that old shed thing over there'.

The old shed thing is an outdoor privy, inside of which is Ronnie Brody, playing the part of an old countryman. He is comfortably installed, trousers down and reading a newspaper, when the Mills bombs thump against the door. In close up we see one of them roll under the door and, because this was a comedy sketch the bomb that rolls inside is a real one and blows the privy to pieces. Ronnie is seen, still seated, his clothing in tatters holding a flaming newspaper.

Because we were filming this sequence in a real cottage garden it would have been impractical to blow the lightweight scenic privy apart with pyrotechnics or practical explosives and so I devised a method of pulling it apart using fishing lines and bungee elastic. The thin nylon fishing lines were knotted together inside the privy and below the knot I hung a powerful magnesium flash. This, when fired, destroyed the knot allowing all the component parts, the roof, the sides and the door, to fly away. Ronnie was no longer inside of course, but was standing with the rest of us watching the demolition. It was a typical Dave Allen gag and very much the sort of thing the viewer enjoyed; it could be repeated in a thousand different ways and still produce a hearty chuckle.

I never met any of the writers, but their ingenuity on *The Dave Allen Show* was impressive. Writers get far too little credit for their contributions and yet it is their work and their imagination that is the basis for all drama, comedy and documentary TV – even the newsreaders speak lines written for them by someone else.

Some of the sketches for which I was responsible gave me particular satisfaction. The tall, stained glass church window that had to shatter into a thousand pieces when a female chorister sang a sustained high note – and Dave as King Arthur ending up impaled on Excalibur, the sword that rises mysteriously from a lake. But the most memorable sketch, and one that has been shown several times since, was the Stonehenge sequence in which the huge stones tumble like dominoes when Dave yawns and leans against one of them. The imitation Sarsen stones, ten feet high and made of timber and hardboard dressed with sculptured expanded polystyrene, were delivered to the location field and laid on the grass in rows. Each was hinged to a large base plate and it was left to my colleague, Bob Slatford and I, with a day in hand, to erect them in the familiar circle. One or two were bridged by stones laid on the top, but the others stood singly, much like the ones at the real Stonehenge. I dared not rely on the 'domino effect' to topple them, it would have been far too risky. This was a gag that had to work first time and while it had to look as if each stone fell when struck by its neighbour it involved quite a complicated rig. Each stone was pulled over by a nylon fish line and heavy industrial elastic, and was released by a detonator fired by the stone before it. It took a long time to set the stones in the right orientation and to work out the distance each must fall before the detonator restraining the next one fired. But we had a day in hand so we were able to work things out without too much hassle. It was a good day in every respect. The weather was sunny and the larks sang in a blue sky and all was right with our world. There was even a good pub not far away.

We left the field that evening feeling satisfied that we'd done a good job and as we drove off I stopped the car to have a look at our handiwork standing proudly on the skyline; had this been Salisbury plain people might easily have confused it with the real thing.

The following morning, Bob and I got up early, had breakfast and drove to the site. The weather was still fine and we looked forward to an easy day and a lunch in that pleasant country pub. But somehow or other we had missed the field. I stopped and looked around – it looked like the same field and I was sure we were in the right area, but where was Stonehenge. We found the farm track we'd gone up the day before but of our imposing monument there was no sign – until we reached the field. The stones lay scattered around as if some giant hand had reached down and played skittles with them. We couldn't believe it. The bases that had been fixed to the ground with lengths of steel rod were now torn up and the lines that had been cut to length and tied off to ring eyes were broken and tangled. The detonators and batteries were, of course, safely in my car, but who could have perpetrated such wanton vandalism? We were due to film that afternoon so we had to move swiftly. Everything had to be set up again from scratch.

Half an hour later, in response to a frantic phone call to the PA, the scene-van drove up carrying the tall step ladders we didn't think we'd need again. 'Did you hear the wind last night?' asked Charlie. 'We wondered if it would have affected your stuff.' said Fred.

I said that Dave Allen was a nice bloke and one example of his thoughtfulness remains in my memory. We had been filming at Ealing Studios and the place was a mess. Broken pieces of expanded polystyrene, burnt wood and piles of peat littered the floor and as it was our responsibility to clear it up ('You made the mess and it's your job to get rid of it' maintained the scene crew before they all trooped off to the pub) we had to thoroughly clean the stage. Everybody except Dave Allen had vanished leaving Jack and me to deal with the problem. Picking up a broom, Dave stayed behind to help us.

G i a n t   S p i d e r s

Doctor Who appeared on my schedule once more, this time it was Jon Pertwee's swansong *Planet of the Spiders*. A number of spiders featured in this story and several of them had to be animated. It was decided that they should have a leg span of about eighteen inches with a body length of approximately eight or nine inches.

They were designed and made by Ian Scoones and myself from expanded polystyrene carved into the body shape. Aluminium wires were inserted to form the legs, and the wires were then wrapped in glue-soaked tissues to fatten the leg sections. This left the joints free so that the legs could be bent into the correct postures.

After painting, bristles cut from a paint brush were applied to the legs to simulate black hairs. The effect of this was to make them look horrifyingly realistic. As usual, when making props of this kind, we had studied photographs of the real thing to ensure that our spiders looked authentic and not at all like the ones bought in joke shops.

Many people have a loathing of spiders and the effect of our monsters on various people in the studio was quite remarkable. Some people would not go near them while others even believed them to be real spiders that had been stuffed – despite the fact that no real spiders of that size have ever existed.

A fact worth investigating is the therapeutic effect that making such spiders might have on people afflicted with arachnophobia. I found that after making them, my own normal distaste for spiders evaporated entirely and I was able to handle any indigenous spider without adverse effect. Even now when they land on my clothing or in my hair I experience no feelings of revulsion whatsoever.

For sequences in which the spiders had to move, we had two methods. Spiders that were static but had to flex their legs were worked by hand from beneath, the special legs being hinged at the body. The other method was to employ Boris the walking spider made by Mat Irvine. The legs had independent links fixed to a crankshaft which, driven by an electric motor, made them move alternatively up and down. Locomotion was achieved by fitting small motor-driven wheels below the body. Up and running this fine prop reproduced the effect of a scurrying spider to perfection.

S o m e   M o t h e r s !

Despite his successes in such stage shows as *Billy*, *Barnum* and *The Phantom of the Opera*, television viewers remember Michael Crawford chiefly as the hapless Frank Spencer in the series *Some Mothers do 'ave 'em*, but this is to be expected when, proportionally, few people go to the theatre and television audiences are counted in millions.

I came to the show without really knowing who Michael Crawford was or whether the script was funny. However, I did know who Michael Mills was and I knew him to be a hard man, a director not given to suffering fools gladly. Perhaps it was Jack's experience on the Scottish location that made him hand the series of six programmes so enthusiastically to me.

In the end I was to be responsible for many of the programmes, other episodes being taken over by my colleagues as the availability of personnel and schedules dictated. Some of the classic episodes were undertaken by Peter Day who, as our first assistant, had plenty of experience and was both imaginative and capable.

The scripts varied in the number of effects required as well as their complexity. While some merely called for simple props others demanded elaborate and often dangerous stunts. In one sequence where Frank, as a learner driver, had to drive a car along a jetty, through a steel barrier and into the sea, was almost certainly more complicated than viewers realised. But the episode in which a chicken house collapsed was easy to make and child's play to operate. Such is the nature of visual humour that each drew an equal amount of happy appreciation from the studio audience.

In the episode with the chickens, our task was simply to provide a wooden shed that collapsed. Frank was supposed to be looking after a neighbour's hens, but unsurprisingly his caretaking soon develops into a major disaster. The chicken shed was made of lightweight components that had to fall apart in an extended routine. First the ends fell out, then the front fell in and finally the roof collapsed. Frank, who has gone inside to sort things out, is left with his head sticking out of a ventilator. The studio audience, as well as laughing at Frank's futile attempts at poultry keeping, might have wondered how the destruction was achieved. It seemed to be operated by remote control, but in fact the collapse was achieved by my colleague, Bob Slatford, and I who were hidden inside the shed and simply had to push and pull it apart.

Bob and I had gone in there before the audience entered the studio and now, silently awaited our cue. Our first action was to push one of the hens out of the small door in the front. It flew out accompanied by loose feathers which we flung out after it. Next we pushed out the ends and released more of the birds. Finally we pushed out the front and dropped the roof over Frank's head. Of course the audience laughed, they were enjoying Frank's inept handling of the situation – this was exactly the sort of thing Michael did so expertly. Bob and I, trapped under the front, were not as fortunate as the chickens and had to stay there until the end of the scene allowed us to creep out. Prudently we took the cardboard boxes that had housed the chickens, hoping they might have contained an egg or two, but we were unlucky.

The chicken shed was a simple prop involving only a few elementary catches and hinges, but the presentation was the important thing. Had the audience seen us enter the shed, the gag would have been signalled; they would have known we were there and would have been waiting to see what we were going to do.

The aforementioned car driving into the sea was a different matter. A prerequisite was that for this very expensive and dangerous stunt, the vehicle should stay afloat. It was not something that we had tackled before and in order to ensure that it would ride the waves and not plummet like a rock, we filled every available space in the car with aerated foam. Door panels were removed and the cavities filled with the chemically foaming compound; we squirted it under the seats and around the engine and even packed the wheel arches with the stuff. But nothing short of total immersion would prove whether it really would stay afloat. Accordingly, we arranged to try it out on the day before we were due to film. Unfortunately this allowed us only one bite of the cherry because if the vehicle had sunk we would have had to recover it and rethink our strategy. But the thinking would have needed to have been very good indeed because there was nothing that we could have done to increase the buoyancy – there wasn't a spare inch of space left. Our task was not an easy one; the car, a Hillman Imp, would be required not only to support its own weight but would be carrying two men and two lots of underwater survival gear. Furthermore the electrics and battery had to be fully submersible and able to function the next day when we were due to record the entire sequence. We got advice on this from the tank regiment at Bovington, where the drivers habitually take their vehicles through deep and muddy waters. A second requirement concerned the angle at which it entered the water. A car driven at speed over a jetty would tip nose first because the front wheels would start to fall before the rear ones. I had to ensure that we could counteract this effect and so, in order to flatten out its trajectory, I arranged for a ramp to be constructed at the end of the jetty which would fling the front of the car upwards. This would, of course, have had the same effect on the rear wheels cancelling out the effect and so I had to devise some means of getting rid of the ramp before the back wheels passed over it.

'If in doubt, use explosives' – a philosophy I had learned from ICI. Their advice came in handy now. I supported the ramp on stout wooden pegs and blew them to pieces with detonators activated by contacts in the path of the front wheels. By the time the back wheels hit the ramp, albeit a mere fraction of a second later, the supports had disintegrated and the ground was flat.

Our stunt arranger for the series was again to play a vital role; he would play the part of the driving instructor and would be seen only as a shadowy figure in the front passenger seat. It would have been his job to clap an underwater mask over Michael's face if the stunt had gone wrong. The second mask was his own; because it was considered that a drowning stunt man was likely to be of little use in a sinking car. We calculated that this gear would have kept them both alive long enough for the rescue boat, which was standing by with a crew of trained underwater divers, air bottles already strapped to their backs, to get them out of the car. With this organised, I thought we had covered every contingency but, inevitably, I had not allowed for the unexpected – the hand of fate.

The rehearsal went fine. I could not fault it in any way. The car shot off the jetty, lifted up at the right angle and landed more or less flatly upon the water. It was copybook stuff and I was well pleased and inclined to be a tad self-congratulatory. The little Hillman Imp, loaded with our plastic foam, was so buoyant I was sure that we could have supported a Bailey bridge on the roof without it sinking more than an inch or two. We had tied a rope to the back of the car so that we could haul it back to shore and that operation also went without a hitch. Mind you, it was rather like towing the *Queen Mary* and with only the three of us to heave on the rope it came ashore in its own sweet time.

Now all we had to do was to manhandle it up the beach and onto hard ground. Alas, this was the problem I hadn't bargained for. It was a shingle beach composed entirely of pebbles and the wheels just would not go through them. We enlisted help, and eventually had four or five men trying to push and haul the car up the slope. It was hopeless and progress was restricted to a few inches at a time. Nearby, however, was the chap with the tractor, a contingency laid on for the following day. Seeing our difficulty, he suggested that he tow it up the beach to the flat strip of concrete at the top, an offer I was delighted to accept. It was getting late and we still had some work to do on the car. The sea water would have to be drained from the foot wells, the battery and the electrics checked and the engine and exhaust tested and run. The tractor driver walked down the beach, fastened a stout rope to the back of the car and, making sure he had a clear path, reversed the tractor and dragged the car onto to the concrete strip. But even with the tractor applying all its power, the Hillman Imp still protested, its wheels biting deep into the shingle. We could see the strain on the tow rope as it straightened like a steel rod. Eventually both vehicles were on the hard standing and we could get to work making the Imp ready for the following day. Putting a plastic sheet on the wet seat I got in and turned the ignition key. Nothing! No whirring noise from the self-starter and no coughing as the petrol fired. I turned the key again and again but it refused to start. Despite all our careful waterproofing and carburettor sealing it wouldn't even turn over. I went to the back of the car (Hillman Imps are rear-engined) to check the electrics – and what I saw nearly brought on a seizure. The strain on the back of the car during the tow had been too much for the sheet metal bodywork – the engine mountings had been torn out!

It was a nightmare to eclipse all nightmares. The engine was now at an angle, and the shafts connecting it to the rear wheels had come adrift. Other structural damage had occurred but I couldn't take it all in. I closed my eyes and breathed deeply, a measure that is supposed to ward off nausea and vomiting – but it was touch and go. I looked again and the sight was even worse. On the following day, the film crew would be ready for action, Michael would be made up and on the jetty, the stunt man and the underwater team would all be equipped for the great event and the sightseers would be gathering on the shore – but there would be no car! Perhaps the gag could be rewritten to show Frank running along the jetty and jumping into the sea, but I didn't think this would appeal to Michael Mills who wanted a car to be driven at speed along the jetty; and a car was the one thing we didn't have.

We phoned the A.A. asking if they knew anyone who could fix the body work and the engine mountings, replace the half shafts, the carburettor supply pipes, the fuel pump and the electrics and have the car sweetly tuned and ready to go by seven o'clock the next morning. They were sorry, but they thought one of their contacts could get it done by the following Wednesday. In desperation I phoned the police. I knew they would laugh and I was about to hang up when they said they knew just the people. I could not believe my ears and suspecting that they hadn't understood me I said, 'Did you say you *did* know someone?' They repeated that they did and gave me the phone number of two chaps who had a workshop and just loved dealing with problems of this kind. I thought they were taking the proverbial, but no. Apparently these blokes specialised in accident repairs. They would collect the car, transport it to their workshop, labour throughout the night and have it on site next morning tested and ready for action. Could they stay and watch the filming? *Could they stay?* I would willingly have built them a private stand bedecked with flowers, supplied with arm chairs and provisioned with Champagne had I the luxury of time!

But that was all a long time ago and I regret to say I have forgotten their names. However should they ever read this, a thousand more grateful thanks and I am still willing to supply the Champagne.

That evening Ian and I saw the Hillman put aboard a recovery truck before we left for our hotel. Still trembling with the combined effects of shock and relief we made immediately for the bar where we drank long and deeply – it worked better than the deep breathing. Nevertheless it took almost three hours and a great deal of money before our own damage was repaired. The next day the Hillman Imp was driven to the site humming like an expensive watch. The sequence was filmed in a series of single takes in which everything worked and nothing had to be recorded again. The little Hillman Imp performed like a star. And Ian and I, because we had to drive back to London, celebrated with no more than a pint of shandy each. Collecting our gear we said 'Cheerio' to both Michaels and had had the supreme satisfaction of seeing the Mills one smile.

Head over Wheels

As I have already hinted, when things go wrong actors react in different ways. Some recognise that props and equipment can occasionally malfunction and are prepared to wait patiently while technicians struggle to put them right, but others, the whingers and whiners, are less accommodating and lash out at everyone within earshot.

Michael Crawford was an accommodating type and would wait calmly until things were put right; he would go for a walkabout rehearsing his lines in a quiet voice until everything was ready. During the whole series he never once showed the impatience or irritation that he must have felt. And, of course, things did go wrong as I've shown in this book (in fact I wonder if anything ever went right). Take the episode we filmed in Dorset, the sequence that involved his driving a car over a cliff.

As a novice driver, Frank Spencer was supposed to have taken his wife Betty out for a picnic, but unused to reversing on grassy slopes he backed the vehicle down to a cliff edge where he finished up with the rear wheels hanging over a fifty foot drop to the sea. The trouble started when Frank and Betty were picnicking on the grass and (in the script) it starts to rain. Other picnickers scurry around packing up their bits and pieces and driving off. Frank and Betty remain, but she complains that the rain is now getting worse and so they get in the car and drive away. And that's when he slides the vehicle towards the cliff. Sod's Law dictated that because it was supposed to rain and spoil their picnic, the sun shone in a cloudless blue sky. We couldn't disguise the fact that it was a glorious day because the hard shadows showed quite clearly that it was a sunny day.

The off-screen drama started when it was discovered that a hired dog wasn't at the location. This dog was supposed to climb into the car uninvited and, because this upsets the balance of the perilously poised vehicle, was essential to the plot. But neither the dog nor its handler had shown up. There was obviously a reason, but without a dog we were stuck. The PA was despatched to find a substitute. All that was required of this dog was that it should sit or lie still on the back seat of the car and look friendly. Trained dogs are seldom found sitting around awaiting a call to star in a TV comedy but the PA found one. He'd started off by driving to the farmer's house (or was it the local pub?) and there, sitting outside was a black Labrador. Its owners were contacted and were delighted to lend it. They brought it to the site and introduced it to the cast. What a wonderful animal that was. It stayed where it had been put without a bark of protest and when Michael called on it to climb over the seat, it did so with such intelligence and understanding that we felt it must have been rehearsing all its life for this opportunity to have its fifteen minutes of fame.

The vehicle chosen for the stunt was a Morris Minor and it was my task to design a rig that would not only support it safely with half its length overhanging the cliff edge, but also contriving some means of rocking it up and down. Because my design involved some heavy engineering, I had enlisted the services of a firm of metal workers in Surbiton where, in their large and well-equipped workshop, they had constructed a channel-iron base and a trunnion mounting which, when the car was bolted to it, enabled it to be see-sawed dramatically, apparently teetering on the very brink of disaster. A length of steel tube clamped to the under-side of the car and protruding between the front wheels enabled it to be operated with almost fingertip control.

We were filming on grazing land and Ian Scoones and I had brought a spade and a mattock with which we intended to cut two trenches sufficiently deep to accommodate the rectangular iron frame. I was banking on the fact that buried in grass and soil it would not be seen. The frame was massively heavy and quite long, extending several feet beyond the front of the car. This I felt to be an insurance against the entire shebang tipping up and dropping into the sea. Stunt arranger Stuart Fell, who had again been booked to advise Michael on his more dangerous commitments, arrived at the site early and was able to see the car and the location where it would sit on the cliff top. Stuart was a chum with whom we had worked many times before and it was nice to have his opinion on what we were proposing to do. In *Some Mothers*, Michael Crawford, who overtly performed all his own stunts, inevitably took risks, but he never took foolish risks and hanging by one hand from the rear bumper of a car suspended over a sheer drop onto rocks and sea would have qualified as a very foolish risk indeed. Stuart, who knew all about such things, fitted him with a safety harness to be worn under his costume and a wire cable which, hidden inside his sleeve, could be attached to the specially strengthened bumper bar. It meant that Michael, while still performing dangerously, would, if things went wrong, drop only to the length of the steel strap.

That morning we were going to position the car and bury the iron frame. 'Michael Mills had already shown us where he wanted it and so we set about measuring and marking out the trenches. Anxious to get started I took a mattock, spat on my hands and, intent on removing the first sod, whacked the blade into the ground.
'Clang!'
The shock wave almost fractured my arm. Although it was painful and took me by surprise I assumed my mattock had struck a very large flint or piece of stone. While I massaged my arm, Ian took over and, rolling up his sleeves, picked up the mattock and took an even mightier swipe.
'Clang!'
Both his eyes appeared to have swivelled inwards towards his nose. Realisation dawned rather quickly; this part of Dorset was made of granite, solid igneous rock composed of quartz, felspar and mica and

had only a vestigial topping of soil and grass. This was something we hadn't bargained for. We prodded around in other places, but it only confirmed our worst fears – the car, which had been planned to teeter on the edge of the cliff, would be performing more like a low-flying aircraft. We had one hope and that was to cover the frame with tufts of grass and earth. This would camouflage it by raising the height of the ground under and around the car. Having decided on a policy we gathered up the tools and moved to another part of the field.

The spot we chose was a long way from the cliff top but it turned out to be exactly the same. We dug around, here, there and everywhere and failed to prise away anything more than a handful of grass. The entire field and the next one and the next were of the same composition; there was no usable turf in this part of Dorset. In desperation we collected thin wisps of grassy soil hoping that if we could get enough it would hide the ironwork or at least disguise it on the camera side. But even in this quest we were out of luck. Despite the paucity of top soil, every meagre, miserable, square inch of grass had developed roots that penetrated crevices in the granite and clung tenaciously to it with a strength that made carbon fibre look like embroidery silk. We sweated and prised and we shovelled and swore, but at the end of an exhausting thirty minutes we'd gathered not quite enough to fill a carrier bag.

And so the car was eventually filmed with just a few miserable bits of dead grass spread around the sides of the iron work. It's possible that had we journeyed further inland, say as far as the next county, we might have discovered lusher pastures but time was short and we were almost due to start filming. With the car bolted to the frame we tried the rocking motion and were relieved to find that it worked; even Michael Mills gave one of his brief smiles. The filming went smoothly and I don't think we had to retake anything vital. It should be explained at this point that Frank Spencer was supposed to have secured employment as a fertiliser salesman and the car he was driving came with the job. Now, on the cliff top with the car likely to plunge into the sea, Frank is certain that if he could remove the two heavy sample bags of manure from the boot of the car, the front end would stay down. Telling Betty to climb on the bonnet he makes his way over the roof in an attempt to reach down and open the boot lid. He almost succeeds but, of course, slips over the top and disappears. Frantically Betty tries to see what's happened to him. She daren't get off the bonnet so she screams 'Frank, Frank!' From a camera viewpoint below the cliff we see that he is hanging from the bumper. He shouts for her to stay where she is. Michelle was unhappy with the rocking motion and the fact that the car was on the edge of a high cliff; she had nothing to hang on to except the wiper blades and she was on a polished surface. She asked me if I would hold her ankles, a job that seemed to me considerably more attractive than prospecting for turf.

Ian had secreted himself inside the car with two open bags of peat. He was to ease these bags out when Michael, hanging from the rear bumper opened the boot. But Ian discovered that the wind, although fairly gentle, was blowing from the sea and into the car and during the action it covered him in peat dust temporarily blinding him. Michael was equally afflicted when he pulled the bags out and dropped them into the sea. His reactions on being deluged in simulated manure were hilarious but not entirely as scripted. Try shouting 'I think I've done it Betty' with your mouth and nose bunged full of peat dust and you'll find that your voice sounds more like a CD player swathed in blankets. Having successfully jettisoned the fertiliser Frank has to get himself back to the safety of the cliff. But in seeking a new handhold he grabs the exhaust pipe. Slowly this breaks away, bending under his weight. It was, of course, a specially contrived prop, hinged at the far end and supported by a steel cable which could be lowered in stages from inside the car. It looked very scary and with Frank's dawning realisation that his handhold is coming adrift, had viewers wondering if he really was going to plummet into the ocean.

Meanwhile Betty was shown spread-eagled across the bonnet, but the picture cut above her knees so that my firm but gentle hands were never revealed. Although the rest of the sequence was filmed miles away and days later, Frank is seen still hanging onto the exhaust pipe and Betty is still on the bonnet when a coach load of rugby players passes along a coastal road higher up the field. They hear Betty's cries of distress and, stopping the coach, they dash to help. Quickly forming up on either side of the car and doing the old heave-ho routine, they lug it back up the hill. Frank, still clutching the exhaust pipe and unseen by the merry rugby team, is pulled along the ground behind the car. Realising that even a hefty rugby team would have difficulty in doing such a thing we'd hired a Land Rover equipped with a winch to tow the Morris Minor up the hill. This would free the actors to mime the pushing and heaving bit. Fitted to the winch was a very expensive climbing rope that I treasured as part of my personal equipment. All was going well until the car reached a flat bit and the enthusiastic rugby team swept it forward. My climbing rope went slack and Michael Mills, with his seafaring knowledge, hastily flung a couple of turns around the winch. It caught and the journey up the hill continued. Unfortunately my rope kinked in the middle and from then on became an ex-climbing rope.

The final scene showed the Morris travelling along a leafy lane. Frank and Betty, back inside, agree that all's well that ends well. The camera pulls back and we see that the car is strapped to the top of the team's coach. What is not apparent is that Ian and I have become two members of the rugby team.

We had hired a crane to lift the Morris Minor onto the roof of the coach, but despite having its wheels clamped securely to the coach, the springing of the car made it bounce up and down. It was lunch time and Ian and I had one hour to solve the problem. It had taken nearly thirty minutes to get the car up and locked in position so we hadn't all the time in the world. To make it appear as if the car was roped to the roof of the coach I used what was left of my climbing rope. Since this was merely set dressing we bunged some wooden blocks under the springs and had the coach driven to the rendezvous. There were two ventilators on the roof of the coach and through these Ian and I could see the under-side of the car which, although not as temperamental as it had been, was still behaving badly.

When we reached the location Michael Crawford and Michelle were already made up and waiting. We were ten minutes late and everyone seemed to think we had been taking our ease in a pub. Our protestations that we had been working were met with unfeigned scepticism. We didn't argue because it invariably happened that we would have to spend our lunch breaks repairing something or making something or even reinventing something. This was the fate of everyone in who worked in Visual Effects.

The PA was standing by with a step ladder and Michael and Michelle climbed up into the car. Michael, accustomed to these sort of stunts, was confident and anxious to get on with it, but poor Michelle was unhappy. From up there it looked a long way down, besides which the car appeared to be tied on with a bit of nylon clothes line. She couldn't see the four large clamps holding the wheels and if I'd thought about it I would have shown her before the journey commenced. While they got into the car the rugby team boarded the coach, the camera car took up its position and on the cue for action we all moved off. Ian and I stood in the aisle and by poking two iron bars through the ventilators were able to dampen some of the oscillations, but it was hard work and we were only partially successful.

Years later, people still remember the 'car over the cliff' episode and, those of us who were instrumental in bringing it to the screen, are still rather proud of the fact that we contributed to the show's success. My reward was holding on to Michelle's ankles.

To Go Downstairs

To show Frank Spencer playing a raw recruit in the Air Force was to test viewers' credulity to the limit; how could the gormless Frank have passed the first hurdle – filling in the application form? But several of the plots depended on the assumption that he had actually got a job (or was seriously being considered for one) only for everything to fall apart during the rest of the show. But such was the brilliance of the writer, Raymond Allen, that the scripts were always believable. Who would doubt that Frank Spencer had joined the RAF?

There were many funny gags in that episode and I remember having to provide a hot water bottle that would spurt a jet of water on cue. Standing by a window he attempts to empty it and appears to be relieving himself, (hearty guffaws from the ex-service men in the audience with long memories.) But my main commitment was to provide a tall wooden locker in which Michael Crawford would hide and then topple down a flight of stairs. I had the feeling that of all the stunts he had performed so far this might prove his last. It was horrendously dangerous, combining the worst elements of a white knuckle ride and a car crash and I was more than concerned that it might also finish my own career.

I discussed it with the producer Michael Mills and his comments were not reassuring. He sat back in his chair and said 'You can do it, Bernard.' in a tone of voice that was reassuring but at the same time might have been construed as sarcasm. Was this a challenge or did it show a remarkable faith in my ability to solve any problem? Knowing Michael Mills I felt sure it had nothing to do with my past achievements. He was testing me, but I knew that had I said that I considered it too dangerous he would have accepted my judgement.

Because this was television, it was unnecessary for Michael to be in the cupboard as it crashed down the stairs – a cut shot would have saved him from harm and the end result would have been much the same. But I knew that Crawford would never have agreed to such subterfuge. With the two Michaels showing such faith in me I was on my own, out on a limb and up a shark-infested creek without a paddle!

From its position at the top of the stairs the locker had to tip over, slide all the way down without stopping, crash through a landing, tip over once more, finally breaking through a wooden balustrade and falling several feet to the floor below. I tried to picture what it would be like for a person inside a cupboard going through that sequence. Turn over, crash, slide, crash, turn over, crash, turn over, land on solid floor and finally what was left of said person would climb out and carry on with the performance! I read through the rest of the script unable to concentrate; all I saw was a picture of Michael in a wooden coffin being smashed to pieces, every bone in his body fracturing progressively and his brain being churned into scrambled egg.

As an effects designer I had always claimed that I would subject myself to any stunt or dangerous effect before handing it over to an artiste – but not this time – not on your (or anyone else's) Nellie! I don't know what traumas Michael endured in *Barnum*, but I doubt if there was anything more frightening than that locker sequence. The first thing I had to consider was a method of cushioning him from the multiple impacts – something that would protect him and absorb most of the shock. Foam plastic wouldn't do because point sources compress the foam in the immediate area and provide very little protection from impact. It wouldn't have safeguarded his elbows and knees which would compress the foam locally and come hard up against the wooden sides. He would need to be encased by something pneumatic – something like the modern automobile air bag.

After much thought I decided to use the inflatable cushions employed by sufferers from piles and bought two dozen from a very surprised chemist. Pneumatic cushions become progressively more resistant the more pressure you apply to them. We had the locker delivered to our workshop and were able to take a more reasoned assessment. We started by inflating the cushions with an air compressor and gluing them to the inside and top of the cupboard, after which we sprayed them black so that they wouldn't be seen. As an afterthought, I decided to hang two brown coats over the cushions to give additional protection and to provide useful camouflage. Besides which it would have seemed odd if Michael had climbed into an empty cupboard.

Most importantly, something had to be done to prevent him from being thrown around during the double rotation. A safety belt would have held him securely, but because he had to open the door and climb out this would have been impractical. I doubted if he would be in a suitable condition to fumble with a safety belt clasp. We decided to give him two grab handles and two foot restraints. We'd finished the job by that evening, but I couldn't help noticing that with its lining of black cushions it looked horribly funereal.

One job remained: someone had to test it. I was working with Ian Scoones and Rhys Jones and incredibly Rhys volunteered to act as a guinea pig. He climbed inside and we shut the door. Then, making quite sure he was ready and well prepared we slowly pushed the top of the cupboard until it toppled over and banged down on the concrete floor. We expected Rhys to climb out and when he didn't Ian and I quickly un-latched the door. We saw him lying on his side and looking like the victim of a hit and run driver; we bent down and helped him out. He'd gone into the cupboard a young man eager to help; he was lifted out, an old man with only a few days to live. His hair was sticking out all over his head, his tie had somehow twisted to the back of his neck and his face was suffused with an unhealthy flush. When he was capable of speech we asked him, somewhat unnecessarily, how it had felt. He looked at us pityingly and didn't answer. Rhys had traversed an angle of ninety degrees before hitting the floor – Michael would be called upon to go through a hundred and twenty before impacting the equally solid wooden stairs. We got to work on more padding for his head and strengthened the foot restraints. But it was never tested again by us. Later that week, we showed it to Michael Crawford and asked him if he'd like to try it. He shook his head and replied that he would do it only once and that would be on the night of the show. I hoped he would live to tell us what it felt like.

The reason for Aircraftman Frank Spencer to be hiding in the locker was that there was sudden spot inspection of his barracks. Frank's kit was untidy and in order to escape punishment he has to dive into the cupboard and close the door. The script explained that all should have been well had not Frank given an involuntary response when his name was called. Hidden inside the locker, he stamped on the floor, came smartly to attention and shouted out his last three numbers causing the locker to tip over and fall down the stairs. We had raised the cupboard on two blocks of wood. One, on the stair side, was removable from behind the scenery. Our instructions to Michael were that when he responded to his name and jumped to attention that he must throw his weight slightly against the up-stage side of the cupboard so taking pressure off the removable block enabling us to withdraw it. That evening the studio audience saw Michael get into the locker – they saw it fall down the stairs and they saw what was left of Michael climb out.

The viewers at home saw the same thing, but what they didn't see were the means of achieving an impossible fall, one that defied the laws of gravity. Imagine if you will a box of matches sliding down a sloping ruler. When it comes up against an obstruction (the landing) it comes to a halt. However fast the box of matches is travelling, nothing on Earth will make it turn over – all its weight is on the wrong side. And this was what we were faced with. The cupboard sliding down a flight of stairs would be subjected to the same laws. It would come to a jarring stop when it hit the landing – and so we had to fake it.

Underneath the Balsa wood landing we had built and installed a large iron cradle which could be rotated by means of a long lever. This would rotate the cupboard through an arc and send it on its way. It was important to time this very accurately or it would appear to stop momentarily at the point of impact. Ian was on the lever and although we had never been able to rehearse it, he got it right – absolutely spot on. The locker slid down the stairs, crashed through the landing, turned over, smashed through the balustrade and dropped to the floor. Knowing how Rhys had fared we had put a thick box spring mattress on the floor (we assumed that because the sleeping quarters were upstairs this would not look out of place) This was necessary not only to cushion Michael against the final impact, but to save the floor from damage. I didn't want to be asked why I had permitted a stunt in which Michael Crawford ended up in hospital and, worse still, I had mutilated the studio linoleum.

The studio audience applauded wildly as he climbed from the cupboard and got to his feet, but it seemed to me that he hadn't the faintest idea where he was, or what he was doing. The sound of clapping enabled him to locate the position of the audience and he turned and took a few staggering steps across the mattress before recovering and carrying on with the act. When it was all over he limped over to me and offered the expected words of praise. '****' he said.

A   R o o f   J o b

Unfortunately, the location filming on this occasion was scheduled only for a single day, no overnights and no drinking – which meant that Ian Scoones and I had to start out hours before the crack of dawn in order to get to there on time. It was going to be a busy schedule and because we had a lot to prepare we daren't risk delaying our part in the operation. Driving to Norfolk in the early light of what was apparently going to be a fine day was a pleasant experience. We passed through tiny villages where the dogs, the cockerels and the milkman were the only living things awake. We drove through landscapes of large open fields and far horizons and saw the sun come up through an early morning mist. If the contractors had done their job and provided us with access to the church roof then everything should be straightforward.

Ian Scoones, who is an excellent map reader, had guided me away from the main roads in favour of the pretty route. I was glad of his expertise because I am notoriously lacking in orientation skills and can lose my way on a zebra crossing. Our destination was a small village with a large church. Sadly, it was also a redundant church and with too few worshippers to warrant even an occasional service it had been deconsecrated and was now scheduled for demolition. Ideal for our purposes we had booked it for the location filming.

The sequence we were about to film was the one in which Frank Spencer, garbed as an angel, was to be flung through the church roof. If this sounds bizarre even for the witless Frank it was the pay-off to a sequence which would later be recorded before a live audience. In the studio he is seen taking part in a Christmas nativity play where he has been cast as the Archangel Gabriel, a role which calls for him to float down from heaven on a wire. Predictably things go wrong and while he is being hauled up above the stage, his wire is over-counterweighted and he is catapulted straight through the roof of the church. On location we were going to film the next part of the sequence where we see him burst through the roof from the outside – his body, costume, props and everything were to be flung upwards through the slates. As a stunt this would prove to be as dangerous (but arguably not as painful) as the locker-down-the-stairs sequence because it meant that Michael would have to crawl around on the very steep, and very high roof, grabbing the ridge tiles and hauling himself upward until he is sitting astride the apex and calling for Betty. The sequence was to finish with him being rescued by an RAF helicopter.

Like most of the personnel chosen to be BBC effects designers at that time, we were young and totally undaunted by the risks we took – this was clearly part of the job, but we were very conscious of the fact that there were other demands on our youth and stamina. For example, we were expected to carry loads that would have ruptured a camel. Cumbersome props and equipment that had to be transported in blazing sun or pouring rain across fields and to the tops of high buildings; we were not supposed to have a fear of heights nor complain when we were exhausted, thirsty or hungry. But the important bit, it seemed to me, was that we had to take responsibility for dangerous stunts involving highly paid actors – and that day in Norfolk was going to test our ability to cope with every one of these in full measure.

Norfolk is a flat, and to me, beautiful county, without the trees and hedges which are a feature of my own county that one can see for miles. We spotted the church quite easily from a long way off. When we got close to it we could see that it looked exactly like the photographs we'd been shown back in London, but it was bigger than I had imagined, quite a bit bigger. We went inside. It was completely empty – no pews, no font, no vicars and no communion wine; it was bare of everything except the scaffolding tower which had been erected to enable us to climb up to the ceiling. Sensibly someone had thought of incorporating a platform two thirds of the way up. We ferried our gear from the car and got to work. The contractor had made a large hole in the ceiling and removed the slates and, thankfully, had cut a section from one of the joists. Communications were working well. We hadn't noticed it outside, but when we climbed up to the ceiling and stuck our heads through the hole, the wind seemed quite lively. This was Norfolk and it was to be expected, but it was worrying. The helicopter would have to hold station while the rescue of Michael took place – no easy task in a frolicsome wind and the winch line he would have to grab and attach to his safety harness might prove a trifle frisky. To complicate matters he would be wearing angel's wings and a large Happy Christmas sign. I tried not to feel pessimistic, but I hoped God wouldn't object to my uttering a short prayer in one of his deconsecrated buildings.

Our first job was to paint pieces of hardboard to resemble roof slates. We mixed some scene colours and, laying the rectangles on the church floor, got to work with a large brush. Leaving them to dry, we climbed back to the top of the tower and positioned a few balsa wood timbers across the hole. Was it my imagination or was the wind becoming stronger?

The final stage was to cover the hole with our dummy slates. Working from the top of the tower I fixed the balsa wood battens and then, half out of the hole, I duplicated the layout of the real slates until I'd almost closed up the aperture. To finish the job I would have to position the few remaining slates from the outside – which meant scaling the long ladders left outside for us by the contractor. Despite our careful work in matching the colour, the newly roofed area could clearly be seen as a patch, but it didn't matter because the director's intention was to cut the shot from Michael going up on the wire in the studio to his explosive emergence from the slates on the roof. Being a rapid transition this would keep the action moving and ensure that the viewers would have little or no chance to examine our handiwork.

Laying the final slate, I heard a vehicle arrive – it was the camera crew. They opened the church door and went in calling out cheery good mornings and other pleasantries but the moment they opened that door the wind swept into the church, blowing away our artificial slates and depositing them all over the Norfolk countryside. It happened so quickly and so unexpectedly I was powerless to do anything. While Ian and a couple of volunteers searched the land around the church for grey rectangles I stayed on the roof re-fixing the balsa wood. I struggled with the temptation to put the original slates back and tell Michael that he must brace himself and close his eyes, but this mood passed. Michael needed a soft area of lightweight slates supported on loose rafters of balsa wood. The imitation slates, even if some were to be lightly glued together, would have to be free to move the moment his head came into contact with them. It was obvious however that the wind coming into the church would keep blowing them away. The solution, we decided, was to tie the slates down with thread. That way they would offer little resistance to Michael's head but should be able to withstand the pressure that built up inside the church whenever the door was opened.

Ian and his helpers returned having recovered every one of the slates. Working from inside and outside, we set them out again. However, this time we tied them down to the rafters with fine nylon fish line. I left one slate off to serve as a safety valve and release some of the internal pressure, knowing that it was unlikely to be noticed as Michael crashed through the roof.

When star and director arrived I explained what we were hoping to do. They had been concerned by the wind and had already phoned the flight controller at the RAF station to check on conditions. The flight was still on so we fixed a time to shoot. Ian and I climbing down from the roof, went to the coffee table, and found that the unit had got there first and cleaned it out; the urn was dry and the only food left was a sandwich that had fallen under the trestle table.

The slates stayed in position and now, with the church door firmly closed and someone posted outside to keep it that way, we were ready to commence filming. Michael was to be hoisted through the roof by two stunt men and now the four of us made our way to the top of the tower. The stunt men went first, Michael followed and I brought up the rear. It was cramped up there, but the two throwers were confident they could pitch Michael out with sufficient velocity to match the preceding (but as yet unrecorded) interior shot. The cue was called and I swung out and away from the scaffolding to give them more room. 'One, two, three, heave!' and he'd gone. The slates flew away in the wind but it no longer mattered. If the cameraman had got the shot we wouldn't need them again. Michael had angled himself towards the ridge and was now able to clamber up and straddle it. He would have to wait up there until the camera was repositioned and the helicopter had flown in from its holding position. The next part was going to be more dangerous. Climbing out of the hole I was able to make final adjustments to his wings (a thick sheet of expanded polystyrene cut into rudimentary feathers) but it was the Happy Christmas sign I didn't like. This was hung over a large stone finial and was being whipped around by the wind. The plan was for Michael to catch his leg in the cord and to take it up with him as he sailed away. The cord was of woven nylon with a breaking strain that could have landed a whale and I didn't like it. However, as long as this cord was free of obstructions or impediments that might snag it at the moment of lift off. All should be well.

But the wind kept whipping it around and I was haunted by the thought that if it became wrapped around the finial while it was attached to Michael's ankle, the helicopter pilot would be lifting a one-legged actor. I kept trying to gauge the wind which now seemed favourable and so, on getting my okay, the director gave the cue. The helicopter dropped the line which Michael caught successfully and then, hanging below the helicopter and still calling for Betty, he was flown away. I was lower down on the roof paralysed with fear. I forgot to mention fear when I listed the things we were expected not to be troubled by, but it's too late now.

A   S o r t   o f   E p i l o g u e

There had been rumours of changes and reorganisations for several weeks but management was playing its cards close to its chest and we weren't told anything and, more humiliatingly, we weren't consulted. Jack and I discussed the implications because we were the most vulnerable section and had suffered many relocations and upheavals since we had first come together; now there was obviously to be another. We were certain of this, because rumour is seldom without foundation and although we didn't know the details, the implication was strong enough to cause us concern. Eventually Jack was summoned to Cliff Hatts' office and told of the plans. We were to be moved to 250 Western Avenue, a factory site in a part of North Acton that had no shops or facilities of consequence and a place of little charm. What it did have were the new purpose-built rehearsal rooms with a good restaurant and nearby, an excellent pub.

Cliff Hatts had succeeded Richard Levin who had retired some years earlier and he had taken over Richard's office. I don't think Cliff was the instigator of our move, but when the BBC had acquired the island site in Acton they had inherited the empty buildings. Now they were looking for suitable units to fill them. They had already relocated the Drama Script Unit to a suite of offices that, coincidentally, was the site chosen for the Visual Effects complex. This was a happy coincidence for me because the Drama Script Unit was headed by Christopher Wade, a lifelong chum of mine who had been part of that small group in Germany responsible for creating the wartime entertainment unit. He and I had met and become friends there and although we couldn't have known it then, it was to be a friendship that would last a lifetime. Within a year we had both been honourably discharged from the RAF, chosen identical overcoats at the Cardington demob centre, and eventually both joined the BBC where Christopher (Robin to his wartime chums) became Head of the German section of the overseas service at Bush House while I went to Research Department. A few years into our careers we both joined television. And now we were to be together again in the same building, a fact that brightened our lives and made relocation to North Acton less dispiriting. Now we were able to have the occasional lunch together, drink together and discuss work together and, although we both fumed at being away from Television Centre, we were often required to attend meetings there – and inevitably if our meetings coincided we would lunch with mutual friends and colleagues in the club.

Moving to Acton offered an unprecedented opportunity to reorganise the Visual Effects section. We could expand our activities and take on new staff and, for the first time employ a permanent store-keeper – someone who would issue materials and organise the stock effects. But there was a price to pay. While we were assured that we would continue to operate as the managers of the section, the overall administration was to be given to John Cooper, one of our fellow senior designers. Jack was furious. After so many years it seemed we were still regarded as disreputable hairy-armed mavericks, more suited to working in muddy fields or sweeping up the workshop than running our own section. What did John Cooper know about special effects anyway? I saw Jack change; he became tight-lipped and morose. Life had gone full circle and we were back in the period when the redundant engineer was deputed to take over our section. The difference was that while in those days it had been easy to deal with the situation, now the organisational structure was far too complex to offer any hope of a managerial change of heart. Later on, when I got to know John Cooper as a friend, I found that he was uneasy in this role and no happier than we were by the arrangement. Although he had been flattered by this elevation from scenic designer to administrator he was equally a victim of the system.

I went to Acton to see the proposed site and found that it consisted of a large old factory with separate areas originally used as machine rooms. It also had a suite of offices on two levels. It offered ten times more accommodation than we had at that moment, in fact it was considerably larger than any premises we had ever worked in and, best of all it had its own capacious car park. I walked all around the area inspecting the offices, the toilets, the workshops and the store rooms. It was an excellent site, but being over two miles from Television Centre meant that we would once again be isolated from the studios. Admittedly we still had the Puppet Theatre to use as a base while working on a programme, but contact with the directors, designers and the servicing departments was now more or less confined to the telephone. We discussed its potential long and hard but I could tell that Jack had lost interest. At a meeting with John Cooper (Jack didn't go) I learned that future plans included the provision of vastly improved workshops, a state of the art model stage, administrative offices, computerised accounting and many of the other things we had dreamed of for years. But they had come too late for Jack who made the decision to retire early. He knew that he would receive a very adequate pension, reduced only slightly by the loss of two years' service, and he felt he'd endured enough. He realised that we'd have all the responsibilities of running a large organisation but none of the fun. He saw that the new kids on the block – the special effects designers we ourselves had taken on – were capable of using techniques far more advanced than the old fashioned methods we'd espoused for so long. New and sophisticated processes were evolving, exotic materials were being discovered and, above all, advanced camera techniques and computerised images were now in use. These were subjects about which Jack and I had only a vestigial knowledge. We had to bite the bullet and accept that we had become yesterday's men.

Because he was leaving I would take over his chair, inherit the coffee maker and the empty hospitality decanter and would run the outfit from a tiny dark office overlooking Western Avenue with its quadruple lanes of incessant traffic. I would be well supported by the lovely and efficient Anne Baugh who would control the accounting and, with her own small staff, organise the day to day administration of the designers and sort out some of their problems.

In the workshop, as well as the new machinery and equipment, there was to be a welding bay and a purpose built fibre glass workshop and studio for John Friedlander, our sculptor. It was to have its own air conditioning system, a big drying oven and ample room for large creative work. John had always been short-changed in the allocation of space, but he never complained. Now, he too was to be given very adequate, almost luxurious accommodation. Furthermore he was to be given an assistant. In the main workshop there would be large open areas for the designers to use and, when their own benches wouldn't suffice, there were to be two large flat stages on which they could lay out bigger or more complex items. Each designer was to have a shared office equipped with individual drawing boards, filing cabinets, tables and chairs. Under other circumstances, and at an earlier period, such luxury would have seemed unbelievable. Final proof of the section's new status was a copy of the Factories Act displayed on one of the machine shop walls.

And now our twenty-five year partnership was about to end. Poetically, it should have finished where we first met and shared drinks to celebrate its beginning in the White Horse, but neither of us felt like conjuring up the past to that extent. Jack was retiring and I would do the same in two years' time. But in the meantime I was to take over the new setup and all its problems, a responsibility that without him to debate and plan the details, with wouldn't be the same.

From the small group that had formed the nucleus of our original department the section had grown to employ forty two people. And here we were in the club at Television Centre, occupying our usual settee near the window and morosely sipping our beer. Jack would be leaving at the end of the week and the section had organised a grand farewell party to give him a good send off. But, to me, it felt more like preparing for a wake than a celebration. Sprawled on the settee I knew that we were both remembering the happy days – the excitements, the triumphs and the splendours, but we didn't speak of them; in fact we said very little. From time to time colleagues came over to ask Jack if it was true that he was bowing out and when he told them that it was, expressed genuine surprise. They wished him 'good luck' and, feigning envy, told him he was a lucky bugger and how they too would like to leave the rat race. 'It isn't like the old days any more' they all opined, and reminded him that from now on he wouldn't have to cope with the traffic and could stay in bed and perhaps do a little gardening before sauntering off to the pub – all the clichés. Why is it that people think retirement is so bloody marvellous? We sat there until the bar closed. I now faced life without him and he faced the fact that he was free to do absolutely anything or nothing at all as the mood and the day dictated. It didn't seem right and neither of us was happy.

Our string and elastic philosophy was clearly outmoded but we'd pioneered the techniques. If occasionally we'd got it wrong we nearly always managed to bluff our way out of trouble. One thing was certain, for twenty five years we had thoroughly enjoyed our role in television and wouldn't have changed it for any other – not even that of Director General (although his pension would have come in handy). We had made wonderful friendships along the way and not only with our own colleagues and designers in the section, but with the directors, the floor managers, the girls in the library, the firemen, the contractors and, of course, the stars of entertainment. But above all else, we had enjoyed working with each other. Shortly afterwards, Jack and Gladys sold their house in Surbiton and moved to a peaceful village in Oxfordshire where they bought a delightful disused vicarage. However, although we no longer lived near each other, we discovered that we hadn't finished our association with television. We were to meet up again on several occasions when we were invited onto several primetime shows to talk about our careers in the BBC or to demonstrate various special effects.

One of our most memorable reunions was the farewell party to mark the end of Lime Grove. Now surplus to requirements, the building was to be demolished and the site given to a housing trust. On the night of the party we arrived well before time (not wishing to miss out on the drinks and the *vol-au-vents*) and gave ourselves up to an evening of nostalgia. It was held in Studio E, home of so many memories. Primed with glasses of sherry we tried to remember the names of our colleagues as they came through the studio doors. But we were troubled by the fact that although we knew their faces we couldn't always recall their names. We decided that more introductory drinks were required and for a short time this did seem to help. Shamefully they remembered ours so we had to fall back on the tried and trusted 'Chum' or 'Dear' according to gender (and we didn't always get that right). We resorted to whispered conversation. 'Do you know who that chap is?'
'Who?'
'That chap over there; I can't point him out because he's looking this way, but he's got a red wine... no, he's put it down. You must know him. He was a producer I think, or was he a writer?'
'You mean the one talking to the two girls?'
'No the one behind him, talking to old thingy... Oh bugger, I can't think of his name either.'
In the end we gave it up and concentrated on the food and drink. We listened to the speeches and the tributes and shed a tear or two. Where had all the years gone? I recalled the tin bath and the dry ice which we had first used in this very studio. Jack suggested that we ask Frank Holland if he had really given us the worst gas hose in stock. But because Frank was the original custodian of the bath and had taken rather a shallow view of us and our activities at the time it might have recalled old enmities – and Frank was by now one of our oldest chums. I had asked my hired-car driver to arrive at midnight, but he waited for me

long after that I fear. I was drunkenly determined to be the last person to leave – the very last BBC employee to quit the building and to metaphorically put out the lights and lock the door. And I achieved my ambition. Sitting in one of the armchairs provided by the thoughtful organisers (who probably assumed that to have worked at Lime Grove we must all be in our nineties) I shook hands with departing guests and continued to toast the building until everyone else had left. The caterers were collecting the glasses and sweeping up crushed *vol-au-vents* but they made sure that I was provided for. On the table beside me were two uncorked bottles of Champagne.

When I was certain that I was the only member of BBC staff left I climbed unsteadily from the armchair and looked around. It was an emotional moment. This was the studio that I had entered on that first day – the day I left my fibre glass work to visit the studios – and this was the studio in which I appeared before the cameras in my own programme with Neville Duke, the famous test pilot. And now Lime Grove was finished; kaput, done with, surplus to requirements.

Although I had been retired for many years it seemed on that night that I had never been away. I held on to the back of the armchair and raising one of the bottles, gave a histrionic farewell to The Grove, a melodramatic gesture that brought on a choking fit and caused me to pour half a bottle of Champagne down the front of my shirt. I was rather pleased actually, this seemed a stylish way to leave.

I tottered downstairs to reception which was, of course, unmanned. Gone were the lovely receptionists, gone were the telephones and the appointment books and gone were the commissionaires. I crossed the road to where my driver was patiently waiting. I turned and looked at the old building for the last time and saw, or imagined I saw, ghosts from the past waving to me from the windows. The next day the demolition men moved in.

And that brings me, appropriately, to the end of my story.

A f t e r w a r d   b y
M a r t i n   W i l k i e

Bernard left the world of television a richer place than when he saw its first flickering beginnings. He managed to steer through a career peppered with chance, mishap and success. But most importantly, he did so with great enjoyment for the industry and the people around him. His journey was not only fascinating to him, but to many who shared parts of it along the way. He embraced the challenges it threw up and he relished in the merest nod of appreciation from cast or crew when it all went well. And, like all fellow effects practitioners, he also knew the trial and torment required to create the impossible, and the dark hours when an occasional '*special defect*' became the butt of all jokes, on and off set.

His pioneering position as co-founder of the BBC's Visual Effects Department along with Jack Kine was, as you have read, as accidental as it came. His real drive was simply to be part of this great new industry that he had found himself on the outskirts of when based at the BBC's Kingswood Warren Engineering Department. This glimpse of the real 'showbiz' world beyond oscilloscopes and Bakelite was a natural progression from his wartime days writing, designing and producing shows as part of ENSA in the RAF.

Bernard and Jack found that the cards dealt them an unbelievably responsible hand in making such masterpieces as *Quatermass* and *Nineteen Eighty-Four* the real, live televisual gems of their time. It is difficult to appreciate in this new mass media world the huge impact that a simple effect made on audiences then. Tens of millions watched live programmes huddled around their small black and white TV screens. These dramatic moments became the stuff of conversations the next day in factories, at bus stops and in boardrooms across the country. Yes, the 'string and sealing wax' approach was inevitable but they embraced what was around them and relished their new found roles with the energy and respect the job deserved.

Jack and Bernard had their ups and downs trying to steer a department through all that the BBC's management threw at them, on top of making shows glitter with faultless effects. Jack, as well as being an exceptional artist, was the great mover and shaker of the two. He helped reinforce the department's prowess within an established industry more used to the familiar Design Department. This was a pretty closed world before two men in smart suits, white coats and bow ties brought 'effects' firmly into the mix. In parallel, Bernard created the department's technical backbone with his blend of engineering and imagination. He also gifted the industry the much thumbed 'effects bible' *The Technique of Special Effects for Television*, first published by Focal Press in 1971.

Bernard left his post as head of the department in 1978. He and Jack had moved their rag tag of belongings from Lime Grove to Television Centre in the early sixties and after Jack retired, Bernard oversaw the move to larger, better equipped but somewhat divorced headquarters in London's North Acton. The department was now the largest TV Visual Effects Department in the world and boasted many new and innovative skills and facilities. In this purpose built 'Magic Factory' sculpting skills were as important as welding, electronics were as important as carpentry. Well-organised magazines brimmed with precisely arranged pyrotechnics, a model stage brought outer space to inner London and racks of materials could help whistle up a giant

Goodies Dougal dog in an instant, well almost. But the vital component remained the men and women brought into this unit under Bernard's wing. This highly skilled team was to produce many names that would go on to create some of the most accomplished special effects in both TV and film.

His own work was inevitably restricted as administration grew, but he still relished designing and executing physical work that ended up being seen in the nation's living rooms. Having been there for the first series and throughout its long, and quite unexpected run, he created his last creatures for *DoctorWho* in 1974 with some suitably frightening spiders. They were perhaps based on the ones he often removed from his old Tudor cottage in Chipstead?

Back at home he created a smaller version of his Television Centre workshop set up in a converted flint barn at the top of the drive. Times have certainly changed. Back then neighbours grew rather blasé to explosions, smoke and very odd contraptions appearing in this quiet corner of rural Surrey. The need to build and test effects at home wasn't an option many designers had, and it ether pointed to the inner desire to ensure everything went 'alright on the night' or the extra pressure of running the department. An earlier heart attack in the late sixties probably points to someone seldom able to switch off from his work.

The farm regularly saw new pyrotechnics tested on film to assess their smoke output or likely camera flare. Perhaps this was a better location than the roof of Television Centre after all! This quaint old barn produced many studio props including the flapping bamboo wings for endless 'birdmen' featured on *The Dave Allen Show*. Two new-style hover movers were memorably strapped together to test a floating coffin for another Dave Allen sketch in which the inventor of the hovercraft was taken to the churchyard. Michael Crawford's explosive microphone and Vesuvius Suit was fully tested here one Sunday morning before Bernard's lunchtime pint with chums at the little pub up the lane.

Recalling my brother's and my own childhood we naturally assumed everyone's dad regularly cast latex limbs before cutting the lawn or set up a flamethrower to see its glare after dark, just in time for bedtime stories. We remember vividly the shock of walking into the barn one morning to find an Indian mutineer strapped over the mouth of a cannon. Just another day at the office for a BBC effects man!

Actually running the department probably wasn't the career route Bernard would have chosen. He cut his teeth in TV during an era launching such names as Morecambe and Wise and David Attenborough. It was an era when he could share a pint, and a giggle, with the likes of Eric Sykes and Spike Milligan. His creative spark was one that had always pushed him to offer his writing and comedic side to productions as shows developed. Judging by the discovery, after his death, of many rejection slips from the BBC of scripts, jokes and formats from the fifties through into the seventies. This either points to an impenetrable hierarchy at the BBC or simply a run of rather poor jokes!

But Bernard struck a chord with Dave Allen and during the long run of his popular 'sit down' comedy and sketch show, some of Bernard's material did make it to the screen. But in those days you were what you were, and being part of the design department should have been enough for most.

His last production for the BBC took him to Jamaica for a children's drama and perhaps swapping North Acton for the Caribbean helped cement the need for a change after 30 years at the Beeb. When he left the corporation he was able to call on many contacts to continue a career in creating effects for independent productions but still that latent talent must have been pulling on his conscience and that pack of lucky cards. He went on to write for the likes of Russ Abbott and the Grumbleweeds for ITV, and wrote many technical articles for the emerging video production industry.

His effects notoriety then took him to Germany, many decades after being part of Eisenhower's SHAEF group at the end of the second World War. With nothing but wonder for the delights of Cologne he began working for their equivalent of the BBC, West Deutsche Rundfunk or WDR. Drafted onto a production called *Plattenkuche*, or 'Record-Kitchen', meant dealing with all manner of 'crazy' effects to back up their gregarious comedy and music act programme. With gentlemanly tact and sporadic German he would often advise simple ways of improving the shot or tightening the punchline. A year later he was writing for the show, a year after that he was embraced as a co-producer by Rolf Spinrads, the show runner. His career in Germany extended into the late eighties and he helped bridge the language gap of many a discussion between English speaking bands visiting this important European pop show, such as Roxy Music and Blondie.

When not abroad, he still found that his BBC connections drew him back into familiar territory. He had been instrumental in providing the all-important Daleks for the *Daily Mail*'s 1968 'Boys and Girls Exhibition' at Olympia, when *Doctor Who* and Dalekmania was still at its peak. His involvement with the exhibitions spurred a lifelong friendship with Lorne Martin who later ran these events for BBC Enterprises. Lorne left the BBC and took *Doctor Who* exhibitions on independently and Bernard remained a key contributor to their success. He later became chairman of Experience Design and helped the company create many media based exhibitions and events.

Bernard stepped off stage after a remarkably good run and a very swift illness one afternoon in May 2002, with great grace and good timing it has to be said. He was 82 and left his wife since 1949, Barbara, two sons Simon and Martin and two grandchildren Amelia and Hugo. His enjoyment for the media he found himself in has left us with some ground breaking shows and memorable TV moments. If one of the techniques from his book or jokes from his scripts has helped anyone else get on board the world of the entertainment then his days at both the workbench and typewriter was time well spent. He certainly enjoyed it and I hope you have too. My great thanks also go to Matt West, Robert Hammond and the team at Miwk (another chance meeting), for finally bringing Bernard's notes to print.

A f t e r w o r d   b y
M i k e   T u c k e r

In the opening paragraphs of this fascinating memoir, Bernard describes how he entered the world of television when there was only one channel, and the BBC was breaking new ground in how programmes were made.

I never quite had that experience, but when I joined the BBC in 1985 (at which point there were four television channels), I was lucky enough to catch the very tail end of what I genuinely believe was a golden era of British television, and got a taste of what those early pioneering days must have been like.

A major milestone in my journey to becoming an effects designer was the discovery of an earlier book of Bernard's – *The Technique of Special Effects in Television*, published by Focal Press. Bought for me as a Christmas present when I was in my mid teens, this guide to the intricacies of special effects quickly became indispensable to me in terms of expanding my knowledge of the craft, and confirming that *this* was the industry that I wanted to be part of. Within the densely written text were fascinating drawings of special effects rigs, photographs of model ships and spacecraft, descriptions of exotic devices like cobweb guns.

I took inspiration from that book, and adapted the techniques described (in a slightly more Heath Robinson manner) to create the effects for the amateur science fiction and horror films that I used to make with by school mates, filming in local woods and quarries, using clockwork super 8 cameras.

When I finally joined the BBC Visual Effects Department as a holiday relief assistant, I found that Bernard's book had been invaluable in introducing me to the terminology and working practices of the department – working practices that Bernard had been instrumental in developing.

Within the discipline of television special effects, Bernard – along with department co-founder Jack Kine – was a true pioneer, and the working environment that the two men created within the BBC was unique, not just in terms of the ground-breaking work that was created, but as a training ground for dozens of special effects designers still working in the industry today.

When I founded The Model Unit in 2005, I was determined to retain some of the spirit of what Bernard had helped create, and it never fails to raise a smile when we use a technique described in Bernard's book to create an effect for a modern production.

The Technique of Special Effects in Television remains an indispensable publication in regard to the craft of special effects; I hope that this memoir will become an equally indispensible publication about one of the architects of that craft.

Mike Tucker
Miniature Effects Supervisor
The Model Unit
July 2015

ALSO AVAILABLE FROM **MIWK PUBLISHING**

THE LIFE & SCANDALOUS TIMES OF

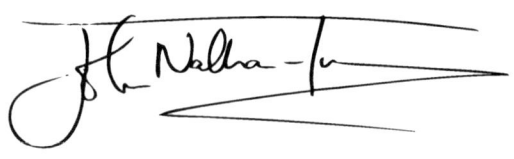

by Richard Marson

For more than a decade, John Nathan-Turner, or 'JN-T' as he was often known, was in charge of every major artistic and practical decision affecting the world's longest-running science fiction programme, **Doctor Who**. Richard Marson brings his dramatic, farcical, sometimes scandalous and often moving story to life with the benefit of his own inside knowledge and the fruits of over 100 revealing interviews with key friends and colleagues, those John loved and those from whom he became estranged. The author has also had access to all of Nathan-Turner's surviving archive of paperwork and photos, many of which appear here for the very first time.

"Extraordinary. A great piece of work. I read it in two days' flat, I couldn't stop. I've never seen a biographer enter the story like that, it was brilliant and invigorating. It really is a major piece of **Doctor Who** history and the history of an entire industry. An entire age, really. In the end, I think the book is clear - we have to forgive JN-T. That ending - he didn't deserve that. And I think by writing about it, you have made something elegant and even beautiful out of such a wretched mess. And I think that's very kind of you indeed. This book says a lot about JN-T but it says a lot about your good and kind heart too."

Russell T.Davies (Writer/Producer)

ISBN 978-1-908630-13-1

ALSO AVAILABLE FROM **MIWK PUBLISHING**

DRAMA AND DELIGHT

THE LIFE AND LEGACY OF
VERITY LAMBERT

by Richard Marson

For five decades, the name Verity Lambert appeared on the end credits of many of Britain's most celebrated and talked about television dramas, among them **Adam Adamant Lives!**, **Budgie**, **The Naked Civil Servant**, **Minder**, **Edward and Mrs Simpson**, **Eldorado**, **G.B.H.** and **Jonathan Creek**. She was the very first producer of **Doctor Who**, which she nurtured through its formative years at a time when there were few women in positions of power in the television industry. Later, she worked within the troubled British film business and became a pioneering independent producer, founding her own highly-successful company, Cinema Verity.

Within her profession, she was hugely respected as an intensely driven, sometimes formidable but always stylish exponent of her craft, with the stamina and ability to combine quantity with quality. Many of her productions have had a lasting cultural and emotional impact on their audiences and continue to be enjoyed to this day.

But who was the woman behind all these television triumphs and what was the price she paid to achieve them?

Combining months of painstaking research and interviews with many of Lambert's closest friends and colleagues, *Drama and Delight* will capture the energy and spirit of this remarkable woman and explore her phenomenal and lasting legacy.

ISBN 978-1-908630-33-9

ALSO AVAILABLE FROM **MIWK PUBLISHING**

SCRIPT DOCTOR

The Inside Story of **Doctor Who** 1986-89

by Andrew Cartmel

"There are worlds out there where the sky is burning, and the sea's asleep, and the rivers dream. People made of smoke, and cities made of song. Somewhere there's danger, somewhere there's injustice, and somewhere else the tea's getting cold. Come on, Ace — we've got work to do!"

Andrew Cartmel was the script editor on **Doctor Who** from 1986 to 1989. During his time on the show he introduced the seventh Doctor and his companion Ace (Sylvester McCoy and Sophie Aldred) and oversaw forty-two scripts written by eight writers new to the series.

With a clear mission to bring proper science fiction back into **Doctor Who**, he formulated what was later termed 'The Cartmel Masterplan', re-introducing the mystery to the character of the Doctor as the series celebrated its twenty-fifth anniversary and beyond.

Script Doctor is his memoir of this time based on his diaries written sometimes on set and sometimes not even in the diary itself but on the back of scripts. Illustrated with 32 pages of photographs, many of them not published before, this is a vivid account of life in the **Doctor Who** production office in the late eighties.

ISBN 978-1-908630-68-1

COMING SOON FROM **MIWK PUBLISHING**

MAC

THE LIFE AND WORK OF
MALCOLM HULKE

by John Williams

Malcolm Hulke wrote some of the best-loved **Doctor Who** stories and novelizations and his work continues to be influential long after his premature death in 1979. All the various manifestations of **Doctor Who** since then, including the New Adventure novels, the Big Finish audio adventures and the 2005 series have returned regularly to his creations, particularly the Silurians and Sea Devils, but also to his abiding ideas and themes.

Despite this enduring influence, little is known about the man himself aside from his background as a member of the Communist Party of Great Britain and the bare facts of his career as a writer. That career involved writing for some landmark television series including **Armchair Theatre**, **Pathfinders in Space**, **The Avengers**, **Crossroads** and, of course, **Doctor Who**. Hulke also had a flourishing career in non-fiction writing, most notably when he used his many years of experience to produce Writing for Television in the 1970s which became the standard text in its field.

Hulke was the writers' writer. He was always professional, never missed a deadline and would take pride in turning his hand to anything. Although engaged in an intensely solitary profession he constantly forged alliances either with other writers such as Eric Paice and Terrance Dicks, or enthusiastically engaged with socially significant group endeavours such as Unity Theatre or the Writers' Guild. All these aspects of his life will be explored in depth and add to the picture of a complex and paradoxical individual.

ISBN 978-1-908630-09-4

ALSO AVAILABLE FROM **MIWK PUBLISHING**

WHOAH!

Eight years of bizarre cartoons from the pages of **Doctor Who Magazine**

by Jamie Lenman

...the earth was invaded by a horde of sticklebacks?

...Jackson Lake thought he was Mr T and not the Doctor?

...the TARDIS crew met Posh and Becks?

From the pages of Panini's Doctor Who Magazine comes a complete collection of Jamie Lenman's comic strip, published under the name 'Baxter'.

Collected here for the first time, these are presented in a full-colour hardback book and includes some unpublished early drafts, rejected ideas and commentary from Jamie.

Miwk Publishing will be donating £1 for every copy sold to Giggle Doctors – Theodora Children's Trust (http://uk.theodora.org/en-gb)

ISBN 978-1-908630-73-5

ALSO AVAILABLE FROM **MIWK PUBLISHING**

TIME & SPACE & TIME

TRUTHLESS BILGE ABOUT EVERY **DOCTOR WHO** STORY **EVER**

by Robert Hammond

"...You'll probably cherish this proudly silly little book. Lap it up and laugh it up."
Doctor Who Magazine, issue 480

Who sent Phillip Hinchcliffe a special rug and nine goslings?

Why did Palitoy lose £26, five shillings and sixpence?

Who wasn't keen on 'dumb little lizards'?

Who wanted a French monkey puppet?

Read this book and find out...

£1 from every copy of this book sold will be donated to the PDSA
(People's Dispensary for Sick Animals)

ISBN 978-1-908630-71-1

COMING SOON FROM **MIWK PUBLISHING**

THE

WORZEL

BOOK

by Stuart Manning

When a former Time Lord swapped time and space for the mystery of the countryside, one of children's television's most unusual personalities was born. Jon Pertwee's portrayal of the anarchic scarecrow Worzel Gummidge won him a new generation of viewers and would become his most enduring character.

The Worzel Book traces the journey of Scatterbrook's scarecrow, from the days of early radio and the novels of Barbara Euphan Todd, through to the hit ITV television series and its eventual resurrection in New Zealand.

This is the untold behind-the-scenes story of a much-loved TV classic, featuring over 40 new interviews with cast and crew, including Geoffrey Bayldon, Jeremy Austin, Bernard Cribbins, Barbara Windsor and Lorraine Chase, illustrated throughout with over 200 photographs in black and white and colour, many previously unseen.

ISBN 978-1-908630-60-5

ALSO AVAILABLE FROM **MIWK PUBLISHING**

THE QUEST FOR PEDLER

THE LIFE AND IDEAS OF DR KIT PEDLER

by Michael Seely

For many people, Kit Pedler is best remembered as the man who created the Cybermen for **Doctor Who**, a real life scientist who was brought in to act as an advisor and bring some science to the fiction. The Cybermen were his ultimate scientific horror: where the very nature of a man was altered by himself, by his own genius for survival, creating a monster. Pedler was that rare animal, a scientist with an imagination. He liked to think 'What if...?'

Together with his friend and writing partner Gerry Davis, he created the hugely successful and controversial BBC1 drama series **Doomwatch**, which captured this fear and frightened the adults as much as the Cybermen scared the children.

Resigning from the Institute, Pedler turned his back on the world he had spent his adult life working in, and spent the rest of it campaigning for a real Doomwatch, to stop the unnecessary and cruel animal experiments in the laboratory (which he himself had seen in his earlier academic days), experiment in what we would now call eco-friendly housing, alternative technology and began to change his own relationship to the world. This lead to his book *The Quest For Gaia*, published in 1979 where he envisaged how a Gaian life-style would work in the post-industrial age. He also designed and built a nuclear bomb in rural Kent.

With contributions from his family, friends, colleagues and critics, this book tells the story behind a fascinating, charismatic, complicated, and demanding human being; a natural teacher who didn't just want to pontificate about the problems facing the world in a television or radio studio, but actually do something practical about them..

ISBN 978-1-908630-12-4

www.miwk.com/

www.facebook.com/MiwkPublishingLtd

www.twitter.com/#!/MiwkPublishing